The Black Ace Gang

A Novel
by

Charles A. Lewis

authorHOUSE®

AuthorHouse™
1663 Liberty Drive, Suite 200
Bloomington, IN 47403
www.authorhouse.com
Phone: 1-800-839-8640

First published by AuthorHouse 4/28/2008

ISBN: 978-1-4343-4322-2 (sc)
ISBN: 978-1-4343-4323-9 (hc)

Library of Congress Control Number: 2008902824

Printed in the United States of America
Bloomington, Indiana

This book is printed on acid-free paper.

Dedication

This book is dedicated to that first peer group to whom we bonded when we were young; in a time when our spirit was bright and breathing deeply, and when a smile came effortlessly. To these never-forgotten friends that we trusted—and the trust that was returned. May we always be worthy.

Foreword

Kids are different from the rest of us. There are obvious differences: size, too much energy, short attention spans; but that is not what I mean. I am talking about other things, such as the unique ability to see deeply into the heart of a situation. Not through logic and thought, because that process gets in the way.

Kids use what some call "beginner's mind": a deep unspoiled openness that permits them to see and feel things with a pure truth, not clouded by preconceived ideas. It is a distinctive gift that makes kids alive and complete with the inhaled breath, wrapped by an individual second. Embracing existence, without analysis. Unburdened by the past or future. Then they grow up.

Day One

This is the story of ninth graders growing up in the late fifties. I have been elected to tell the story. My name is Bob Parsons. As things go on, you will see why I became the narrator. This tale, although edited to flow as a story, is in essence the events as they happened.

My family had just moved about twenty-five miles. In this day and age that does not seem like much of a distance. But to those of us who lived in an area called Fred's Creek, where relatives' houses had been scattered about since many years before the Civil War, it was at least a long way culturally to now be living near the banks of the Ohio River, in a town called Boaz, among other residents of an almost-completed subdivision. Traveling down from the ridges and hills away from Fred's Creek was in many ways a big move.

We had been in our new home all summer. Like all fourteen-year-old kids, I had found my way around the back paths, shortcuts that only kids know. Now familiar with the territory, I had an accurate gauge of time and distances that goes with traveling by foot, a sense that is lost on those riding in automobiles. Coming here from Fred's Creek, where I was well known by everyone, having visited their homes countless times, Boaz and its unfamiliar people were quite exotic. An outside observer would see an ordinary boy walking down an ordinary street, but to me there was the feeling of moving about in a foreign country.

Today was the first day of school: my first day in a new school. Mother and I had earlier in the summer made a trip to enroll and meet the principal. He looked at my grades from Fred's Creek. They were not good at all, but they seemed to make him happy. He told mother about the great strides education had made. How the new educator must be able to meet the children's needs on different levels, teaching each according to their abilities.

I remember no direct references to a "slow learners' class" and would not have understood if there were. When trapped in a room with serious-talking adults and no window to at least escape through with my eyes, I had a tendency to fog over and wait for my release from the dull confinement. So while me not understanding would be normal, my mother was a different story. She was aware of social status and appearances and would have protested if she had detected any hints of stigma. She was the first on both sides of her family to graduate from high school. Her rural background did not get in the way of her ambitions, and she was happily anticipating the social mobility promised by a new house and town.

The term "special education" was not used back then, but there was a growing movement in schools with multiple classes of the same grade to group them according to how quickly the students learned, with so-called slow learners in one class, and "fast learners" in another. This was done at the discretion of the principal and teachers, using as their basis, grades, behavior, attendance, and physical appearance. The explanation to anyone who asked—and they would have had to ask—was, "They will all learn the material, but some will naturally learn it faster than others." The new approach to grouping students was not mentioned when I enrolled.

This morning I left the house, walking out past the newly built fieldstone markers at the entrance of Maplewood subdivision and across the main road that ran to the Boaz downtown area, where the junior high school was located. I immediately broke the first of many rules that mother had given me.

"Don't go over the hill and down by the river. That's where all those trashy people live." Those who lived down along the river were called as a group "river rats" by everyone else.

My first destination was Jerry Joe's house so we could walk the railroad tracks to school. Jerry Joe Culpepper was from a long line of river rats and did not know who his father was. His mother said his father was killed during World War II. He questioned her occasionally when she was drunk, which was often. He received enough conflicting information to realize that she was either lying or didn't know either.

The question as to who his father could be was not an obsession but the kind of speculation that fills kids' idle time along with many other topics. Jerry Joe was a survivor and had surviving down to an effortless art. He became my first teacher on the monetary aspects of the world.

His house was one of about ten in a row, all exactly alike. At least there used to be that many houses, but a few were missing. Still others were uninhabited with rooflines leaning at odd angles and front doors missing. The row stood along a narrow dirt road with patches of gravel and holes here and there. Poles supporting the back-most foundations of the houses hung out over the riverbank with the big, round rear poles actually in the water. These houses were constructed of vertical board and batons with a vague hint that they had once been painted.

I met Jerry Joe the day we moved in. After helping with furniture and boxes, I took off exploring, heading directly for the river. I stopped at the bottom of the steep bank, squatting with my knees resting in my armpits, amazed by the width of the water, the river smell, and the allure of the foreign Ohio people off on the other shore.

I saw something move out of the corner of my eye. My instincts from hunting took over and caused me to remain still. I watched a tall kid come sliding down the bank and squat beside me. He remained quiet, looking out over the water.

"What you doin'?" he said finally.

"Lookin' at the water."

"Where you from?"

"Fred's Creek."

"They don't have no water to look at in Fred's Crick?"

Turning to look at him grinning at me from ear to ear, there was nothing that could have prevented me from grinning back. I shook my head no, which made him laugh out loud.

We became friends. He took me the next day to the country club and introduced me to the caddy master. Before the day was over, I became a caddy, carrying a bag on each shoulder and trying to figure out what to do next.

Jerry Joe stepped in, smoothing things over when I committed glaring errors, such as standing directly behind the golfers when they were about to swing. He attended to the pins on the putting greens, made signs for what club, and when to hand it to the golfer, and whispered instructions while they were teeing off. He got me through the round without me being yelled at and with me getting only a few disturbed looks.

The golfers each gave me a quarter tip. That, added to the $3.75 counted out by the caddy master, brought my earnings to $4.25. It was a huge sum to me. I was receiving fifty cents allowance each week. I was now a professional caddy, not bad for a kid who didn't know what "fore!" meant that morning. The fact that Jerry Joe got a dollar tip from each of his golfers did not bother me. We each splurged on a quart of chocolate milk.

This morning I turned the loose doorknob at Jerry Joe's house and went in without knocking, knowing he would be asleep on the gray couch in the house's main room. The only other rooms were behind two dirty green doors, one leading to the bedroom and the other to the toilet in the rear, over the water.

He lay sound asleep where I expected. He was in the habit of staying awake for extended periods that ended abruptly by lying down about anywhere and falling into a deep sleep. I pulled a stained handmade quilt from a long body that was wearing holey jockey-type underwear. Looking up, his wide mouth spread into a grin, and saying nothing, he came up gracefully from the couch, which spouted stuffing and had a mildewed odor.

He pulled on the pair of new blue jeans that he had been wearing for a couple of weeks. They had yet to be washed for the first time.

Then he added a T-shirt that didn't quite cover his belly button. He walked to his mother's purse, which was sitting on the table in what could be called the kitchen area, and unsnapped it to dig around until he pulled out a pack of cigarettes. Putting one in his mouth and one behind his ear, he moved to a black cooking grate that was attached to the wall and found a kitchen match that he swiped on the wall. It made a distinctive popping sound when the head ignited. He held the flame a couple of inches below the cigarette until it lit, while at the same time he was moving to a position in the middle of the floor. Then, puffing smoke while closing one greenish blue eye, he aimed and dropped the still-burning match cleanly through a knothole between his feet and into the river.

"You stay outta my purse, Jerry Joe!" said a woman's voice from behind the bedroom door.

"I'm only gettin' a cigarette. Don't have a shit fit for Christ's sake."

"You heard 'er," a man's voice said.

"Shut up, Cecil, or I'll take a tire iron to your dumb ass!"

There was no answer. We started to leave. I said, "I gotta pee."

Jerry Joe made an exaggerated gesture in the direction of the toilet door with his cigarette hand. He headed out the door, carrying his shoes to be put on outside, while I went in. I looked down into the commode that was connected to a short open pipe. Through it you could see directly into the river. When peeing and aiming correctly, so it did not hit the side of the pipe, you could watch a straight line traveling all the way to the water. I loved this for some reason and did it at every opportunity.

We headed upriver, walking on the railroad tracks at a fast clip, not talking about much, scouring the weeds on the hillside that rose at a sharp angle up to the main road. We were looking for a hint of reflected light or an outright sighting of an empty soda bottle, or pop bottle as they were called, because this find would bring two cents deposit at Gibson's, an old-time grocery, hardware, and clothing store. Three empty bottles would buy a Three Musketeers candy bar with a penny change. We were amazed that people tossed money right out the window. This was the same route we traveled to caddy, but today we would walk into the Boaz Junior High building instead of passing it by.

Ahead uphill, behind a Texaco Station located close to the school, we could see, sitting on a wooden pop bottle storage case turned on end, a person who hated school as much as the two of us, Mike Masters. Mike's usual ambition was to be a juvenile delinquent, but today he looked to be waiting for us, and he was.

Mike was wearing a long-sleeved, white dress shirt with the sleeves rolled to the elbow and new dress shoes and slacks, both black. He wore long sleeves the year-round because he was not happy with his skinny arms. He combed his oiled dark hair straight back on the sides of his head. The style was called by most a "DA"—short for duck's ass. You could see the comb marks swept back like wings to meet in back. On top, his hair was short and stood up uniformly straight, creating a flattop that remained held in place by a wax specially designed for that purpose.

We negotiated the path up the hill. Mike rose to his feet, fell in beside us, and walked to the school with a sour look on his face that was caused by pimples and family pressures, along with general teenage angst. Mike's problems stemmed generally from the fact that it is hard to be a tough guy when your father is a trauma surgeon and your mother is a high school English teacher. He had managed to get into enough trouble to make some headway in that direction. At unguarded moments he displayed a gentle smile that would have embarrassed him had he been aware of it.

We entered the gymnasium that was attached to the back of a two-story, red brick structure displaying many large paned windows per room. Bird droppings stained each of the gargoyles framing the front entrance. Built in the early twenties, it had changed little, except that the floor of the gymnasium had been warped during the 1928 flood. Tan, foot-square tiles were laid over plywood to become the new surface of the basketball court.

The bleachers, to the left and right of the back entrance and facing the stage across the gym floor, were full of fidgety kids waiting for the principal to read names and reveal their homeroom number so they would know who would be their classmates. The older kids, ones my age, were milling around out on the gym floor and trying to look casual, giving the appearance that this procedure was all beneath them.

The size of the school and the number of kids was heady stuff to me. The Fred's Creek school was cinder block, four rooms, with a gravel parking lot. An uphill sloping field that was used for recess was surrounded on three sides by hills with trees. A basketball goal with a wooden backboard was nailed, not quite as high as it should be, to an oak tree.

One room was first to third grade; another was fourth to sixth, and the next, seventh to ninth grades. The fourth room was used for the kids to blow off steam when the weather turned bad and they couldn't go outside. To me this new school was very sophisticated. I was joking around with Jerry Joe and Mike but was secretly hoping not to get lost and embarrass myself.

My friend the principal was up on stage and reading the names of the students. He gave us an occasional unnatural smile, as if suddenly remembering again the "be friendly" instructions from his principal's training. There were five groups of ninth graders left after the lower grades were sent on their way. The 9-5s, the "fastest" learning group, were called and left for their homeroom. In descending order the kids in the rest of the classes left, until all that remained were the 9-1s.

"As group one you will be required to report to room 207 each morning. Today you will go to this room to receive your textbooks. If you need help finding your other classrooms, ask your homeroom teacher, and she will help you find each room, if you are new to our school that is." He repeated the same set speech for each class's benefit.

Before the principal began reading the 9-1s names that included all three of us, Mike headed for room 207 and waved for us to follow. The rest of the twenty or so class members followed along, and the principal seemed not to notice that we were leaving. He was now in the gymnasium with four or five stray students, standing at the podium, and still reading names from the paper in front of him.

Our homeroom teacher was a short, elderly woman. She was wearing a high-necked, plain, black dress with a white embroidered collar and had short, gray, pin-curled hair. Glasses attached to a silver chain draped from her neck. She pronounced her words clearly and slowly while calling the roll. She seemed to get louder when she addressed me.

"Bob, we are going to sit you on the front row so you can hear. If I say anything that you do not understand, just raise your hand. I will repeat it. OK?"

She nodded her head up and down while talking. I nodded in sync. This seemed to make her happy.

I soon discovered that my mother had visited both the principal and this teacher on a follow-up trip after my enrollment. Mother explained to them about my hearing problem. When I was younger, an ear doctor had examined me because when mother called me to the house, I would ignore her. I do not think it ever occurred to her that my hearing was fine. It just seemed that at the moment she would call me, I would be absorbed in doing something. I did not like being interrupted. When asking me if she could be heard, I would lie.

"No, ma'am."

The trick was used often. A hearing aid had been discussed, but my father was against it. He quietly looked at me with squinted, sky-blue eyes, suspicious of the whole affair.

We were not kept at school the entire day but only assigned lockers and issued books, plus other first day formalities. It was my first combination lock. I concentrated to learn which way the dial turned and memorized the combination. It was my locker, a place to keep stuff; no one else could get in, and I loved it.

With these things completed, Jerry Joe headed for the country club to check on available caddying jobs. Mike, who caddied once in a while, went along with him, mostly to see if there was a caddy's game of pitching coins that would satisfy his gambling interest.

New students were supposed to attend an orientation meeting that was being held in the library. After finally finding the library and entering, I was amazed by the many books lining the walls. Fred's Creek school had few books other than textbooks. Most were old, thick, and full of dry historic facts. The few fiction books they had were mostly donated. They included a book of short stories by Mark Twain, most of *The Bobbsey Twins* series by Laura Lee Hope, *Hopalong Cassidy* by Clarence E. Mulford, and Zane Gray's *Riders of the Purple Sage*, my favorite. I read it several times and still remember the beginning.

"A sharp clip-clop of iron-shod hoofs deadened and died away, and clouds drifted from under the cottonwoods out over the sage."

When I walked into this library, the long shelves of books made me stop and stare.

There were several new students. We eased into random seats along the rows of large, much-used tables and sat quietly, not making eye contact.

A teacher walked over, introduced herself, and explained to us how important the art of "learning to work and play well together" would be to our future. She said getting off to a good start in our new school was what we should concentrate on at the moment. Asking a lot of questions was suggested. Learning to share and waiting our turn to speak was emphasized.

With a mimeographed handout to take home, which explained how to purchase the school's accident insurance, the school's sickness and absentee policies, and a schedule for the Parent Teacher Association's meetings, the pep talk was over. We were free to leave.

I walked slowly to the door, still scanning the books, and stopped before the young teacher who was sitting at a desk beside the door, inking and stamping "Property of Boaz Library" at random on the page tops of new books taken from a stack. She finally sensed my presence and looked up with a questioning expression.

"Uh, ma'am, is there some way I could, sometime maybe come in here and read one of those books?"

Her eyes narrowed in thought, trying to understand what she heard. "New student here at Boaz?"

"Yes, ma'am."

"Where'd you move here from?" she asked.

"Fred's Creek."

She slowly began to think I was serious.

"You can come in anytime after today; we'll check out a book to you, you can keep it for one week. If you don't finish, you can keep checking it out until you do. OK?"

"Thank you, ma'am." I started to leave.

As an afterthought, she asked, "What class are you in?"

"I'm in the 9-1s," I said, proud to know my assigned class. She gave me another steady, curious look but said nothing as I smiled, slowly backing out the door.

The path I traveled back to my locker turned out to be correct. The combination worked the first time I tried it. After backtracking to the gymnasium, I bolted out the door and over the hill to the train tracks, running at a steady pace and watching so my feet would come down squarely on the cross ties.

The farther I traveled upriver, the more affluent the residential areas became. The tracks passed between the country club's back nine and the river. There was a much-used path that ran from the tracks through the rough to the fairway. I left the path to cross a couple more fairways, traveling the distance, always on the watch for golfers. The two I was looking for were sitting on a bench up the hill behind the country club's white stucco main building that sprouted green-and-black-striped cloth awnings. This was where the caddies were told to stay when waiting for a job.

Mike and Jerry Joe were practically the only ones around, since the prospects of getting a job at this time of day on Monday wasn't good—maybe a "drunksome" later on. That is what we called a group of members who were hanging around the club bar, drinking, kidding, and finally deciding to play three or four holes for a considerable sum of money. The tips were good, especially if your member won. Mike sometimes would go scout in the bar for potential drunksomes because his family was a member and he could go inside.

Jerry Joe saw me coming across the fairway and began walking back and forth in front of the bench with his knees lifting high. His neck, with protruding Adam's apple jerking, made his head go forward and back, while he flapped his arms in rhythm like wings, imitating a goose. This was an often-used comic act on his part. It was impossible not to laugh. He spent his life around a group of unpredictable drunks and had a gift for physical humor, used to disarm people. It was obvious that he could handle almost any situation.

"Hey, dumbass! Get up here! We got places to go and people to see!" he yelled my way, cupping his hands around his mouth.

We talked mostly about school, the unfair burden we thought it to be. Then we decided to go over the hill to look for lost golf balls that we could sell back to the golfers and generally passed the time by searching the tall grass running parallel to the fairways, using sticks we had found along the way. We were having a three-way sword fight when Mike stopped to scan the country club's' surroundings, which were close to empty because Monday was for most of the employees a day off.

Mike looked at both of us.

"Let's go," he said, while leading us back in the same direction that we had come from.

"What we gonna do?" I asked.

"We're going to go see Kay," Mike said. He flicked a cigarette back over the hill and started up a gravel path that led to the groundskeeper's building beside the first fairway, in the trees, hidden from golfer's view.

"Who's she?" I asked.

Jerry Joe laughed by snorting through his nose. "She's a he. Think he's got one, Mikie?"

"I'd say it probably doesn't work. Nothing else on him does. I told you about him, Bob, he's sick," Mike said.

Mike was now walking slower, looking left to right like a burglar about to pull a job. As it turned out, that is exactly what we were doing.

He reached for a pole, one of several leaning against the building's corrugated siding. Poking it into a loose flap, he pushed open the handle of the swing-out metal window, squeezed himself through, and then walked to slide open the big door on the end of the building. Mike was after one of the four golf carts that were sitting in a row and pointing out the door. Made by Harley Davidson and powered by gasoline, they were a new addition to the club. They had become a source of ill will between caddies and the club, because caddies thought the carts would take their jobs. The club was trying to keep up with modern times.

We caddies had gone on strike in protest of the carts; we stood by the club entrance and yelled at members as they drove in. A number of the caddies were in there twenties. A few were still older, so we were not the ringleaders, but we enthusiastically yelled at every opportunity. The strike lasted most of one Saturday morning. A compromise was reached. No new carts would be purchased. They were noisy and the members didn't like them anyway. We went back to work.

It was my first picket line. The caddies felt they had won. Excitement filled the air with the announcement. Some caddies were belligerent the rest of the day, but things quickly returned to normal. The experience made me feel a kinship to my grandfather, who had fought against lowered wages and for the union back in the Fred's Creek area, even though he was not a coal miner himself.

Mike motioned for us to push as he climbed into the seat to steer. We paused to slide the door closed so no one would notice the missing cart. Stopping and peeking around the corners, we made it undetected back to the footpath.

Not made for carts, the footpath was steep and rough, and when the momentum of gravity took over, Mike traveled faster, bouncing downward into a fairway. Jerry Joe and I ran behind him, laughing. We watched the hair that was combed back on the sides of Mike's head bounce up and down. The cart finally came to a stop. He reached to his back pocket and combed the hair back into its proper place.

We pushed the cart to a hiding place in the trees between the fairways. Mike raised the motor cover. After looking for a minute, he unscrewed a small bolt and held it up for us to see.

"This is the 'governor.' Keeps the carb from getting gas so it'll only go so fast." He gave a sly grin and tossed the bolt into the weeds. "Now we see what she'll really do."

Mike liked cars. He knew about engines and only went to school because of a deal struck with his parents. If he attended school regularly until he was sixteen, they would let him get a car. His parents, along with the teachers, decided he should repeat the eighth grade in the hope that he would improve academically, but if anything it made things worse. He got into more trouble, not less. Mike was a year older than me but the same age as Jerry Joe, who had been kept back for bad grades, due mostly to nonattendance. They would both be sixteen in the spring.

Mike sat back behind the wheel, adjusted the hand choke, and said, "Pull."

Jerry Joe pulled the starter cord several times. After giving it more choke, adjusting, and pulling, we were off, with me beside Mike in the seat. Jerry Joe was standing behind where the golf bags normally rode. We cut across the empty fairways and rough and headed upriver on a gravel road that ran parallel to the railroad tracks. The cart went surprisingly fast.

Jerry Joe stood on one foot, held his arms extended behind himself, and yelled over the engine noise, "I'm the hood ornament!"

Mike cut the wheel suddenly. This made Jerry Joe grab on so as not to fall. We all laughed. Life was great fun.

The road crossed the tracks. It went on down to the country club marina, located along the river, but instead of following this road, Mike turned up the actual train tracks. The balloon tires made a smacking sound when hitting the cross ties as we traveled squeezed between the rails. Something under the cart was banging on the cross ties, but it soon came loose. The engine noise became louder. We came to another road crossing and left the tracks to take this road inland and stopped facing the gate to a large fenced field that held a herd of big-bagged Holstein milk cows, covered with black-on-white pinto markings. I jumped out to handle the gate. We continued, bouncing through the field with the cows paying little attention.

Ahead was the biggest barn I had ever seen. Behind it was another, identical. We continued on, now passing a series of, white, square-bricked buildings, that combined looked like a small factory, with many pipes going in and out from one structure to another. Among the pipes I saw a sign that said Schultz Dairy. Behind one building was parked a row of milk-delivery trucks.

We were moving toward an old three-story residence. It pointed out to the distant main road with the long driveway traveling at an angle away from our sideways approach. Attached behind the house was a newer-looking addition. After another gate, Mike drove onto a road that went to the back. The addition turned out to be a metal-and-glass-enclosed swimming pool. We stopped. I followed the others as they entered through a door and into the pool area.

At one end of the pool, sitting in a small wooden Adirondack chair, was Kay, with dalmatians lying one on each side, sprawled like throw rugs. Their raised heads looked briefly at us, but we were of little interest, so they reclined again.

Describing Kay is difficult; he was short, about four feet tall, and his spine curved decidedly to one side, and that kept one shoulder perpetually higher. His legs were short, out of proportion to the puffed-out rib cage of his upper half. His high-topped brown shoes had flat soles like baby shoes, and they were left untied most of the time. He had long fingers. His thumbs were undeveloped, useless, and jiggled when he walked. His hand held a pencil between the first two fingers as he wrote, more like scrawled, some words on paper held by a clipboard. What caught the attention first was a large prominent forehead that showed tiny blue blood vessels forking beneath delicate white skin. His light brown hair was combed forward and cut into bangs.

"Where the hell you people been? We got stuff to do. You know that?" He looked at me. "Who are you?"

"Bob."

He made a dramatic flourish with his arm. "What'd you bring him for?"

"He just came," Mike said. "When did you finally get back?"

"Yesterday."

Kay had spent much of his life in hospitals, some overseas, but most of the time at and around the Cleveland Clinic, sort of home base for decisions as to what to do with him next. He needed periodic operations to stay alive. At birth the doctors had told Mr. and Mrs. Schultz that he would not see his sixth birthday; he was now fourteen.

"When do you go back?" Mike asked.

"I ain't goin' back because I overheard the quacks saying they did all they can do." He looked at each of us and said with casual finality, "I'm a goner, fellas." Then he added, "I'm starting a professional football team. You interested? Jerry Joe, you're big, pretty fast, how about it?"

"How much I gonna make?" Coaches at school wanted Jerry Joe to play sports. He could dunk a dodge ball because it was small enough for a firm grip. Obviously, the basketball would soon follow. But the idea of attending practice, doing all of that work without pay, made no sense to him, so he grinned and shook his head and said, "I gotta go caddy." That was that.

"I'll have to see you run the hundred yards though, and throw a few passes first," Kay said.

Kay pulled a new stopwatch from the front pocket of the bib overalls that he wore all the time because his almost nonexistent waist would not support regular pants. He showed the watch to each of us. His eyes narrowed when he looked at me.

"You ever play any football? Son!" Kay sprayed spittle when talking loud, which was often. I had just learned not to stand directly in front of him.

"Some," I said, casually wiping my face, although my exposure to sports, or at least to sports that use a ball, was limited. Most activity in Fred's Creek had to do with fishing or hunting and gathering.

"He's got a gun," Mike said.

"I got three guns," I corrected.

"I meant the pistol," Mike said.

"You got a pistol? Let me see!" Kay said.

It was my first bit of respect. I was crestfallen to admit that it wasn't with me.

"What the hell good is it if you don't have it with you? What if you had to shoot somebody? What then? Huh?"

"We go to the river and shoot it sometimes; you can go next time," Mike said. "Come on outside, we want to show you something."

The prospect of shooting seemed to overcome his cynicism, but he ignored Mike and went back to football, discussing his new professional team. They would be called the Boaz Browns. It was obvious that he had given the project much thought.

He finally turned on his belly and slid awkwardly from the chair while still talking. He headed outside by leaning his body forward and churning his legs to keep up, holding his arms out for balance. He moved like a penguin. Over his bib overalls was a black jacket with the name "Browns" sewn onto the back in orange cloth letters, a result of attending Cleveland Brown's football games. It had made Kay a big fan.

The dogs suddenly jumped up, prancing along beside him, making noise when their nails struck the cement encircling the pool. Kay went around the pool, banged against the exit door that had no latch, and went through still talking. Looking over and seeing how we had arrived made him stop. He stood still for a second, then began waving his arms and pointing.

"Uh-oh, I know where that come from!" he sprayed.

"We just borrowed it, a little while," Mike said, grinning about as much as he ever did. Jerry Joe did his snort laugh. I laughed too, as proud as if I actually had something to do with it.

"Let's go!" Kay said.

To save time, Jerry Joe picked Kay up by the underarms and sat him in the middle of the seat between Mike and me. We headed back the way we came. Kay had a gravelly voice except when he laughed. It then jumped to a high falsetto. He squealed with laughter while holding tightly to the round chrome bar running across the dash of the cart.

A round person of about thirty or so, wearing a dirty khaki uniform and a three-day beard, was walking from the first barn to the second. He grinned from ear to ear when he saw us coming.

"Vernon, come to the club, pick us up. If you tell anybody, we'll kick your pussy willow ass!" Kay said, with the ease of command that came from ordering older people around his entire life.

Vernon nodded. He changed directions and headed toward the old car that was sitting in a driveway beside the barn. He lived on the farm with his twin brother, the car's co-owner. Their mother worked at the main house.

We headed out and around the cow field. Mike held the engine wide open. We were traveling fast when I caught a glimpse out of the corner of my eye of something black and white running beside us. I thought for a second that it was a cow but glanced over to see the dogs keeping up

"Come on, Otto. Come on, Lou!" Kay shouted their names.

We were back traveling downriver on the railroad tracks, after several trips around the field, when Kay wanted to drive. The wheels had no clearance between the rails and were actually touching on each side. Even if he wanted to, Kay could not drive off the tracks

16

until the next road crossing up ahead, where the tracks were buried level with the road to allow automobiles across.

Mike sat with his foot on the gas pedal. Kay guided the tires back and forth between the rails, pretending he was in a parade, laughing, and waving to an imaginary crowd.

The engine sputtered, went a bit farther, sputtered again, and did a nosedive. It rolled to a sudden, quiet stop.

"Probably the gas," Mike said. We watched while he broke off a weed and stuck it into the tank. When it came out dry, he said, "We'll move it off here and walk; it's not that far."

We three lifted, and straining, could almost get the back tires above the rails, but the front end, with the engine, was much heavier. It would not budge; it was like trying to lift an automobile.

Kay sat behind the wheel with his arms folded, making a pouting face, but finally giving in to the inevitable, he held his arms up. Jerry Joe reached down and lifted Kay into his own arms like Kay was a ventriloquist's doll. We had gone a few steps on the tracks when the dogs sensed the problem first, giving a whine almost in unison. They glanced in Kay's direction. Jerry Joe, up ahead, looked around. Using Kay as a pointer, he indicated down the tracks. Now we all were aware that a train was coming.

"We have got to hide!" Mike said.

He pointed to the weeds on the up-sloping side of the tracks and began heading that way. I started too fast. One of my feet lost traction on the round river gravel that was lining the bed of the tracks. Regaining my footing seemed to take forever. That made me the last one into the tall late-summer weeds. We sat, not moving or talking; all eyes were glued to the black steam engine belching a plume and coming on fast. Even the dogs instinctively felt some impending doom. They sat quietly beside us with their heads held low.

It happened like catching a fly with your bare hand. You see it sitting. Swipe at it and it disappears. You don't know if you caught it or it flew away, but we knew the golf cart was caught. The only remaining sign after the surprisingly quiet "poof" heard over the noise of the engine was a loose wheel with tire that bounced about as high as the trailing open cars that were piled high with coal. The cart had disappeared.

A long silence followed. Jerry Joe started giggling, and then laughing.

He said, "I ain't had so much fun since the hogs ate my little brother."

He did not have a hog or a little brother. We all had heard him say it before, but right now it was funny.

I was walking, laughing with tears in my eyes, shaking involuntarily, and holding my jaw clinched to keep my teeth from chattering and was glad that no one was noticing. I stuffed my hands into my pockets so no one would start noticing. We walked on to the club, laughing, shaking our heads, and being amazed.

Then occasionally Kay would yell, "Poof!" The laughing would start again.

For all his bravado, Kay had limited stamina. He tended to be either on or off, pacing himself, summoning up a burst of energy when needed. We made our way very carefully to the club parking area, in order not to be identified and connected with the incident. We quickly loaded into the waiting automobile, staying low inside, while Vernon drove out the front gate slowly. He was whistling. Kay, Jerry Joe, and the dogs were in the backseat with the now-curious dogs hanging their heads over the front seat, drooling on the rest of us. Kay ordered Vernon to get home quickly. He needed a shot. Kay received shots for pain.

Vernon stopped in back of the house at the swimming pool door. We all piled out.

"Vern, you didn't hear nothin', see nothin', and you don't say nothin', understand?" Kay said.

Kay was slapping a palm with the back of his other hand for emphasis, while we all stood at the parked car. Kay was stiffly bent back so he could look up at Vernon, who had become aware that there was a problem about the golf cart, but he was not exactly sure what.

"And don't smell nothin," Jerry Joe said.

Kay turned to Jerry Joe with a mean look. The rest of us snickered. We all went inside and walked around the pool and into a large kitchen that had two adjoining big, black stoves that were fit for a restaurant. Assorted large copper pots and pans were hanging from the long rack attached to the ceiling.

Veada, Vernon's mother, was sitting at a wooden desk in the corner of the kitchen, sipping coffee in the quiet house. Her face was lined. She sat still, like a person who physically worked hard, with a contented look and no wasted motion.

"You all want somethin' to eat?" she said.

"Got any ice cream?" Jerry Joe asked.

"We got some. Chocolate?"

"Yeah." Jerry Joe looked at us.

We, along with Vernon, nodded our heads in agreement, while Kay walked on through the kitchen without speaking. Veada reached for the desk telephone and called the nurse to meet Kay in his room.

"Go on, sit in the dinin' room," Veada said to us.

We paraded through a large dark door, hinged to swing both ways, and into an area with an elaborate mahogany dining table. It was centered in a long, tall, and somewhat narrow room. Veada flipped a switch that brought to life the electric lights hidden under globes in the chandelier, which hung at the exact center of the table. The table stood bare except for white cloth doily placemats lying in front of each of the many chairs. The four of us sat across from one another at the end closest to the swinging door.

There were several black-and-white pictures carefully arranged to line the wall behind my chair. I turned to look at them. Close to me, in a dark wooden frame, hung a picture of a dozen or so men posed with a team of draft horses. Cleats extended from their horseshoes. They were harnessed to a sled and standing on the frozen river.

The men held a variety of large saws and tongs, stiffly positioned in front of their chests, posing for the camera. The picture reminded me of stories I had heard of how my great-grandfather had often left Fred's Creek to find work. One of those jobs was cutting ice from the river. I moved closer and looked more carefully and was struck by the uniform serious expression on the men's faces.

They all had full drooping mustaches except for one person in the back, who was holding nothing and leaning casually against one of the poles attached to the wide wooden runners of the sled. His light hair, reaching almost to his shoulders, was hanging from under an old, dark snap-brimmed hat, turned down. He was warmly smiling and looking directly into the camera. An unlit, homemade, oblong cigarette hung from the side of his mouth.

Veada backed through the door with a tray holding stemmed pewter goblets piled with chocolate ice cream. She served them in a serious manner after first removing the doily placemats in front of us and replacing them with long spoons on heavy, brown cloth napkins.

"What's that picture of?" I asked, pointing to the picture of the men and horses when she came around to me.

"That's one a the Schultz business things they did—cut ice. They'd cover it with wood chips from the sawmills and put it up in the caves till summer, and then they'd sell it. The 'frigerator came along and stopped them from cuttin' ice, so they built a icehouse," she said with a laugh.

"I thought so," I said. The fellow smiling in the picture looked familiar, but I could not place him as anyone I knew. We started on the ice cream.

Kay came in and walked by a serving cart stored in a corner. Without slowing down, he grabbed a large cushion from one of the lower shelves. He stopped at the chair on our end of the table, placed the cushion on the chair to raise himself to a respectable level, and climbed up with some help from the chair rungs and Veada. He then scooted around till he faced the front.

"You want some water or somethin'?" Veada asked him.

"Water," he answered and waited for her to leave the room. "Now, we been in this house all afternoon if anybody asks. That's our alibi. You got it?"

We all nodded. He did not discuss the golf cart much after that because Veada stayed within earshot. Kay started in about his new football team again.

His seat at the end of the table positioned him under a full-length painting of a man dressed in a grass-green military uniform of the late 1700s, with large gold buttons and epaulets. He stood at parade rest, with his right hand tucked behind his back and left hand resting on the hilt of a large sheathed sword, attached to his waist by a wide cummerbund. The vest, tight pants, and cummerbund were bone color. A pair of dark-brown riding boots rose to his knees and were ringed at the top by wide black leather bands.

Veada came back with the water for Kay. She stood close to me.

"Who's that?" I asked under my breath, pointing, while Kay talked on.

"That'd be Kay's great-granddaddy."

"He was in the army?" I asked.

"No, the uniform was s'pose to be just for fun. Kay's grandmother and uncle had it painted."

"Adopted uncle! Adopted step-uncle, I think," Kay said.

"No, just adopted," Veada corrected, laughing. "They got together and traced the Schultz family back to a Schultz that came with the Germans to fight for England in the revolutionary war. They said the name Schultz came from the person who rode in front of the army and carried the flag on a long spear. In Germany, a long time ago, they called the spear a Schultz."

"Prussians or Hessians or something. Not German!" Kay turned his body to look at everyone individually, for emphasis.

"I thought he was a blacksmith?" Jerry Joe said with a sly grin, knowing that Kay thought that blacksmith was too common a job title to be given to his ancestor.

"He was a farrier! They're the same as a veterinarian is today, and they put on horseshoes too," Kay said. "You people need to understand that a person who carried the flag at the head of an army was called the Schultz," Kay said, in a way that suggested that we should already know this information.

Veada continued the story with occasional interruptions from Kay. She was happy at having someone new to listen to this, what she considered interesting history.

The story was told. A mercenary army hired by England to fight the colonial upstarts recruited the original Schultz. His job was to take care of the horses. He traveled from Germany with the army. The mercenaries were defeated at Trenton, and this enterprising original Schultz quickly got a job with the Continental Army, taking care of their horses. When the war ended, he was given a small land grant for his good service and walked across the mountains carrying his deed. From Pittsburgh he traveled down the Ohio on a raft that he helped some like-minded people build.

He found his land, sold it for a good price, and was walking the shoreline back upriver when he entered into a place that is now the town of Sharpsburg. He decided to buy a horse to make his trip back East shorter. Before he could leave, he sold the horse for a profit and inadvertently became a dealer in horses, then cattle, and finally anything else that people wanted to buy or sell. He eventually married. His grandson built a livestock holding pen on purchased land that was overlooking the river. The land was today still in the Schultz name and still held a functioning stockyard business, but was now leased out to others.

Kay's grandmother, with research help from Kay's adopted uncle, hired an artist from Cincinnati to paint the flattering likeness of Kay's great-grandfather. She asked that the German uniform be added because of his immigrant Schultz ancestor.

They learned during the research that the original Schultz had such a lowly job with the armies that his chance of wearing a uniform was slim to none. The uniform was finally added anyway, by Kay's grandmother, as a light-hearted afterthought while having dinner with the painter.

At first the old man did not care for the uniform, but over time he warmed to it. In the end, because of admiring comments from business associates visiting from New York, he liked it more than he would admit.

"Ever'body called him 'King Kay' behind his back, but not to his face because he'd not like it." Veada said.

"You ever see him?" I asked, trying to put time into prospective.

"Lord yes, he hired my husband on the farm when he was a young boy and my husband always said, 'He raised me from a pup.' When we married, I started up this job here in the house. Some say he was a hard man, but he was fair to us," she added in an honest fashion.

"Said he didn't like the uniform making him look like he was fightin' against George Washington is what they tell me about it," Kay added.

Things rambled after that: Kay, Jerry Joe, and I, crawled under the table so Kay could show me how he and Jerry Joe pretended to camp out when they were very young, by draping sheets and pretending that under the table was the inside of a tent. Their names, along with a number of crude stick pictures, were scrawled on the underside of the table in assorted crayon colors.

Jerry Joe talked Vernon into giving us a ride because it was time for Vernon to pick up his twin brother, Herky. At the mayor's request, Herky was on loan from the farm to the city of Boaz. Kay's father had sent him to work as a janitor and handyman at the city hall in an attempt to keep the city's budget in check.

Jerry Joe got out at the Texaco station to visit. I rode to the entrance of Maplewood where Vernon made a U-turn to head back upriver.

I went in our front door and on to the kitchen.

"How was school?" Mother asked.

"OK."

"What did you do today?"

"Not much."

"Where are your books?"

"In my school locker."

"Well, don't you have lessons to get?"

"Not the first day, Mom."

"I expect to see some tomorrow. Now get washed up quickly, your father will be home in a minute. You almost missed supper."

"Yes, ma'am." I walked to the bathroom, past my two younger brothers who were on their bellies in the front room. Their hands propped up their chins as they watched television.

Day Two

This morning, walking to the entrance of Maplewood subdivision, there were three plans from which to choose. One was the same as yesterday: over the hill, pick up Jerry Joe, and head upriver to school. Two, I could stand with the other kids, wait for the school bus, and ride upriver to school. The third was traveling the few miles downriver to Sharpsburg by riding the City-Lines bus. They ran every thirty minutes at this time in the morning; the cost was ten cents. Another option when choosing Sharpsburg as a destination was hitchhiking, but that would break one of Mother's rules.

"Someone might knock you in the head." Hitchhiking to save the ten cents would be my personal choice, but this morning, to avoid potential trouble at home and also at my new school, I decided to wait for the school bus.

Sharpsburg was a much bigger town than Boaz. It had a number of new manufacturing plants. Some of these factories made chemicals. My father had been at one of the chemical plants for a few years now. He had started work the day it opened. Sharpsburg straddled the mouth of the Big Piney River where it flowed into the Ohio. The area had its first permanent European residents around 1750.

If you floated down Fred's Creek, it emptied into the Big Piney. Several more miles of fast-flowing water would bring you to

Sharpsburg, at the Ohio River. This "floating trip" is something I was planning to do someday, to emulate my grandfather's trip years ago atop one of the rafts of timbered logs that were guided by men riding along on top. They floated the logs on river currents to be sold as far away as Cincinnati or Louisville.

Boaz would today be called a bedroom community. Many of the more affluent people making a living from businesses or factories in Sharpsburg lived in Boaz to escape the noise, mess, and stink the factories were creating. There was a small marginally middle-class population living in Boaz. Maplewood subdivision would count as a growing addition to this group. The subdivision was built on what had previously been agricultural land. This brought a sprawling Boaz closer to Sharpsburg. But in general, the people of Boaz were either rich or poor.

Many middle-class people do not understand the symbiotic relationship between the rich and poor. The two groups have a mutual economic need, and to some extent, an emotional need, that neither would easily admit. In addition to this, they make each other's lives interesting and sometimes in ways that neither cares for. My family was the beginning of the horde of burgeoning middle class that would infest the entire region in only a few years. It would apply a strain to this generations-old economic symmetry.

I bounced up the bus steps and slid into a window seat for a view in the direction of the railroad tracks that ran down below, across the oncoming traffic. The river was out beyond. A girl in my 9-1s class slid quickly onto the seat beside me.

"Ywour Bwob," she said, using a matter-of-fact tone. I nodded, looking sideways in her direction, not knowing what to say. She didn't live in Maplewood's new houses but on a hill that rose quickly behind. She was one of about six or seven children who were thin and about a year apart. They all had carrot-colored hair, thick, unruly, and parted in the middle. Another distinguishing characteristic was the many large freckles on pale skin.

Exploring my home's surrounding area, climbing this hill, I had discovered a few houses randomly scattered along the hillside. They were wooden structures, old and small, and most had matching washtubs hanging on nails beside the front door.

She continued watching me intently with pale blue eyes that were set close together over a pug nose. One nostril was wet. To avoid her stare, I looked out the window.

The bus pulled back out onto the road. From the window I could see the "Trampman" walking upriver on the tracks. His name was Garvin. He had an arm missing and often carried a burlap bag slung over his shoulder. He stayed, sometimes, in the house at the opposite end of the row from where Jerry Joe, his mother, and Cecil lived. Occasionally local children were told that if they were not good, the Trampman would catch and stuff them into his bag, and they'd never be seen again.

He and Cecil drank together. They discussed the world, mostly with Cecil listening while sucking long draws from a cigarette at the corner of his mouth. Garvin would talk on about man's plight on earth, with his beard-covered chin pointing out in a defiant manner. The black beard grew high on his cheeks almost up to his dark eyes. He wore, most of the time, an army-colored baseball-style hat that was pulled down tightly to just above his ears. It made the hair growing down his neck stick out.

The bus turned onto the short street separating the Texaco station from the school. It continued to the rounded unloading area located in the parking lot behind the building. We left the bus and walked as a group to the back entrance.

The same girl, now walking beside me, said, "Gwood-bwy, Bwob."

For some reason a strange nervous jumping sensation started in my stomach when she mispronounced my name.

I mumbled "OK" and walked to my locker, keeping my eyes on the floor in front of my feet.

It would be just Mike and me today. We figured that Jerry Joe had gone on to the country club. It was Ladies Day and plenty of caddying jobs should be available. I had time to again locate the library, because the bus schedule made us arrive early. I moved along the rows, slowly studying the books, till I heard the bell for homeroom. Then walking to the front desk, I signed my name carefully on the card, taking solemn responsibility for the chosen one. I had pulled from the shelf

James Fenimore Cooper's *The Deerslayer.* I hurried to homeroom and began reading.

This morning the teacher left me alone, spending her energy on the rowdy laughing group that included an occasional shriek from my carrot-headed friend, who was sitting directly behind me. She turned first one way, then the other, to take in all the action. Mike sat in the back, reading the *Hotrod Magazine* that he had been carrying rolled in his back pocket, while occasionally combing his hair. I had to sit up front, one of the drawbacks of my "hearing problem."

Before the bell rang signaling us to move on to our first-period class, in came the principal. Our homeroom teacher announced his arrival with great importance, as though he were a visiting dignitary.

He said, "Good morning, class. For the next two days we are going to be giving a test to all the ninth graders, including you people. I must say to you that you do not have to study for it, so you mustn't be afraid," he said with a laugh. The teacher, following his lead, laughed. The girl who had followed him into the room, holding in her arms the stack of tests and in both hands many sharpened pencils, leaned back and laughed loudest.

"Penny, will you hand out the tests, please?" the principal directed.

"Yes, sir." The girl pushed her glasses back on her nose with her wrist. She quickly began the process, with the seriousness of an usher passing church communion. After the tests were distributed, she held up one of the pencils.

"Please use this especially designed pencil so that the grading will be correctly done."

"Yes, yes, I must tell you, this is called an intelligence quotient test," said the principal. He moved his praying hands from under his long chin and pointed them, still together, at the class in a practiced manner.

"Education has made great strides. We here at Boaz Junior High School are staying abreast of these developments and are making these remarkable things available to you, our students."

He suddenly walked to the kid sitting beside me, pushing back shut the test booklet he was thumbing through.

"No, no, Mortie, do not open until we say time!" Retreating, he walked backwards, awkwardly moving big feet and glancing behind himself. After a last quick bouncing sideways step, he continued, "We will complete one-half of the test today and the additional one-half tomorrow morning. Scientific studies say we all think best in the morning hours, so we will take full advantage of this knowledge." He laughed again, followed by the teacher and assistant.

"Penny," he said, "is a student assistant from the 9-5s." He indicated her by the movement of his hands. She gave a slight bow. "She will be here to bring you a new pencil; if needed, that is. I might add, the questions are in different order on different tests, so looking on your neighbor will bring only the incorrect answer."

Explanations completed, he left our homeroom teacher holding her wristwatch in front of her face for a dramatic moment. She jerked it down.

"Begin!"

Staring at the booklet, I gingerly flipped it open: $7 + 4 - Y = 2$ was accompanied by four possible answers. I was immediately convinced that it must be a misprint. They had put a letter in a math problem. I stared, $7 + 4 = 11$. If you take 2 away, that's 9. There was a 9 and 13 among the answers. I chose 9 and darkened the circle. Then I attempted to figure out some of the other problems, guessing at the rest.

"Word Meaning" was the next section. I felt better about choosing the definitions closest to the word given. The kid beside me picked at a sore on his arm with the special pencil. Most of the other students looked around giggling. Mike was off in another world, sitting in the back row reading his magazine, with the test unopened.

There was eventually a break in the test. Everyone escaped to the restrooms. Penny stopped patrolling the aisles. She had been walking her beat with hands clasped behind her back, casually rolling up onto the ball of her foot with each slow step.

She quickly moved beside the classroom door to scrutinize those exiting, looking carefully at each student—checking for the unauthorized removal of test copies. This was followed by a close count of the unfinished booklets on each desk.

Natural curiosity is the only answer I can give for me trying on the test instead of daydreaming out the window as was my usual approach to this sort of thing. Even with breaks, we completed the first half of the test before lunch. The teacher let us talk among ourselves. When the volume inevitably rose, she would look up from entering names in her black grade book to say, "Caution!"

Lunchtime finally arrived. Mike and I were heading across the main street to Stanley's Drive-in Restaurant so we could stand in line at the walk-up window. Before crossing the road, a new black Buick slowed to a stop in the yellow No Stopping Zone. The crosswalk guards were students and wearing school issued AAA badges. None of them were from the 9-1s. They motioned for the car to drive on. Their arm movements became more emphatic, and soon they began blowing whistles.

"Shut up!" Kay shouted out the window from the backseat. He waved for us to get in. Mike slid in next to Jerry Joe, who was sitting beside Vernon, the driver. I took the back seat with Kay, pulling the door shut.

"What you doin' here?" Kay asked me. Getting used to him, I just shrugged a silent answer. We pulled away, traveling in a downriver Sharpsburg direction and began discussing the golf cart incident.

Kay was holding his hands with palms pointed out, about as high as he could raise them, moving them out, then in, to emphasize the points.

"If we just shut up, don't say nothing to nobody, it'll all blow over! Vernon, you keep your mouth shut too, do you hear me?"

Vernon looked in the rearview mirror and nodded and grinned, showing yellowed buckteeth, until his eyes were almost shut. He smelled faintly of cow manure as always.

"See this guy here?" Kay said to Vernon, pointing at me, "He's got a gun and he'd druther shoot you as look at you!"

Never before being the bad guy, I felt an involuntary mean look spread on my face.

"Show him your gun," Kay urged.

"It's home," I said.

Kay leaned over and started slapping at me. I put my arm up to block the attack, but his attention quickly turned to things he thought more important.

Vernon was lazy. Like all genuinely lazy people, he remained unperturbed by verbal abuse. He possessed a clear picture of who buttered his bread. He would grin, nod, agree, and do what he was going to do in the first place, nothing. He smoked if handed a cigarette and drank under the same circumstances. The only things he spent any effort acquiring were the candy bars that he lived on almost exclusively. He could tolerate Kay with little effort, something most adults could do only for short periods. Vernon had become, by default, the one looking after Kay when the highly paid nurse was having one of her many long, quiet breaks in a third floor apartment back at the farm.

The rest of Vernon's time was spent in the barns with the cows that he seemed to genuinely care for. He gave each a name, even if they did have numbers branded on their hips. He had calved most of the herd personally. Vernon's father had been for many years the hardworking foreman of the farm's dairy operations. He was found dead one evening sitting in his barn office. The doctor said he died of the progressive diabetes that he refused to have treated.

We rode along. Jerry Joe had caddied earlier, eavesdropping on the women golfers chatting about the golf cart incident. The caddy master thought it was related to the summer strike. Jerry Joe picked up no clues that anyone suspected us to be responsible for the "vandalism." We were vandals.

This report gave us all a feeling of relief, then Kay went on to explain today's mission—why we were traveling down the road to Sharpsburg—without bothering to ask any of us if we would like to go along.

Acquiring uniforms was the reason for the trip. Football uniforms for Kay's Boaz Browns football team, or more realistically, numbered T-shirts with the team's name. They were to resemble Kay's Cleveland Browns jacket as closely as possible. We were headed to Della Culpepper's house to negotiate her services in their making.

Della was Jerry Joe's great-aunt. Della had taken responsibility for Jerry Joe's mother when Della's younger sister suddenly disappeared, never to be heard from again. Jerry Joe was born soon after to this young daughter of Della's missing sister.

Jerry Joe considered Della to be more of a mother, and his mother, being so young, became more like a sister. He still spent nights with Della when it was convenient.

She took in sewing for a living, among other things. During her younger years, she lived in Boaz, down along the river, working as a domestic. This meant she cleaned the houses around the country club. She still road the bus to Boaz, working special event parties at the country club. For some people she still worked private parties at their homes. She now lived in Sharpsburg, in a part of town close to the river, and had a small well-kept house on the border between what was considered a bad neighborhood and an almost-bad neighborhood. The next street over was called Bloody Row by most, named for some long-past occurrences.

She fixed hair without a beautician's license and sold half pints of liquor out of an alley window till late at night. This, of course, was also without a license. Occasionally she rented out the spare bedroom but only when money was tight. Her hair was dyed about the color of a beet. It did not match her green eyes, but the hair did match her fingernail polish. A chain smoker with stained fingers, she lit one cigarette from the last.

While Kay and Della argued over how long it would take to make the uniforms, Jerry Joe looked at me and grinned, making his eyes jump up and down. Then slowly and smoothly, from his seat in the chair by the window where Della sat at night to sell her wares, he pulled a half pint from beneath a round table that was covered by a low-hanging tablecloth, where many more bottles were discreetly stored. He slowly pushed the small, narrow bottle deep into a back pocket.

Kay had known Della all his life. In fact, she was present when Kay was born. Jerry Joe was less than a year old when the event happened. Della and family were living at the farm. As part of her job, she watched the two boys play together when Kay was home from the hospitals.

One day she and Veada got into a fight about who would do which job. Della went to Kay's father. At her insistence, he moved the Culpeppers to the house where she now lived.

Della and Kay argued back then. They were arguing now. She said she would start on the uniforms today, but it would cost more for a "rush job." Kay started squealing like he was hurt.

She shook her head and looked at me. "You got to quit runnin' with these two, that one is crazy," she said, pointing to Jerry Joe, who sat making an exaggerated face like his feelings were hurt. "And this one here is meaner'n snot!" she continued, while giving a quick jerk of her thumb at Kay.

I had met her a time or two during the course of the summer when traveling with Jerry Joe and Mike on trips to Sharpsburg for a movie or to play pool and go roller-skating, or sometimes when we were broke, just to walk around and watch about anything that happened to be going on. During one visit she fed us boiled new potatoes with gravy and sweet ice tea. It was good.

"My granddaddy was from up to Fred's Creek, you know," she told me. I had heard the story before during my summer visits, but I nodded my head like it was interesting news.

"He never was around much, Grandmomma said. But she always told us that he brought her flowers. Grandmomma thought he was 'hot shit.' Momma did too, but I guess he finally quit comin' around."

"Quit jawin', let's get this deal done. I got more important things to do!" Kay yelled, bouncing in his chair.

"All you got to do is find someone to wipe your butt like I use to!"

"Get me your gun, Bob. I'll take care of her my own self!"

I was not in the habit of hearing such loud threats. Talk of this sort in Fred's Creek culture would indicate the start of a serious fight. My instinct to hide was overcome with better judgment when it became obvious that everyone, including Mike, was laughing. The bargain was almost struck. Kay argued that he needed the uniforms this evening. She said in a few days, with the added rush charge. They finally agreed on two or three days, but each still complained about the other's stubbornness.

We left with both still grumbling and drove along the narrow alley that ended when it stopped at Market Street, which was considered Sharpsburg's main drag. Market Street ended in a downhill direction when it came to the river. There stood a large dock, equipped with a coal-loading bridge-like structure that had railroad tracks. The coal cars, with trap doors in the bottom, could be pulled across the bridge. Each car in turn would be opened to drop coal directly into the barges.

We turned away from the river and went uphill on Market Street, approaching the beginning of the commercial district. It included on this lower end Pinky's Pool Hall. We pulled into the Lucky Strike Bowling Alley's parking lot, located across the street from Pinky's. Several times, Jerry Joe had suggested the bowling alley as a place we should stop to eat lunch. Up further ahead on one side of the street was the seven-story Sharpsburg Savings and Loan, the tallest building in town. It stood across from the Blenhime Hotel, the second-largest building in town.

As we approached the parking lot, Kay had this sudden idea that he would hire me as his personal bodyguard and also as a player on his football team. He questioned Jerry Joe about my athletic abilities.

Jerry Joe said, "He runs about as fast as anybody can."

Kay slyly explained to me that if I would start carrying my pistol, which he decided he wanted to go shoot, he would hire me. I would be paid for two jobs.

All during his explanation we made our way inside to a table overlooking the bowling lanes. We sat eating, watching the few people who were bowling at this time of day. When crowded, it was a noisy place, and even more so when you considered the roller rink on the second floor that would open later in the day. Kay waited until Vernon had put ketchup and mustard on his french fries. Still talking about football recruiting, he became excited and inadvertently spread the mixture all around his face, hair, and clothing. You could not watch Kay eat.

Mike ducked a french fry launched from between Kay's fingers.

Kay yelled, "Shut up, pimple farm!" He talked with his mouth full.

They continued to argue. Vernon sat with his face bent close to his banana split. Jerry Joe had other things on his mind, and picking up a milkshake, he motioned for me to follow him to the well-worn stairs at the front of the building, located just inside the entrance. At the top stood a big door. He knocked several times. We listened for footsteps.

Finally it was opened by a girl with dark brown hair that was combed something like Mike's, without the oil or flattop. The hair on top and down around to the sides was swept straight back. It all came to a point about where the back of her neck began. She was wearing a white T-shirt with the sleeves rolled up a couple of turns. One sleeve, up almost on her shoulder, bulged with a pack of Camels that was showing through the stretched material.

Her name was Gloria. The best way to describe Gloria is to say that she was two or three years older than Jerry Joe, head over heels in love with him, and was always glad when he came by the skating rink where she worked. When not working, she came looking for him in her car, sometimes along with a hefty fellow employee named Linda. The four of us would go for rides. Big stuff for a kid like me who still had a bicycle with handlebar streamers.

Neither of them said anything. Jerry Joe and I walked behind her, watching well-defined legs and hips pushing against tight blue jeans, legs made solid by many trips around the rink while policing rowdy young skaters. She lifted a leg to sit straddle of the bench in a tightly packed screened room that smelled of feet mixed with shoe polish. It had rounded windows that opened out to the public. She resumed polishing a pair of shoe skates, taken from the rows hanging on the wall, sorted by size. She dabbed from a tin, rubbing a circle of black polish with her bare fingers.

She was being casual.

"What's goin' on?" she asked, thinking he was going to borrow money like he did sometimes when the caddying jobs slowed. She would give it to him. Today he only bummed a cigarette.

"Why ain't you two in school?" she asked.

"Lunch," Jerry Joe said.

He sat the chocolate milkshake on the window counter and laid the cigarette on the bench in front of her, with the lit end hanging out over the edge, and pulled the liberated half-pint from his back pocket to remove the top.

Jerry Joe was a kid like me and would jump around like a monkey just to make people laugh, but when it came to taking a sip of whiskey; he took a quick nip like a seasoned veteran. After the nip, he wiped his mouth with a finger and handed it slowly my way without looking. Emulating him, I secretly used my tongue to plug the bottleneck in order to keep it from running into my mouth. This would avoid the coughing incident that usually came when I tried to drink the stuff. I knew his offer could not be refused, or it would give an unmanly impression to Gloria.

With the taste on the end of my tongue, I tried not to make a face.

Acting as adult as possible, I said, "We might be goin' to shoot my gun, directly, up at the caves."

Gloria looked up at Jerry Joe from under thick, unplucked eyebrows that almost grew together. She blushed, and then looked out the door and off across the empty skating floor to the platform holding the organ where Sammy, the manager, played for the weekend patrons.

"Any women goin'?" she asked, still looking off.

"May be," Jerry Joe said.

She jumped up quickly and punched his arm a good blow. He staggered back, pretending to be hurt. We all three laughed. Jerry Joe returned the bottle to his back pocket and picked up the cigarette that had been knocked to the floor.

A few weeks earlier, on a Sunday afternoon, Gloria and her friend Linda had been sitting on the curb of the service area parking lot, behind the country club. Jerry Joe and I were finishing a caddying job. Walking down the eighteenth fairway, we saw them waving. We waved back and were embarrassed when a golfer said, "Who's that?"

When we finished with the golfers and came over to talk, they displayed for our approval bottles of pop, potato chips, and smiles with lipstick. A quick unanimous decision was made to go for a drive in her old car that routinely needed the hood raised. The battery cables had to be jiggled before it would start. Our undiscussed destination became the caves.

"The caves" is a geological formation located upriver from Boaz, where the hill descends rapidly, almost straight to the river, except for an enormous, flat boulder sitting mostly in the water. It could be walked out upon. A person walking across the boulder could drop rocks straight down, where they would hit the flowing water about six stories below. Most visitors would just sit and have a panoramic view of the river bending in both directions and observe the frequent boats, most pushing a long line of coal barges.

If you walked along the nearby road that ran uphill, the trip would end at a long level area. There were three individual cave entrances, and each went a long distance back down into the hillside where they eventually intertwined. This area was located about two miles above the Schultz Dairy and Kay's house. You could see while standing on the boulder the Boaz water tower downriver, rising in the distance. Kay's family owned this land. Herky, Vernon's brother, came by periodically to pick up the trash, and Kay's father was in the process of deeding this land to the state to be used for a park, on the advice of his lawyers, fearing liability.

We parked, then sat in the car to talk, and drank the pop and passed around the potato chips. Jerry Joe and Gloria disappeared down out of sight in the front seat. Linda, I guess since I just sat there, draped her strong forearm around my neck. She started kissing.

One or two unavoidable games of spin the bottle was about the extent of my romantic adventures. Even then, when the bottle pointed to me, there was a walk to a private darkened room for the kissing. Noises began coming from the front seat, drawing my attention. Linda, outweighing me by fifty pounds, moved my hand so it lay on her breast. The hand along with the rest of me began trembling. She stopped kissing and looked at me.

Then she leaned over to whisper, "Let's go out and sit on the rock."

I gulped, whispering back, "OK."

She did not mention the shaking. I was grateful for that. Then, for a lack of anything else to say, I began telling her about the place where we were sitting. The information came from one of the old state history books at Fred's Creek school.

The Shawnee used this vantage point to spot the settlers' boats coming down the river. They would signal hidden canoes that held up to twenty warriors each. The warriors would converge, capturing the people on board. A few they scalped, others they kept to work as slaves and then traded them at a later date for the return of captured warriors. Some of the people captured decided after a time to stay, and became members of the tribe. I was jabbering.

I explained to her what the name Shawnee meant, but I had not read about this in the book. Uncle Lester told me. His grandmother was Cherokee. She had told him that the Cherokee and Shawnee didn't get along, a dispute over hunting land.

When the first exploring Europeans asked the Cherokee, "Who lives over there?" The Cherokee answered, "Shawnee."

At that time the Native Americans did not attach names to themselves as a collective group, because they knew who they were. It seemed silly to invent words for something already obvious to everyone present. So when asked, the Cherokee answered the explorers, using the name they called the people across the river, "Shawnee."

It means, roughly translated, "People who do not know who is the father."

Uncle Lester's grandmother would laugh at the joke that her people had made. When asked what Cherokee meant, she would never answer.

Linda liked the part about the name, seemed interested, and listened to me rattle on. We eventually returned to town. She kissed me good-bye.

For some reason I said, "Thank you."

While walking dazed into the Maplewood subdivision, I wiped at something greasy on my mouth. I was surprised and stopped to stare at the lipstick on my fingers.

"Kay says let's go," Vernon yelled across the skating floor from the open door at the top of the stairs. Gloria followed us to the door. She was trying to get Jerry Joe to stay. He could rent the skaters' shoes when the rink opened, a job he did sometimes, but he said no for today. We loaded the car and drove on up Market Street to turn onto the road back to Boaz.

During the ride back, they talked me into a corner. There was no respectable way to sidestep the situation, except to stop at my house for the pistol. The only possible way out would be if Mother were home. I was supposed to be in school, so that would be enough to avoid stopping.

Father rode in a carpool, driving every other week, to save on gasoline. The family Packard wasn't parked in the carport. It wasn't Father's turn to drive. This meant that Mother was out using her newly acquired driver's license.

After trying the locked front door, I slowly eased around the outside of the house and to my room. Pushing open the window to raise myself into the bedroom, I remembered to move carefully so as not to kick the new "miracle" aluminum siding. We were told that it would "never rot or need painting." It would, however, easily dent as we kids had quickly learned.

With the pistol, holster, and belt concealed under my shirt, I made a quick casual exit out the front door and back to the idling Buick.

The next stop was Gibson's grocery, located about halfway between Maplewood and the Texaco station. The stop was for a couple of boxes of ammunition. The signal to quit shooting the gun was always when we ran out of bullets. There were never any leftover. Kay gave me money from the front pocket of his bib overalls. Vernon decided to go in with me. We headed in while Kay played with the empty gun. The others watched.

Vernon filled his pockets with candy bars after counting out the correct amount of change on the glass candy case. He was partial to Almond Joys. I paid for two boxes of .22s and added a Three Musketeer for myself, plus four cold eight-ounce Cokes. I decided to pay for the added purchases with what should have been Kay's change.

Kay pretended to shoot people out of the window while traveling the main road through Boaz. I refused to load the gun for him until we were at The Caves and he was out of the car. He threatened to pistol-whip me but didn't.

The pistol was a six-shooter, made by High Standard Arms Co. Uncle Lester had traded for it and had given it to me when I was nine, not unusual in the Fred's Creek area, as a rite of passage. Considerable effort was spent in teaching me the dos and don'ts of gun handling.

"Don't ever point at nothin' you ain't going to shoot," Lester said. Lester was really my great-uncle. He married my grandfather's sister. My grandfather also married Lester's sister. One brother and sister married to another brother and sister was not uncommon in rural areas, where available partners were not plentiful. Their children and my mother would be considered "double cousins," except Uncle Lester and Aunt Nellie had no children of their own. But they had raised a boy.

The story was told. Aunt Nellie had admired the baby during a trip to the feed store when she went inside to buy some horehound candy. She was sucking on a piece after choosing which sacks containing chicken feed she wanted to buy. The sacks were made of cotton fabric, and each was decorated with a different print. Most were of small flowers. Dresses or aprons and sometimes sunbonnets were made from the material when the bags were emptied.

While sitting inside the store and waiting for Lester to load the truck, she held the baby for a while, talking to the mother, telling her how beautiful the child was.

The young mother's husband was killed in a coalmine accident about two weeks after their talk. She subsequently signed a release saying in essence that the mine owners were not at fault for his death and received around three hundred dollars for the signature. She left the child on Aunt Nellie's porch with ten dollars pinned to his blanket, along with his few clothes that were folded neatly and stored in a paper bag. She was later seen in Sharpsburg buying a one-way bus ticket to Florida. No one heard from her again. The boy grew up and married my mother.

We piled out of the car. Jerry Joe found several of the new short-necked beer bottles scattered in the surrounding weeds. We both hated the new bottles because the stores refused to give us refund money for them. Blowing them apart seemed appropriate. Kay insisted on wearing the holster, so we put it over his shoulder. It hung across his chest like a bandolier because his waist was too small. He took instructions seriously but had trouble cocking the hammer that was required with every shot. The gun was a single-action model, copied after the old cowboy guns.

He soon learned to pull the hammer back into a ready position by using the palm of his other hand. He used both hands to shoot and didn't hit much but didn't point it at anyone as feared. His head tilted back, and the high-pitched laugh was repeated with almost every noise of the gun. The laughing would eventually make him cough. He would hold his hand in the air for us to wait. Soon, after a quiet moment, he would be ready to shoot again.

Mike was drinking from Jerry Joe's half-pint whiskey bottle, following the whiskey down his throat with Coke. He wasn't very good around alcohol, becoming belligerent, and he wanted to argue with Kay about his new professional football team.

Mike hated football. His older brother had played for Sharpsburg High and was locally famous for his good play. The brother was now away at college and still playing football, so between his parents bringing up the older brother or sister's good grades and the people at the country club asking Mike if he was going to play football, things were starting to rub him the wrong way.

"It's the dumbest thing I have ever heard. Football team. You're never going to have a team, you dumb little shit. I don't know how I keep getting mixed up with crazy people like you. Jesus, I wish I hadn't got dragged down here anyway."

Mike sat talking, rubbing the dust from his pointed Italian-style shoes. His family had moved to Boaz a few years earlier from Pittsburgh, when his father, urged by his mother, had taken the job as head surgeon at Sharpsburg Memorial Hospital. Sometimes Mike blamed the area for his troubles.

Kay was used to Mike. He could hold his own, "You're too damned skinny to play on my team, you grease-ball!!"

"You don't have a team. I can whip your little ass, that's for sure!" Mike said.

"Oh yeah, big man, pick on a cripple. Tough guy, yeah! I can probably whip your butt even if I am a goner. I can whip your ass before then!"

Jerry Joe started jumping around, making his fists rotate like he was a prizefighter, and of course, laughing. I sat reloading the gun, laughing along with Jerry Joe. Mike and Kay realized that they were being laughed at and shut up.

"What you laughing at?" Kay asked. "Don't you think I got a team?"

He was directing his question to me. I then said something that changed the way he treated me. I went from someone whom he mostly tolerated to sort of an advisor.

"Yeah, I think you got a team, but who you going to play against?" I said.

He had not considered the opponent problem. He awkwardly rose from his rock seat and waddled off, carefully weaving between the remains of several wood fires left out on the rock by past visitors. He stopped out at the edge of the boulder, carefully peeking over and down at the water, with his arms folded across his chest. At times he acted like a spoiled baby, and at other times he acted like an old man. He stood quietly gazing, looking up and down the river, thinking, now being the old man, pained and tired.

His energy was spent. The shells were all fired. We decided to go home and were walking the path to the car. Jerry Joe was lifting Kay over the places where he could not walk.

Kay said to all of us when we arrived at the car, "We're going to start a secret organization soon. Don't tell nobody or I'll get you, understand?"

We all nodded yes, but I did not understand in the least. We woke Vernon from his nap, lying in the back seat. All four doors stood open. Almond Joy wrappers were twisted and sprouting from his ears to muffle the gun noise. The Buick cruised back downriver to Boaz.

Kay and Mike got out at Kay's house. Vernon gave Jerry Joe and me a ride, with Jerry Joe doing his best to talk Vernon into taking him on to Sharpsburg. Vernon would not budge.

Before letting me out in front of Maplewood, Vernon sat for a minute, explaining to me why buying a Three Musketeers candy bar was a bad investment. He said they were mostly air. He reached over and squeezed together the half-eaten one in my hand to prove his point.

It suddenly dawned on me that I had probably missed supper. Jerry Joe walked across the street, waved good-bye, and stuck out his thumb. I tossed the remains of the candy bar behind a pile of dirt and cut through backyards and eased the pistol through my bedroom window, then went around to the front and entered.

Father, along with my two younger brothers, was sitting in the front room watching TV on our new black-and-white set. It only received two channels, one snowy, and the other worse. Both channels went off the air at 10:00 p.m. during the week. Television was a new addition to our household since moving to Boaz. The whole family would watch anything without complaining.

"Where you been?" he asked, in kind of a rough tone of voice.

"Went to the club to caddy."

"You know your mother wants you to be at the table."

"Yes sir, sorry." Then realizing that she wasn't home, I asked, "Where's Mom?"

"She's gone to a Tupperware thing down the street, whatever that is. Think they sell pots."

I said OK and headed for my room to clean and store the pistol. Father was easier than mother. As long as she did not go to him complaining about my actions, everything was fine.

He had worked hard in his life, going ashore on Iwo Jima and Okinawa with a military unit that had a high percentage either killed or wounded. He was a genuine hero and was afraid of nothing or nobody, except Mother. When she was happy, he was happy.

His nickname was Tuffy. Everyone, even mother, called him that. Uncle Lester, when telling stories about father's youth, always added at the end of each story, "never lost a fight."

I read the funnies in the newspaper, then the newly arrived *Saturday Evening Post* magazine, while wolfing down the meat loaf mother had left for me along with half a pan of cornbread. I added heaps of Grandmother's Concord jelly, mixed with Aunt Nelly's homemade butter.

Then I generally acted casual, making sure I was in bed and pretending to be asleep before mother returned home, to avoid questioning.

I dreamed of Mo that night. Mo was a catfish that lived at Uncle Lester's house, in his well. He was named Mo after one of the Three Stooges. Uncle Lester loved the Three Stooges. I did too.

Lester had put Mo into the deep, dark well to eat bugs or whatever else might fall down into the drinking water.

"He keeps the place clean," Lester explained. "A little fish piss never hurt nobody."

He let me catch Mo one time, fishing a line baited with cheese.

Lester laughed while he slowly checked Mo over. We lowered him back down; carefully making sure the bucket didn't scrape the sides of the well and knock off debris.

"He's gettin' big. He must be makin' a good livin' down there," Lester said afterward, while shining a light down into the well, inspecting.

I dreamed I was down in the well, swimming around in a circle like Mo. Looking up above to see the distant open light.

Day Three

The next morning, Mother was busy coordinating the family, making sure we left the house on time, and paused only to show us her newly purchased plastic storage container.

The burping feature, "to keep in the freshness," was demonstrated.

She mentioned only once my being late for supper: "Don't do that again, young man."

Happy she didn't say more, I hurried out the door, walking the soon-to-be-paved road to the Maplewood entrance. The girl in my class, standing with the group that was waiting on the school bus, waved. I quickly threw my hand up, ran across the road, and descended past the railroad tracks, down to Jerry Joe's house. Cecil was snoring on the couch with the door to the empty bedroom standing open. I quickly backed back out the front door that had also been standing ajar to avoid an awkward moment, should he wake to see me in the house.

Walking along the row of houses, I saw ahead of me a person's back that could only belong to the Trampman. His turned body was jerking, mostly on the side with the arm. My first instinct was to back away and climb back to the tracks and go around, to avoid his unpredictable nature.

Although listening to him talk, with his easy command of language, was fascinating. Words rolled from his tongue with little effort, different from the men in my life, who were silent much of the time.

"Hey there, young whippersnapper!" he said without looking around. "You ever gut a fish?"

I walked to one side and saw him scraping scales from a river perch that had been removed from the dented bucket sitting by his feet. The bucket contained one dead fish, floating on its side, slowly rotating. Several live ones were at the bottom and swimming in circles. The fish he was trying to clean was lying on a large cross section of tree, used as a table.

"I gutted a few," I said.

"Well, let's see you do one then," he said, with a challenging tone.

I reached for the much-worn kitchen knife he had sticking from the wood. It went through the fish's tail. It was being used as an anchor to keep the fish from sliding away while he scraped at the scales with a small pocketknife.

Picking up the fish, I neatly cut open the belly to dig out the intestines with my fingers and then flipped them over the hill in the direction of the river. I swished the finished fish in the bucket of water, while those remaining jumped around.

"That's not bad, bet you could do the rest," he said.

"I could," I answered.

With assurance, I quickly cleaned the remaining fish, without considering the possibility that this would be a difficult job for a person with one arm. In the meantime, he held down by foot a selected stack of dead branches that were taken from a larger pile. Snapping them into pieces with his hand, he tossed them onto an already-started fire that was gaining strength in a much-used oblong pit, dug not far from the front of the house.

"Want to have a couple of fish with me? That's the least I could do for such a great fish cleaner," he said.

"I would, but I got to go to school right now."

"You know I went to school once, graduated from high school, and believe it or not, went to college—for a while anyway—then I quit."

"Why?"

He developed a frown, but it quickly turned into a laugh. I could see his even teeth deep within the thick beard. "Well, I had other things to do."

"I know what you mean," I said, sensing that it would not be a good idea to pursue the topic.

"Got some beer down in the river, cooling. Should be just right by now. You sure?"

"I skipped school some yesterday," I said, explaining the situation to him in a mildly bragging tone of voice. "Need to go today."

"Suit yourself there, young Rooster, it's just that much more for me. I'll take you one of these days and show you where to find hellgrammites almost anytime you need some. Just like owning a gold mine you know."

Hellgrammites were the best bait known. They would catch fish when all else failed. Knowing a good place to catch the rare, many-legged creatures was a fisherman's considerable advantage.

"Yeah, it is," I agreed, glancing at the cleaned fish spread out on the tree stump.

"Don't take them all! Take some and leave some, so they'll be some baby bugs when you want some more."

"I'll do that. So long," I said and walked uphill to the tracks while he busied himself with preparations.

Staying in school today was on my mind. I was afraid my parents would discover my truancy from yesterday. I walked along the tracks at a steady pace, occasionally flicking a fish scale from my white T-shirt and faded blue jeans and fought back the urge to ascend behind Gibson's grocery to fish for bottles.

Jerry Joe and I had a hidden length of bailing twine with a slip loop and would pitch the string over the chicken wire enclosure where Mr. Gibson stored his returnable bottles. We had developed skill in lassoing the empty bottles by the neck and pulling them up and over the fence, to be redeemed for the two-cents deposit a second time.

Climbing the hill behind the Texaco station, I quickly reached the school and soon was standing at my locker listening to Mike complaining about how much he disliked school. I absently tried to decide which textbook would be appropriate to hide my library book behind, forgetting about the second half of the test we were taking.

Mike was wearing a pink, long-sleeved shirt with the collar turned up. Charcoal pleated pants were threaded with a thin, white leather belt. While talking to me, he unconsciously looked at the girls' behinds after they walked past us. His pants were "pegged," or narrowed at the ankles, as was the new big city style of the day. He reached down to wipe his black, pointed shoes with a cloth kept in his locker.

He then changed the subject to Kay. He liked Kay, admired him and his tenacity, but it would have been embarrassing for Mike to come right out and say so.

"He doesn't look too good. You know Dad says he's growing all wrong, some of him is growing and some isn't, complicated, but it's all bad news," Mike said.

"Is he a goner like he says?"

Mike answered my question by slowly nodding his head.

Jerry Joe came in grinning and walked to our huddle. He had ridden the City-Lines bus back from Sharpsburg, where he had spent the night. He was back in Boaz just to see what was going on with us, and then maybe he would go caddy. We walked to homeroom together, but Jerry Joe left quickly when hearing about the test we were taking.

Our homeroom teacher, like the rest of the teachers, ignored him. They considered him just another river rat, who very soon would turn sixteen and quit school officially. He would then be out of their hair for good.

Jerry Joe walked over to the Texaco station just to hang around but ended up pumping gas for the owner until Cecil, who was supposed to be working there, made his way to the station, probably after joining the river perch and beer breakfast that Garvin was working on.

Jerry Joe's mother and Cecil lived together. She had not returned from work last night, but her being missing for a day or two was not too unusual. She would eventually return, hungover, then sleep all day before walking the railroad tracks back to work at the Nightingale.

The Nightingale was a bar propped by poles, sticking back away from the road in the direction of the railroad tracks and river, along the route running between Boaz and Sharpsburg. You could look through the open front door to see men lining the bar at 7:00 a.m., when the factory's graveyard shifts quit work. Many would stop for a beer to unwind on their way home to sleep. The morning crowd occupied the seats only a few hours after the place cleared from the night before.

When you think of families in the traditional sense, as generational, with the elders being wise and handing down rules to live by, it didn't apply to the Culpeppers. They were remarkably equal from birth. They called each other by first names. If one of them was five years old and smoking a cigarette, nothing would be said, as long as the smoker could come up with their own cigarette. Having children at a young age blurred lines between parents and siblings.

Jerry Joe and Cecil often had loud disagreements. In spite of this, they, as well as the rest of the extended Culpepper family were emotionally close-knit. The townspeople knew, "If you mess with one, you mess with them all."

The second part of the IQ test took up most of the morning, but we finished in time to change rooms for the morning's last period class, geography. That was the room where the maps pulled down along the wall like window blinds. They looked interesting.

The teacher unrolled and quickly rerolled several individual maps by pulling the attached strings. Making a sharp noise, she tapped the one she finally selected, using a long, thin, metal-tipped wooden pointer, and then she indicated to us the Laplands of northern Europe. It was the beginning point of the coming year's study. Later, while giving us a quick run down of our upcoming overall studies, she mentioned a river called the Zider Zee. This name was familiar to me from Uncle Lester's story of crossing and traveling near this river during the war, World War I.

The teacher was continuing her quick sketch of our class travels, mostly in Europe, when a siren sounded. More accurately, an air-raid warning sounded with a loud blast of alternating high, then low, pitches. The origin of the warning was the city building that was located across the street and two blocks inland from the school, up the road beside Stanley's Drive-in. The unnerving sound could be heard all through Boaz.

The class immediately dove for the floor under their desks. The teacher walked quickly down an aisle, yelling, "Duck and cover! Duck and cover!"

Slow to react, I sat frozen in my seat. Noticing this, the teacher stepped around the row, coming my way, and using both hands, she pushed first my head and then my body down under the desk, that was bolted to the floor. My seat, connecting to the desk behind me, was forced to flip up with the movement of my body sliding beneath. I stayed under the desk for what seemed a long while, slowly moving around and trying to find a comfortable position for my knees on the hardwood floor without drawing more of the teacher's attention. The siren finally stopped.

"All clear!" the teacher declared.

We removed ourselves from the floor to our seats. Some of the kids looked out the window like they were checking the weather, but it was more to assure themselves that no bombs were falling.

The teacher read from a worn pamphlet that she removed from a desk drawer. It stated that we should be ready to defend our country against its enemies. We should be ever vigilant of the subversive forces that would undermine our security. Most of all we needed to watch out for the Communists. We ended the drill with the Pledge of Allegiance. It was enthusiastically voiced in unison.

In Fred's Creek we were told about these air-raid drills but had never actually conducted one. The teachers explained to us that the Communists would drop the bombs on big cities. They reasoned that the low rural population of Fred's Creek would not be worth a bomb. Boaz now struck me as one of the big towns that they were talking about. I pledged to be on guard.

Mike and I made a dash for Stanley's Drive-in at the first sound of the lunch bell. Mother had given me a dollar, along with instructions to buy five 20-cent tickets that would allow me to eat lunch each day in the school cafeteria. I had yet to see the inside of the place. It was located in a separate building behind the school and was connected to the school by a concrete walkway that was covered by an almost-flat aluminum roof, held up at intervals by round steel poles.

The only opinion I had heard of the food's quality was Mike's: "It's slop, and the football players throw food at you."

My cafeteria dollar was already spent. I was now using saved caddy money. We ordered foot-long hot dogs and milkshakes. Mike played a pinball machine that was located in a room built onto the side of the regular building. The line of booths along the large windows had filled quickly with kids. The windows looked out onto the parking area, where people sitting in the cars ate from a tray hooked to the driver's door.

Mike could play pinball quite well. Concentrating on the hypnotic ricocheting ball, his thin hands with smooth almost elegant coordination tapped the side of the machine for added bounce but not too hard or it would tilt. He was practiced in snapping the flippers at the exact second needed to send the ball back to the top of the board for maximum points.

He had gotten into one of his many troubles by drilling a hole into the side of a machine with a hand drill "borrowed" from the science classroom. He then pushed a wire through the hole to hit one of the targets. This accumulated points and would eventually register on the machine as free games. Mrs. Stanley, the drive-in owner, caught him in the act.

Every pinball machine I looked at after he told me this story had a metal strip screwed to the inside rails. I was convinced that Mike was the guy who caused this addition. He was not winning many games today. After his last nickel, he didn't feel like playing anymore. Since the hole-drilling incident, he wasn't officially allowed on the drive-in property. No one had recently said anything about him eating at the drive-in, but going to the window for nickels would be pushing a delicate situation.

We crossed the street and headed for the Texaco station, to see what kind of a car Cecil might be working on today. Mike and Cecil would have nothing in common if not for their shared interest in automobiles. Neither owned one. Cecil's automobile, an old Nash sitting on blocks in front of his house without wheels, hood, or engine, did not count. The only thing that worked on his car was a round flattened steering knob that had a picture of an almost naked lady laminated onto it. She sat wearing green shorts and neck-scarf, on an automobile fender, smiling and waving. The Trampman had bolted it to the steering wheel as a joke.

The story was told that "shantyboaters" had left Cecil along the riverbank when he was young. Shantyboaters were people who drifted or moved from place to place by using long poles to guide their floating homemade flat-bottom houseboats. They ate a lot of catfish and carp and were considered, on the social scale, to be even beneath river rats. Most of his life Cecil had worked on engines, in and around the Sharpsburg area. One night while drinking many beers at the Nightingale, he fell in love with Jerry Joe's mother.

Cecil was short, a little bowlegged and pigeon-toed, with a dark complexion and black eyes set deep into a pockmarked face. He was probably at least partially related to the Shawnees who paddled the canoes in the history books. When we arrived, he was leaning against the doorframe of the service station's open lift bay, wiping his ever-greasy hands with a rag that he carried hanging in his back pocket.

Jerry Joe was sitting in front of the station on an old tire that Cecil had recently tossed down, after he had replaced it for a customer. Jerry Joe's fingers were laced together. His arms were extended, with his upper arms resting on his spread knees. He would lower his head ever so often and slowly spit on the concrete between his legs.

They both wore serious expressions, unusual for Jerry Joe but not for Cecil; he did not laugh often. It was obvious that something was wrong. The Culpeppers were normally oblivious to their surroundings. If they had something to say to one another, it would be said. If a big crowd formed during their loud fight, it would be ignored. But these two today were concerned, not fighting.

Jerry Joe explained the reason. The Piggotts had them on the lookout. More to the point, Clyde Piggotts' return had them thinking. Clyde had recently been released from prison and was on their minds because Cecil had, earlier in the day, spotted Clyde riding by the station with his younger brother, Lonny. They were probably heading for the country club to caddy. Jerry Joe's mother had been instrumental in getting Clyde convicted of robbery. Many said the charge should have been murder.

The story was told. She and a man had left a bar in Sharpsburg one late night and were cutting across the American Legion baseball field, going God only knows where, with Clyde and Lonny following. During the course of the night, the man Jerry Joe's mother was with had been buying drinks freely with a wad of money from a cashed check that had included his entire month's pay. He worked on a riverboat. During the last thirty days, he had not been allowed on dry land. The ritual of getting drunk after a month on the boats was a common practice in Sharpsburg.

Clyde and Lonny ran from a hiding spot and grabbed the drunken man. They threw him to the ground and held him there. Jerry Joe's mother escaped under the bleachers, stretching to hide on her belly in the mud. It was dark, overcast, and had been raining on and off. The light was sparse. After looking unsuccessfully for Jerry Joe's mother, they became anxious to see how much money was pulled from the man's pockets and ran to a lighted area where they could see to count.

The incident would not have amounted to much if the mugged fellow had not been lying face down in a puddled low spot near second base and drowned. Jerry Joe's mother ran to Aunt Della's house and hid. The police asked around the next day, and armed with the gathered information, they found her. She, not being good under pressure, told them exactly what happened.

It was a much-written-about trial. Clyde was convicted of robbery but not murder because his defense convinced the jury that the robbed man, being very drunk, drowned of his own accord. Most people considered it murder. They were not happy with the verdict.

The judge sent Clyde's younger brother, Lonny, to the boy's state reformatory. He was sentenced to stay only a year because of his young age. Now three years later, Clyde was out of prison. It was on the grapevine that there would be revenge.

Lonny was recognizable to me from caddying. He never talked to Jerry Joe. Even though Jerry Joe was younger, Lonny would have been whipped if he had started anything. He knew it.

Lonny spent his time bullying the younger caddies. The required minimum age to caddy was twelve, but some lied and started at about ten. They carried one bag until later when they could prove to the caddy master that they could handle two. With the addition of the second bag, they would receive twice the money for each round.

Lonny had not bothered me because of Jerry Joe. He and his buddies often told the new younger caddies that they would not be allowed to caddy until they proved they were men. Lonny would then say that a newcomer looked more like a girl and thought he needed to be checked for a penis. He would badger the youngster, with help from others, until the new kid unzipped his pants and exposed himself to everyone.

Lonny would slowly move up closer, saying that it was too small and he couldn't see it. The kid would hold it out farther. Suddenly Lonny would grab hold of it and take off running. Of course the kid had no choice but to follow.

Lonny would then run around in a circle yelling, "Help! He's after me, get him away from me!"

All but the toughest young kids would start crying. I admit to laughing with the rest. These incidents would be followed by an explanation from an older caddy. The kid in pain was told that this same initiation happened to many young caddies. They were also told that Lonnie was stupid and that in the future to pay no attention to anything he said or did. They followed the advice.

Inspecting each automobile passing the Texaco station for Clyde and Lonnie became a priority for all of us. For the first time, I was ready to head back to school.

There was time before the afternoon classes started to stop at the library and have my daily literary chat with my newfound "book buddy," the librarian. I told Mike that I would meet him in class.

She asked how my book was going, if I liked it.

"Yes, ma'am, it's real good."

"Your book is the first in a series of five books, so you can read four more. The one you're reading he wrote last, but it's the beginning of a whole *Leatherstockings* group of stories."

"So he wrote the beginning last?" I asked with interest.

The bell rang for afternoon classes. I left and walked the hall, anticipating the series of *Deerslayer* books and found a desk that was about halfway back in the first afternoon class. I became immediately absorbed in reading, glad to again have this free uninterrupted time. I was mildly aware that the teacher was talking about something.

The *Deerslayer* explained how, 'the loons speak accordin' to their own nature." The sudden voice coming from the hallway outside of the room was not a loon, but familiar, and before it registered in my mind who it was, Kay came banging into the classroom.

"Where's my seat?" he asked the teacher.

His gravelly voice took on a louder resonance in the closed space of the room. The teacher's mouth opened, but nothing came out. Kay's nurse followed into the room with a sparkling white uniform, sheer white hose, recently polished white shoes, and a starched winged nurse's hat that had an attached gold pin that read, "Registered Nurse." She whispered into the teacher's ear. They went to the hallway for a conference.

Kay scooted belly first up into the seat beside me and turned to sit facing forward with his legs dangling and chin only slightly above the desktop.

"Hi there, schoolmates!" he said laughing. The other students came quickly from their seats to crowd around. He might be a goner, but he had charisma and explained that we were going to have him as a classmate.

He went on to explain the start of his football team. They could try out, and if hired, they would receive money just like other professional teams. Then he flashed his stopwatch for all to see, repeating to the circle of onlookers that he was the team's owner and coach, just in case anyone misunderstood.

Mike walked slowly from the back of the room with hands in pockets and stood behind the crowd, shaking his head, while Kay's new carrot-headed classmate leaned on his desk with her elbows. She stared at him, inches from the side of his face. Kay talked on, totally ignoring her presence. The teacher returned without the nurse and talked the students back into their seats. She tried bravely to resume the class. Kay ignored her, although he did try to whisper, but it came out a stage whisper and could be heard throughout the room.

Mostly private tutors were in charge of his education. He had attended Boaz schools in short spurts over the years and had a standing invitation to attend whenever he wanted. Doctors thought the exposure would be good for him, but he did not care for the school routine, wanting instead to dwell on what was of interest to him, ignoring the rest.

"Thought you was a goner?" I asked.

"I am, but I got a plan worked out now," he said.

"What kinda plan?"

"Boy, are you dumb, no wonder you're in with these boneheads, buddy boy. Hadn't you heard of intramural games?"

"No."

The teacher was trying to quiet him. He waved his hand in her direction, not bothering to look.

"We're going to have my Boaz Browns be from this class; we will kick the other classes' butts!" he spit and laughed.

The teacher frowned. The rest of the class started laughing when he said butt. Her mouth was forming to say something when the bell rang. The sound brought a look of relief to her face.

Kay ignored the bell. "We got somebody to play now!" he said, sitting and looking my way intently, challenging me to dispute his plan.

Shrugging an agreement, I stood up, waiting, while Kay struggled from the seat. We walked together out the door. Mike was behind listening. The girl from Maplewood walked on the other side of Kay, dividing her gaze with the quick back and forth jerks of her head, between Kay and myself. We came to the steps, and I handed her my library book.

Mike and I lifted Kay by holding under his arms. Together we carried him down the stairs. He didn't miss a word and further explained his strategy after the stairs, while continuing down the main hall. He was drawing more than a few stares. We headed for the next class. It was physical education.

The class separated into the girls and boys locker rooms to change. About half of the boys had gym clothes already secured in the wire baskets stacked in rows against a wall. We were told to go to the schoolyard whether we had the clothes to dress for gym class or not. Outside, the male teacher had us stand in line, explaining the required dress, which included shorts, tennis shoes, and white T-shirts.

This was another area where in the past Mike had gotten into trouble. He would not wear the gym clothes. To smooth things, his father had written a medical excuse. The final compromise would still require him to attend the physical education classes, but now he just stood in his street clothes and observed. When no one was watching, he would sneak a smoke in the cornfield that was located down over the hill between the railroad tracks and river.

But Mike wasn't the problem today; it was Kay. He took this opportunity to get out his stopwatch and a whistle tied with an old shoelace. He began giving instructions for his football tryouts while repeatedly blowing the whistle.

The boys' gym teacher, also the football coach, was not happy. They began a yelling contest. The coach pointed to the school building, and both began traveling the distance across the grass. Kay struggled to go as fast as possible on this trip to see a surprised principal, who had no indication that Kay was again one of his students. The nurse was standing back and watching the argument from the shade of the building. She fell in behind, forming a parade that was heading for the office.

Mike bet me that the principal would send Kay home. We laughed as we walked across the schoolyard grass and went out almost to Main Street in order to check the Texaco station, located on the opposite side of the school, for any sign of the Piggotts. All we saw was Jerry Joe pumping gas, checking oil, and cleaning the windows of a customer's automobile.

The lady driving was leaning out the window talking to him while he expertly used the squeegee to remove water from the windshield; then he wiped the squeegee's rubber edge with a rag. He worked at the station when the owner was off somewhere and Cecil was busy repairing a vehicle in the lift bay. Occasionally, Jerry Joe worked all day when Cecil didn't show because he was sleeping one off, or sometimes he worked when Cecil arrived on time but was too drunk to work. The owner would put Cecil on the couch in a small back room of the station until he improved.

Our gym class members were chasing each other or shooting baskets with a dodge ball. Mike and I walked to the side entrance of the building, past Homer, a skinny, pimply, big-eared 9-1s classmate, who was squatting between the shrubs and smoking a cigarette. Homer wanted to drive big trucks and had a metal belt buckle that read "Peterbilt."

With every class attended, he would ask anyone who would listen, "What's all this got to do with drivin' a truck?"

We went in, walked the empty hall, and heard loud voices from the principal's office. Kay was making his share of the noise. The words from behind the door were muffled.

Finally, we could hear nothing. The physical education teacher came out of the office door with a red face and passed us by, swinging his arms fast and taking no notice.

Mike slowly opened the door and peeped into the office. He did not see the principal or Kay, so he stuck his head all the way in to ask the secretary, sitting at a desk in the outer-office reception area, "Where is he?"

She motioned with her thumb to a door with a red cross. The words "First Aid" were painted beneath on the opaque glass. We went through the door quickly, before the secretary had time to ask what we were doing there.

Kay was lying on a cot-like bed, located up against the far wall of the windowless room, with a dark green wool blanket covering him to his neck. His eyes were closed. The nurse was sitting in a straight-backed chair against the opposite wall. She signaled with a finger to her lips for us to be quiet. Kay resembled a baby with his large out-of proportion head and whiter-than-normal complexion. We started to leave, but Kay opened his eyes and spoke with slightly slurred words.

"He said we couldn't do it."

"Do what?" Mike asked.

"Have us a team."

Mike's eyes narrowed. An angry look appeared on his face. "Why not?"

Kay showed a flash of anger also. He was fighting through both fatigue and the shot that the nurse had just given him. "He said we couldn't waste time on a football team."

"Why not?" I asked.

Exasperation took over. "Because we're in the retards and cripples class, you idiots!"

The nurse quickly stood, flicking her fingers to shoo us from the room, shaking her head no. We walked out and down the hall. Mike's eyes were watering with anger. He looked the other way so I wouldn't notice, and I made no indication that I did.

"We're going to get these bastards, you watch," he said.

"What are we gonna do?" I asked.

"I don't know. We could go on strike, like at the club maybe. You know."

I wanted to do something to help Kay, but this strike didn't seem to be a good idea. Mike headed out the main door, quickly banging one of the big double doors open with all his strength. I followed. We stopped at the crosswalk. Looking around, he picked up a chipped piece of the concrete curb.

"I ought to sling this through his window," he said.

Saying nothing, I stood and watched. Finally, he tossed the chunk into the air, made a catch, and then threw it hard into the grass in front of him.

"Come on," he said.

We crossed the road to Stanley's. I stopped by the walk-up window and bought two bottles of Orange Crush while Mike slipped into the room with booths. He was sitting with his back propped against the window ledge. With feet stretched out in the seat, he was deep in thought by the time I got there. We both sat quietly. I was trying to think of something to do but had no ideas. Even the idea that we could think of something to change the situation seemed beyond me.

I was absently looking out the window, wondering what Mother was going to do when she found out that I was on strike, when my eyes suddenly stopped. I saw Lonny Piggott grinning at me from behind the wheel of an old car parked at one of the drive-in stations. He made a motion, using his finger like he was cutting his own throat. My skin suddenly became cold and clammy.

Feeling a shaking spell coming on, I whispered, "We're in big trouble, Buddy."

Suddenly, I realized a new possibility. Since we hung around with Jerry Joe, we may have been added to the Piggott hit list.

Pointing in Lonny's direction with my finger just below the window ledge caused Mike to sit up and look around. This made Lonny laugh even more. He began slapping the steering wheel. The other guy, in the passenger seat, could be none other than the famous criminal, Clyde Piggott. He sat with his head down, occasionally sticking a hamburger into his mouth, and ignoring all three of us.

"What we gonna do?" I asked.

Mike shook his head and shrugged. His eyes were darting around like he was looking for options. Lonny soon answered the question for us by pulling out. Driving by our window while slowly waving, he slowly turned onto Main Street in the direction of the Texaco station.

"Jerry Joe," we said, almost together.

We came out of our seats and ran out the door and up the sidewalk after the car without a plan. But whatever was going to happen, we wanted to be there.

We ran, waving our arms, and pointed ahead to the slow-moving car. Cecil had spotted them already and stood with his greasy Texaco shirt hanging out over blue jeans that had large holes in the knees. He was holding a steel bar that formed a flat hook on one end, used for removing tires from wheels. Jerry Joe was just behind, standing in the station doorway. Both of them stood completely still, carefully watching the slow-moving car pass by and go on down the road.

Mike and I ran across the road. Jerry Joe came out to meet us at the gas pumps, grinning and shaking his head.

"I don't know if they'll mess too much with Cecil."

"What about Della?" I asked.

"They won't mess with her, for sure."

He folded his hand to resemble a gun and jerked it into the air like recoil after a shot. We knew what that meant. During the summer, when we three visited Della's house on trips to Sharpsburg, Jerry Joe had shown us the holes.

Della kept a long-barreled .38 caliber pistol beside the window where she sold her whiskey. Occasionally, when a fight and noise was under way in the alley, she would open the window and squeeze off a round across the vacant lot into the back of a storage building where the city kept road signs and equipment. This would cause the perpetrators to scatter. We always took the time to stop and inspect for any new divots in the cinder-block building. Della had a reputation.

"And they ain't allowed in the Night'ngale neither. Dutch would beat the holy hell out of them," Jerry Joe explained.

Dutch was the Nightingale's bar tender, bouncer, and proprietor.

We felt a little better and were about to laugh with relief when I happened to look around. There, standing at the edge of the school property with his big hands on his skinny hips, was the principal. He wasn't happy. He motioned for the three of us to come to him. Together, we all four walked back to the school in silence. Moving chairs into a row, he orchestrated our seating in the office, then sat at his desk and looked at each of us in a grave and serious manner.

"We work hard here, providing you young men—and I say young men because you are young men—an education, to prepare you for the world out there."

He moved his hand in a rehearsed manner toward the window and the world out there, where he had no doubt seen Mike and I running past, waving our arms.

"It saddens me to think that you are not taking full advantage of this wonderful opportunity. What were you two doing over there?" he asked, with a look that demanded an answer.

"It was gym class. So we were running to get in shape." At least it was an answer. More than he usually got from Mike.

Suddenly Kay pushed open the door, coming into the room. Awkwardly, he scooted a straight-back chair into the line of chairs that the three of us already occupied. Then he moved to stand in front of it. Jerry Joe stood and automatically picked him up and sat him on the seat.

The atmosphere in the room changed because the principal, being politically aware, knew Kay's father was an important member of the community. He became suddenly concerned about Kay's well-being.

"I'm doing much better, thank you," Kay responded politely. "I would like to ask again that intramural football games be allowed in our class."

"Kay, my young friend, you know we went over this. The class was designed for concentration on studies, with no outside interruptions, and that is for a purpose."

"What purpose? It's just a touch football game, for God's sake," Mike said, in a steady tone.

"Now, Michael, you have been raised better than that, and you are aware that language of that nature is not allowed in this institution, and I personally will not stand for it."

"I don't think a lousy, stupid game will hurt anything. I'm going to talk to Dad about this," Mike threatened.

"Me too," Kay said.

"Me too," I said.

He looked my way frowning, trying to remember who I was.

"Well, you children go back to class now. We will discuss this at another time."

Thinking ahead, he saw the possibility of an awkward moment with Mr. Schultz, who was on the county school board. Not to mention Mrs. Masters, a teacher at Sharpsburg High School whom he felt he had had one too many talks with about Mike already. He reasoned that this incident would do his career and political ambitions no great benefit.

He could not at this moment place my parents, and Jerry Joe was irrelevant.

He quickly decided to institute the bureaucrat's greatest tool. Stall, and the problem will eventually go away.

"Yes, we will discuss this at another time," he said again. "Now, you boys, get back to class this minute."

We left the office in single file; the nurse fell in behind. We didn't go back to class. Kay pointed ahead to where we were going as he approached the gym door. He walked straight across the basketball floor instead of going around like the rules written in large letters on the wall stated. He continued out the back door and directly for the Buick. We piled in, with the nurse getting behind the wheel.

Mike had strayed away from the group, walking instead to the principal's Plymouth. He removed the gas cap that was protruding from the side of the older car, while unzipping his pleated pants. He emptied his bladder down the hole. The nurse pretended she was looking for something in her purse to avoid witnessing the act.

She had kept her job longer than most, accomplishing this by avoiding anything that did not involve nursing. She and Kay had an understanding. With everyone now inside the car and giggling, even the nurse, we pulled from the parking lot. We turned onto the short road that divided the Texaco station from the school.

We could see Cecil pumping gasoline into an older car with his foot resting on the running board. He was squinting down the gasoline nozzle to judge when to release the gas flow, while trying to avoid the smoke from a cigarette dangling at the corner of his mouth.

Kay said, "Go to the park."

The nurse turned upriver onto Main Street, then quickly turned back off Main Street and onto the road beside Stanley's. She now traveled away from the river, driving the short distance to the city park. On Kay's instructions, she retrieved a new football and an old orange football helmet from the trunk. Having regained some energy from his rest, Kay began blowing the whistle while she lowered the helmet onto his head.

He gave orders: "Practice! Let's go. Let's go."

The park was about a block square. The city hall, fire department, and police station were all located in the two-story brick building that occupied one end of the open area that had random large trees and picnic tables. An old man in an open-necked, white dress shirt and suspenders was sitting by the building on a wooden park bench, reading an evening newspaper pulled from a bundle that was dropped daily in front of the city building. The paper carrier would soon deliver them from house to house. After finishing with Kay, the nurse walked to where he was sitting. He stood and offered her the bench, but she declined. They both stood talking.

Herky, Vernon's brother, was wearing a stained, black cowboy hat, an old khaki shirt with matching pants, and old, black, high-topped tennis shoes. He was slowly sweeping the walk that ran along the front of the building, where he worked as a custodian. When we pulled to the curb, he began watching us closely but still pretended to sweep. Twenty minutes older than Vernon, his fraternal twin, Herky had different ideas about things, being more serious and less flexible then Vernon.

Their co-owned car was sitting behind the city building. It was one of the things they didn't agree upon; arguing often about what color it should be painted. Herky thought the bottom should be black and the top white, like a police car. He had this idea—it was really more of a dream—that he was now in some way connected with the police force because of his relatively new job working at the city building.

Boaz had a police chief and about eight or nine volunteer nonpaid deputies that he could call upon if needed. The old man who was talking to the nurse lived on the second floor and answered the phone at night in case of emergences. He would set off the fire siren to call the volunteer firefighters. Except for the chief, there was not a paid police force or fire department.

Herky considered himself a volunteer policeman, and Vernon's idea of a red or purple car was not compatible with his vision. In a compromise, each brother took turns painting the car a color of his personal choosing, for an agreed upon period of time, using a paintbrush.

From a distance the car looked great, new even, but up close the brush marks could be seen. Paint was inadvertently dabbed in places that it shouldn't be, like on the glass and bumpers. The repeated paintings had built a thickness that did not enhance the car's visual appeal. It was in police car colors at present, sitting ready to go, pointing out the drive behind the building.

Kay was busy teaching me to fake one way and than cut the other while Jerry Joe threw the ball with accuracy. Most of the time it landed in my arms. I caught it. This delighted Kay and he became animated, pretending to jump. He mimicked my catches.

"This is great!" Kay said, " Mike, after you center the ball, rush back at Jerry Joe so he can learn to pass under pressure. Try and touch him before he throws."

Mike tried but Jerry Joe avoided him and still completed passes.

The nurse walked over to us while Kay was drawing a play in the dirt with a stick. She said she was going home. The plan was that Herky would bring Kay home the second he felt like coming.

Kay was upset because she had interrupted him and he waved her off. "Yeah, I'll bring him home with me, go ahead."

Kay went back to scratching his play in the bare spot.

I was trotting back with the ball after a play when Mike waved his arm, motioning for me to come faster.

"The Piggotts are sitting across the park, don't look." Mike said.

Kay immediately popped his helmeted head up from our huddle, turning his body stiffly, looking all around.

"Those the guys that killed that guy in Sharpsburg?" he asked.

"Yeah, will you quit gawking?" Mike said.

"What they doing here? Let's arrest them or something," Kay said.

"I think they're gonna get me and Cecil," Jerry Joe said.

"Herky, come over here!" Kay yelled.

Herky walked over, carrying his broom.

"Go arrest those guys!" Kay ordered.

"I can't."

"Why?"

Herky didn't want to be involved in whatever was going on but was still flattered that we might think he had the authority to arrest someone.

"I gotta get a warrant first," he finally said.

"Well, go get one!" Kay yelled and waved his arms.

Herky headed for the station to hide from whatever was going on while we stood thinking, not knowing exactly what to do. The Piggotts, at the far end of the park and sitting on a picnic table under an open-sided shelter, got up and began slowly walking to their car, which was parked along the street.

"Cecil needs to know," Jerry Joe said.

He and Mike started walking fast, in the direction of the wanna-be police car. Kay and I were bringing up the rear. Jerry Joe opened the passenger door and waited to lift Kay, still hugging the football, onto the front seat and then got into the back with me. Mike had already slid behind the wheel.

This is another area that had caused Mike some trouble in the past, driving without a license and without the automobile owner's blessing. This car did not need a key; actually I don't think they had one. You just flipped the switch and stepped on the starter button that was bolted to the floorboard. Next you put it in gear, let out the clutch, and pushed on the gas pedal. Mike did. We bounced into the street.

"Step on it!" Kay said.

Mike stepped on it, but when we reached Main Street and made the turn, it was obvious that school was out. The front of the school was teeming with students. The crosswalk guards were in the street. The principal was standing on the sidewalk. With hands clasped behind his back, he was noting with pride the proficiency and safety of the process. The crosswalk guards blew their whistles and then held out the well-worn, hand-printed, six-sided stop signs, causing Mike to use the brakes. We were now stopped at the crossing. Sitting ducks.

"Give him the helmet," I said, pointing to Mike.

Jerry Joe reached over the seat and quickly pulled it from Kay's head. Kay gave a squeal of surprise. Mike squeezed it onto his head, in an attempt to disguise his identity. He sat waiting while we three hunkered down below the windows, trying to stay out of sight. The principal finally looked our way, frowned, and started walking toward the car at the exact same time that the guards waved us on. Mike pushed on the gas. Peeking out the back window, we saw the principal watching us drive away. He continued watching as Mike pulled into the Texaco station. At Jerry Joe's instructions he pulled to the far side, away from the school, to block the principal's view.

Jerry Joe got out. "You all go on, before he decides to come over here. Clyde won't bother us two together."

"You sure?" Mike asked.

Jerry Joe nodded his head. Mike raked the gears to back out. He headed downriver.

"Where we going now?" Kay asked. "We should stay here and kick those idiots' ass!"

"I live on down here a ways. Drop me off maybe? You know, Herky's going to be mad," I said, trying to divert Kay's attention.

"Why? This ain't Herky's car, it's mine," Kay said condescendingly.

The car we were riding in was one of those unclear interdependent areas between the wealthy and the poor. When Herky and Vernon wanted to buy the car, of course they had no money, so they went to Kay's father and asked for a loan and promised to pay the money back a little at a time.

They showed him the car. He gave the previous owner a check and had the car transferred to the Schultz Dairy before tossing the title into his desk. They had yet to make the first payment, but Kay's father now had added leverage. When things didn't go as he liked, he would threaten to take back the car. So if Herky was back at the city building fuming, that was all he was doing.

We turned into Maplewood.

"What kind of houses are these?" Kay asked, looking around curiously.

"I don't know, just houses, new houses," I said.

Mike stopped in front of my house. I got out to the stares of my parents, who were sitting under the carport and drinking iced tea. Mike pulled away, still wearing the orange helmet that had been painted with the same paintbrush that was used on the car. They left slowly, making a dusty U-turn. Kay's head was barely visible above the front seat window.

"Who is that?" Mother asked.

"Kay Schultz, you know, the people that brings the milk."

The clear glass bottles with the name Schultz etched on the sides were well known.

"What kinda car is that?" Father asked.

"1948 Ford."

" I know that. Where'd they get that paint job?"

"Oh, it used to be a police car," I said in a matter-of-fact tone.

"What was that on his head?" Mother asked.

"That was uh, his chauffeur. They were practicing football, and he still had his helmet on. They just gave me a ride home. So's I could, for sure, be home in time for supper."

I headed quickly into the house while hearing Father say, "Rich people are kinda funny, ain't they?'

"Funny, aren't they," Mother corrected.

"Yes, funny, aren't they."

"Well, I'm glad he's seeing better people these days," Mother said contentedly.

Day Four

Mother, sitting across from me at the breakfast table, was absently using a butter knife to scrape on a piece of toast that she considered too dark. After an examination she began spreading it with a small amount of peach preserves. She slowly scraped the preserves from the bottom of a pint jar that had traveled from Fred's Creek.

"Bob, why don't you have a party for all of your new school friends?" she asked.

I was caught off guard. "Party? What kind of a party?"

"Well, I was just thinking." With both hands at once, she guided her thick, black hair, which came down to a little below the bottom of her ears, back behind each ear to keep it out of the way while she ate. "We could have it in the backyard, plenty of room out there, and I saw in the Market Street Hardware—they have these grills that you can buy, that uses charcoal briquettes, cooks everything outside. The magazines say it really enhances the taste of the cooked meat."

"Oh?" I said. My mind was racing to think of a way out of this disaster. "Don't know too many people yet. Maybe we could wait till spring or something like that?"

"Bob, see, you don't understand. This would be a way for you to get to know new children from Boaz."

Father had already left for work, so I had no help and felt the sweat breaking out on my forehead.

I looked out the window and went to desperate tactics. "Mother, please don't make me do this. Please."

She looked at me. "Well, I'll be. Don't you think that that would be fun? I would have given anything to have a nice party with all of these new people in Boaz when I was your age."

With my best, pained expression, I turned so she could see my face, and said, "Please don't make me do this, Mom."

"All right, all right, I just thought that it might be fun; don't get so upset. Sometimes I wonder about you."

"Got to go. I'll be late," I said.

I quickly headed for the door before she could come back with another argument for the party. She would, just as soon as she thought of one.

"Maybe in the spring!" she said after me.

I made my escape, running for the gates of Maplewood, crunching the newly laid gravel under my feet, imagining her at the suggested party. Smiling proudly, she would tell my classmates, "Bobby was such a good little boy."

The usual group was gathering at the bus stop.

My classmate yelled, "Whi Bwob!" and waved.

Throwing up a hand in return, I decided to escape over the hill.

A car coming from the direction of Sharpsburg suddenly pulled off the road, stopping several feet past where I was standing while waiting for a chance to cross. Out of the car came Jerry Joe, holding an open quart of chocolate milk

He flipped his cigarette over the car roof, and it went out onto the road. He yelled, "Thanks" back into the car, before slamming the door.

He came running over to me with a silly grin, "Oh Bobby! Bobby! I missed you so!"

Before I could react, he wrapped his arms around me, pinning my arms to my sides while at the same time picking me from the ground and swinging me back and forth. I felt milk splash onto my back. It ran down the plaid, button-down shirt that mother had insisted I wear today, instead of my usual white T-shirt.

"Well, how you been? I ain't seen you all night!" he said, dancing around while holding me in the air.

The carrot-headed girl jumped up and down, repeatedly kicking both heels up until they touched her behind. She pointed with both hands while shrieking laughter.

She said, "Wook! Wook!"

He finally lowered my feet to the ground. I immediately took off across the road and over the hill to hide my red face. Jerry Joe came running behind me.

"What's a matter? Don't you love me no more?" he said loudly, looking back at the others to make sure they were entertained, and they were.

When I finally stopped running, he caught up. I stood looking at him and shook my head. He snorted laughter. We walked to his house.

He opened the front door and shouted, "'Bout time to roll outta bed, Cecil. Drop your cock and grab a sock!"

"Shut up, Jerry Joe!" a woman's voice said from behind the bedroom door.

Peeking in, we saw on the table a bottle of vodka with about one drink left in it, surrounded by the assorted mess of a late-night lover's reunion.

Jerry Joe shut the door. "She's OK," he said, looking at me and laughing.

We started for the tracks, past Cecil's old Nash automobile. It was perched at an angle while sitting on four cinder blocks, with weeds growing where the engine should be. Jerry Joe started to relax and offered me a drink of milk. I took it and said thanks.

We were walking along saying nothing when something up ahead, behind a tree, caught my eye. Two kinds of people are fascinated by and take careful notice of shadows, artists and hunters. The morning shadows were made by a clear sky holding the rising sun that was coming toward us from upriver and out of the northeast. Something bulging but unseen was behind a tree and making the otherwise matching tree shadow stick out beyond where it should. It changed positions slightly. I tapped Jerry Joe's arm, pointing out the inconsistency.

We slowed crept to see what it was. Garvin suddenly stuck his head around the tree from his sitting position.

He said in a loud voice, "Who the hell do you two think you are! Dan'l Boone or somebody?"

We jumped back. He rolled awkwardly out to a position where he could get to his feet. He seemed delighted that he had startled us.

"Looks like you two young roosters are up to no good this morning, so I'll just go along and see what the hell you're up to." He fell in beside us, walking the tracks, and started humming a tune that I had never heard before.

"As president of Garvin Enterprises, I think this morning I might go on up to the dump and see what the fine citizenry of Boaz have discarded. I'm probably just wasting my time. You know what's up there?" he said, looking at me, since I was the closest to him.

"No."

"Junk! That's what's up there. People don't throw nothing but junk away. I look that place up and down, and there's nothing but junk, junk, junk!" He waited awhile, and then said quietly, "I just don't understand it."

We walked on in silence while he snickered to himself.

"You been up to the farm lately?" Garvin asked Jerry Joe some time later.

"Kay's back home. Mr. Schultz—he's about the same, caddy for him a bunch."

The story was told. A flood had killed Garvin's family. This happened downriver, near a low area called St. Catherine's. He was only a few months old when someone found him in a tree. A sister who was not very old herself was holding him. Their parents were never found.

Kay's grandmother, who was helping with the flood, brought the baby home for temporary care and to be checked by a doctor. An order of Polish nuns, also helping with flood victims, took the older sister with them. Kay's grandmother, along with Veada and Della, became attached to the baby boy, and he eventually stayed, to be raised more or less as a brother to Kay's father. Veada and her husband cared for both of the boys when the Schultz parents were out of town.

Garvin made almost perfect grades in school without trying very hard. He was sent to college, but not long after that he had a fight with his adoptive father and quit school. He left town and was not heard from for a while. He returned home shortly before his adoptive parents were both killed in an automobile accident. After that he joined the army and was gone again.

"You know what I'm trying to figure out right now?" Garvin asked.

"No."

"Well, I'll tell you then. I'm trying to figure out if the universe has a heartbeat."

"You think it does?" I said, not knowing what else to say.

"If it doesn't, that wouldn't be so bad either. There are plenty of things that are worse than nothing, my boy, just remember that."

"I'll do that."

We parted from Garvin, to take the path toward school. He walked on up the tracks, whistling another unfamiliar song.

"What's he talkin' about?" I asked Jerry Joe in a low tone.

His head shook and shoulders shrugged at the same time. "He just jabbers that ah way. I don't know. When he's drinkin' a lot, it gets worse. He'll stretch out sometimes on the track and falls to sleep, big as you please. Cecil pulled him off once, right before a train came."

We stopped at the Texaco station. This morning Jerry Joe would stay at the station to work for Cecil until he decided to show up. Then he would go on to the club and caddy. The station owner mentioned to Jerry Joe that he wanted Cecil to look at the principal's car as soon as he arrived. The engine was running poorly.

I traveled the now-familiar route to my locker.

Mike came into the school through the front door after his mother dropped him off. He began telling me about the phone call he had received from Kay before school. Kay was going to stay home and diagram new plays for the football team, to be used in our games as soon as he could get the school to change the rules. He told Mike that he wanted to see all three of us as soon as possible, on urgent business.

Mike thought Kay had less stamina than on his last trip home. Mike didn't seem saddened by Kay's health, but he was indignant, frustrated, and genuinely angry that something like Kay's condition could exist.

"Hi, Mike!" two female voices said in unison.

"Hi, Susan, Karen."

"Hi, your name's Bob, isn't it?" Karen asked.

"Why yes, Bob," I said.

"Hi, Bob!" they said together.

"Hi."

We had met at the Labor Day weekend party that officially ended the summer season at the Boaz Country Club. Within a week they closed the swimming pool. Mike's mother invited me to attend with Dr. Masters's niece, visiting from Pittsburgh. Mike went with Susan because she asked him. Susan liked bad boys. She really liked Mike.

During summer caddying, Jerry Joe had taught me to go home with Mike for lunch whenever possible. His house was a short distance from the club. The lady that worked for them was a good cook. Mike's mother seemed delighted that we ate like pigs at her elegant dinning table while Mike mostly ignored the food.

There were deviled eggs and tuna fish on toast that was cut diagonally, topped with lettuce, and served on matching plates. Milk was served in stemmed glasses without a hint of Howdy Doody's picture, like the glasses at my house had. While wiping our mouths on cloth napkins, we thanked Mrs. Masters repeatedly when she happened to be home. Best of all it was free.

One day the niece joined us. She was shy and said little. When she did speak, it was in a low monotone that I could barely understand. I mostly nodded and smiled politely. It seemed to do the trick. Somehow plans were made. Mike's mother also invited Jerry Joe to the party. He thanked her but said he would be working that night. He would be working, at the same party, in the kitchen, and getting paid for it.

The party would be held at the marina, located over the hill and directly below the country club golf course. It was a small man-made lake that had a pier and a channel to the river. There were slips that held dark wooden motorboats, slowly bobbing. A covered wooden dock, large enough for a band, lights, and dancing, was the focal point of the semiformal dance. The white coats and pastel gowns created a romantic scene that was as grandly sophisticated as a kid from Fred's Creek could imagine.

I, of course, lacked a white coat. Mike's mother searched back and forth in a closet before handing me one of Dr. Masters's old jackets. It was a little loose in the shoulders, but the sleeves were perfect. It looked OK.

Mother didn't know what to say when I showed her the coat. She was thrilled at my invitation to the party but was taken back by my accepting what she considered charity.

Explaining to her that it was only borrowed and would soon be returned would not do. We made a trip to Sharpsburg that ended with a new white sport coat plus black pants and shoes. I am sure that it was not part of the household budget, but Father never mentioned the clothes, in fun or otherwise. So coupled with a white shirt that I had for church, and one of Dad's black ties, I felt dashing.

Having never danced was another obstacle. Mother became my teacher. The church we attended did not believe in dancing; it was thought to be too suggestive. Grandfather was the preacher. He had planned and built the church building in Fred's Creek many years ago. Mother thought dancing once in a while wasn't so bad. She had sneaked off with Father to dance on the sly. When the Labor Day party arrived, I could pretend to dance.

Susan's friend and next-door neighbor, Karen, attended the dance with her steady boyfriend, Butterbean Boggs. He was captain of the Boaz football team, which more times than not won the championship of the county junior high schools. Son of Sharpsburg's biggest department store owner, he was predicted to play college football. Butterbean questioned the manhood of any kid who did not play on the school team. He ignored Mike and me by addressing us only through Karen. This was not a surprise to Mike. They had crossed paths before.

Mike and Susan slow danced with her face buried in his neck. The cousin and I fast danced. Nobody laughed. Slow dancing made me nervous, but I warmed to it with time. We danced quite a bit, mostly on the edge of the floor area, looking at the strings of bare light bulbs that were woven among the wooden beams that formed the roof over the band. We were taking turns commenting on how nice everything was.

The corner of my eye caught a movement in the weeds that lined the bank that ran along beside the waterway, going out to the river. I looked over to lock eyes at forty yards with Garvin, squatting in the weeds. He held a finger to where his lips would be located under the beard. He shook his head and then disappeared.

Later Mike and I sneaked away while the girls talked during a band break. The men were discussing this year's football team with Butterbean. We caught a ride on one of the golf carts that were heading up and down the hill, across tracks and fairways, to and from the kitchen. The one we were on was heading to pick up additional supplies for the lakeside buffet. The golf cart driver, an older caddy, was wearing a starched, white cotton coat that buttoned all the way to the top. The coat's narrow collar fit tightly around his neck.

Mike knew his way around. I followed him into the busy kitchen, which held a number of people, all wearing white coats. Some were giving instructions. At a middle table stood Jerry Joe's great-aunt Della, carefully flipping over a large rounded Jell-O mold to dislodge a fresh green mountain that stood shaking and showing fruit cocktail suspended throughout. Della had already piled fresh whipped cream around the bottom of several other mounds of assorted colors. The mold imprint made them look like small rounded hills with squiggled ridges that started at the table and ran to a point at the top. She nodded hello but was too busy to talk, and pointed to a line of large sinks.

We found Jerry Joe scrubbing the big pans used for cooking the food. He glanced up and motioned us to move back out the door. He followed, slapping me with a wet hand on the back of the head.

Grinning, he said, "How you like bein' a big shot, bub?"

"It's fabulous," I said, pretending to put on airs. That got me an additional smack in the head. Mike ignored us while lighting two cigarettes, then handed Jerry Joe one.

I said, "There's a sailboat back down there, almost as big as in *The Crimson Pirate*." That was a favorite movie we had sat through twice on a summer trip to Sharpsburg.

"That belongs to the Schultz's; they got a boy. He's away," Mike said.

"Away. Where?"

"Hospital, he's sick."

"Oh? He's got a real sailboat? Could we go look at it when he comes back?" I asked.

"He wouldn't care a bit. I rode it before," Jerry Joe said.

Someone yelled for him. He flicked his cigarette while heading in the door and didn't look back, but he waved to us over his shoulder.

Yelling after him, I said, "I saw Garvin!"

"Take him a beer!" he yelled back from inside.

We rode back to the dance, standing on the back of the same golf cart, balancing between us a chest of beer and soft drinks, covered in ice. The seat beside the driver held several matching food trays that were covered with thick silver lids. We each forced bottles of beer into our front pant pockets and walked casually to near the place along the bank where Garvin had been spotted. We were glad to get the cold, wet bottles removed, and we left them sitting on the ground to walk back to the party.

Except for Butterbean's dirty looks, the pleasant evening faded into a fun night.

As Karen later said, "A good time was had by all."

Mike was still standing beside his locker this morning, talking to Susan. Mostly he was listening.

Karen asked me, "What class you in?"

"9-1s."

She looked a little surprised. She was waiting for Susan to quit talking and grinning at Mike. They finally walked away.

I overheard Karen speaking to Susan, "So-o-o he's in the 9-1s too! Oho-o-o!" She looked toward the ceiling and wrinkled her nose.

With this sudden insight leading to awareness, my face grew hot with embarrassment. My stomach felt a sudden sharp pain. I felt like crying but with monumental effort was able to prevent the tears from forming. I felt for the first time the stigma of social judgment of the 9-1s by the rest of the school. I had never before considered this.

This type of embarrassment, big or small, is a place that all people sooner or later visit, but today was the sudden awakening of a fourteen-year-old kid to a world that he had only recently been exposed to. I was now aware of what people thought of those of us in the 9-1s.

"Come on," Mike said. "What's the matter with you?"

"Nothin'."

I walked ahead of him to homeroom so he wouldn't see my face. I tried to read my book but could not concentrate and ended up staring out the window, wondering if I was dumb.

The morning passed slowly. Between classes we stopped by the bathroom. Mike lit a cigarette, and to get rid of the smoke, opened and swung out one of the several metal windows that were hinged at the top. I spent the time by the door, nervously peeking into the hallway for teachers but saw something coming our way that was worse, Butterbean.

Four football players, wearing white pullover sweaters with maroon *B*s and short flattop haircuts, followed him into the restroom.

Butterbean spoke, "Well, well, two piles of shit, guess finding you in the shithouse would be about right. You two in here playing with each other like a couple a queers?" The others laughed.

He walked over to where I had retreated against the wall. I was standing and looking straight ahead, directly at his mouth.

"Where you from there, Goofy?" he said.

"Fred's Creek."

"That's just what I thought, a goddamn hillbilly, a goddamn hillbilly and a wop, in here hanging around in the shithouse, probably playing with each other. What the hell is this school coming to?"

He suddenly punched me in the stomach. My breathing stopped. It was more of a surprise than pain. I gasped for breath. They laughed louder when I dropped my book and went to my knees.

"Look, he's in love with me!" Butterbean said.

He bent over, grabbed my shirt, and pulled my face close to his.

"If I get a report of you ever talking to Karen again, I'll personally beat you to death. Do you understand me?"

I nodded.

He stood up and kicked me in the stomach. That one hurt. The others pinned Mike by the arms and took turns punching him in the stomach. He kicked one of them in the leg and was hit in the mouth by the kicked person while Butterbean laughed, watching.

Finally he said, "Let's go."

They quickly went out the door, still laughing.

Making an effort to breathe, I tried focusing my eyes on the blurry small, white floor tiles. I finally looked across. Mike was lying in the corner, curled into a fetal position with his eyes tightly shut and holding his stomach. I was beginning to get quick short breaths to restore my oxygen supply and asked a question that caused me to miss a couple of the breathing attempts.

"What's a wop?" I became dizzy again.

Mike slowly pulled himself to a sitting position, leaning against the wall. While holding his stomach with one hand, he combed his hair with the other, as blood from his lip trickled onto his shirt collar. "My grandparents are from Italy."

"You told me about them, they're like Mario Lanza, on the radio."

"Yeah."

"What's a wop then?"

"A bad name, like hillbilly," he said.

I knew hillbilly was a bad name but didn't know that Fred's Creek people were all considered hillbillies until now. "Uh-Italian hillbilly's a wop?"

He squinted his eyes, shook his head, and looked at the ceiling and finally said tolerantly, "Yeah, I guess so."

We sat quietly for a time. Mike pulled himself to the sink and spit water from the faucet. My stomach hurt, but I could now take breaths with less difficulty.

"What we gonna do?" I asked.

"Nothing."

"Nothing?"

"They did this kind of stuff before. Who is everybody going to believe? Not you, you can bet on that, hillbilly." He laughed, and it turned to a cough.

"We ain't queers, neither, I know that," I said.

"I'm glad you at least know something. Let's get the hell out of here." Mike checked his puffed lower lip one last time. I picked my book from the floor. We entered the classroom very late, receiving tardy marks.

"If you accumulate three of these, it will go on your permanent record," the teacher said.

She glanced at Mike's still slightly bleeding lip but asked no questions. He explained to me later that they usually hit you in the stomach because it leaves less evidence.

I took a seat beside Mortie, a heavy kid who appeared to be eating notebook paper. He chewed the paper to spongy consistency. When the teacher turned away, he launched the wad from the catapult—a springy wooden ruler that he held protruding from the edge of his desk. He had quite a collection of paper wads randomly sticking to the ceiling.

I was having a bad day. Figuring out what to do about it was not easy. Telling Father would cause things to get out of hand. Not the way you might think. He would say little to me, but go to the school and punch someone, probably the football coach, maybe others if they got in the way, and Mother would be mortified. A huge ongoing mess would follow. Being the son of Tuffy Parsons carried the responsibility of not getting him upset because of what he might do to those he perceived as bringing harm to his family, although in this case, as you may have guessed, telling him was tempting.

When I was a young kid back in Fred's Creek, we were eating an evening meal around the large table at my grandparents' home, where we lived. The big place at one time had been a boarding house. We sat eating quietly when an old man came through the back screen door without knocking.

"Sorry to bother you, Tuffy, but Marsh is drunk again," he said.

Father rose out of his chair and grabbed a heel of homemade bread from the big wooden cutting board at our end of the table while motioning for me to follow. The rest of the family continued eating.

Being about ten, this was high excitement. We stood in the back of the old man's pickup looking out over the cab and rode down the hill to a cluster of identical-looking wooden frame houses. We stopped in front of the one where people were gathered. When the noisy truck was turned off, we could hear cussing and screaming from within. Father jumped from the truck. At a fast walk, he opened the screen door and entered. Things got quiet.

We heard a thump followed by a loud squeal. A person came out of the door quickly, backwards, and in the process pulled the screen door from the hinges. The screen imprinted itself upon the person's behind. The body, with attached door, hit, slid, and rolled in the dirt, making a cloud of rust-colored dust. Tuffy walked out the empty doorframe followed by a woman who was using a hand to hide the side of her swollen face.

"Lock 'um in they root cellar," she said, pointing to the man lying in the dirt. Several people tugged on his large, round frame. He was dragged into a small room located behind the house that had been carved back into the side of the hill. They locked him behind a substantial wooden door.

During the ride back, Father bent over to my ear and said above the truck noise, "Don't tell your mother."

When arriving home, we sat back down to continue our meal.

When asked, Tuffy said, "Marsh was drinkin' again, but he's OK now."

"What's the matter?" the teacher sitting in front of today's class said. She could not remember my name and looked in her grade book for a list.

"Robert?"

"Ma'am?" I answered, returning quickly from my daydream.

"Are you getting sick?"

I was absently holding my stomach and frowning. The teacher thought I was about to be sick on her classroom floor. She wasn't happy and pointed to the door.

"Go to the first aid station, right now."

I walked out the door and down the hallway, still feeling light-headed and still trying to think of something to do about everything. The steps descended to the first floor. The hallway glistened, smelling of the wax that had been applied in anticipation of the beginning of the school year. Floor traffic had not yet dulled the shine. A big hand suddenly clasped firmly to my upper arm, and I could tell who it was by the voice.

"Your name's Parsons, isn't it?"

"Yes sir."

"What's the first again?"

"Bob."

"Yes, Bob, you know, Bob, I have talked to your mother several times about you. She calls me. Did you know that? Good to have parents interested in their children."

He led me past the secretary, into his office, and shut the door.

With sarcasm he said, "Please have a seat, Bob. Tell me now, why are you meandering about the halls and not in your classroom learning?"

"Teacher sent me. My stomach hurts."

"Ah ha! Some bad food maybe?"

I was nodding my head in agreement when he suddenly rose and went to a tall file cabinet; then he walked back, studying an opened manila folder that said Parsons 9-1s on an outside tab.

His curly, black hair was combed straight back. It was cut short on the sides, around his ears. The white skin showing through this short hair made his otherwise dark complexion seem darker. His ears were flat against the sides of his long head. Bushy eyebrows shaded his dark eyes. His long nose was thin and curled out like a ski jump. The tip stuck out beyond where it should have stopped, like he had told a few lies.

The story was told. He was active in local politics. He was soon to become the candidate for the state representative's seat that would be elected from the Boaz area. The duties would not interfere with his present principal's position. He thought perhaps that somewhere down the road, a more ambitious office would interfere, and that would be just fine with him.

"Now, Bob, I know that going to school is different here than it is up at Fred's Creek, but you should be thankful for all the advantages you have now. Not to say that you should be ashamed of being from Fred's Creek. You shouldn't let that bother you at all, because your future is ahead of you. If you really apply yourself and decide to go on to Sharpsburg High, they have a wonderful trade school program. How would you like to learn to make furniture, or be a carpenter?"

"Grandpa's a carpenter."

"Good, see, that's good. They could teach you to be a carpenter, and then you could go back to Fred's Creek and work with your Grandpa. Wouldn't that be fine?"

He seemed pleased when I nodded in agreement, and he began writing in the folder.

Motioning for me to follow, he eventually ushered me in to see the secretary about my stomach. She was also the first aid attendant. He seemed to forget about my meandering and went back to sit at his desk and continued to write.

The secretary was a hefty woman with a pageboy haircut. The thick bangs made her round face seem rounder. She wore a navy blue suit that had large shoulder pads and was about ten years out of style.

"What's wrong?" she asked, holding her hand on my forehead. "You don't have a temperature."

"My stomach hurts."

She motioned for me to follow and walked into the first aid room.

She said, "Stomach, huh? Pull up your shirt."

I began unbuttoning my new shirt from the bottom, the estimated minimum required distance. She bent over and looked, poking my belly hard enough to hurt.

"Where'd this red mark come from?"

"Don't know." I was as surprised as she was.

"Have you been fighting?"

"No, ma'am."

She stood up and put her hands on her hips. "I was in the Army, young man, and am certified in first aid. I see lots of students in here and know what causes something like this. You fell or you were in a fight, so don't lie to me."

"No ma'am, I wouldn't fight, it's against my religion," I explained, giving her a wide-eyed, innocent stare.

"What religion are you?"

"Sacred Gospel Church, ma'am. My grandfather is the preacher."

She relented somewhat. "Well, OK, you lay down here and rest, and if you don't feel better after lunch, we'll call your parents to come and get you. If you have to throw up, you use this."

She reached into a cabinet and handed me a stainless steel bucket. "Or better yet, if you can make it, go into the water closet."

Lying alone on the cot, with my arms folded, and the bucket sitting by my head, I was wondering what a water closet was. I now understood that being from Fred's Creek made me a hillbilly. I was also a coward for not fighting with Butterbean, and just now with the secretary, I almost got into trouble for a fight where I did nothing but get hit.

I also remembered that being in the 9-1s was socially unacceptable to some, namely Karen. On top of everything else, I had been accused of being a queer. I was not sure what that amounted to but had an idea of what it might be. The air in the room was stale and smelling of rubbing alcohol. My eyelids were getting heavy.

I was suddenly brought back to life when detecting the click of the main office door shutting. It made me sit up. There was something that could be done. I could find out what a water closet looked like. It seemed to be a bathroom without a tub.

A tentative peek showed the outer office empty, so I slowly walked out of the first aid room. Lunchtime had started. I twirled a globe sitting on a filing cabinet and stared at a picture of George Washington. Then I strolled into the principal's office without thinking and was wondering if I was supposed to wait until someone came back. I saw the manila folder on his desk. Flipped it opened. It did have my name on it.

On a sheet of paper and stapled to typed copies of my Fred's Creek grades, mostly Cs and Ds, were several entries that the principal had written: "Borderline intelligence," "marginal social skills," "maturity level below average," "needs discipline," "could benefit from trade school."

So my suspicion of being dumb was confirmed. My reaction was quick anger. I had many things planned for a future time when not burdened by school or parents. It was apparent that being dumb was going to make these things more difficult. I was positive that you could not pilot an airplane or sail big ships if you were dumb.

I sat in the principal's chair and found it would spin. So pushing hard, I attempted to see how many times I could go around with one shove. Soon tiring of the game, I saw something protruding slightly that was hidden beneath a short pile of folders lying at the corner of the desk. Reaching over, I slid out a magazine titled *Police Gazette*. There were red headlines that read, "What Really Happened at the St. Valentines Day Massacre?" Below was a grainy black-and-white picture of dead bodies lying in a row. I put it back and left.

Walking the stairs, not knowing what to do, I found myself looking at the library door and walked in to the smile of the librarian sitting at her desk, reading and eating a sandwich. She laid the sandwich discreetly out of sight.

"Where's your book?" she asked.

Suddenly I remembered that it was on the desk of my last classroom, forgotten during my trip to the first aid room. I had lost it. What else was going to happen?

She smiled again while reaching in the direction of the hidden sandwich and plopped *The Deerslayer* in front of me.

"The teachers bring back library books that they find. I remembered you were reading this one. What page you on?" she asked.

"I'm sorry, ma'am. I was sick, I'm sorry."

"What's wrong?"

"Stomach was hurtin' but it's OK now."

"No harm was done; just try to keep it with you from now on, OK? What page are you on?"

"OK, I sure will." I pulled the book open to where a blade of grass marked the page. "Thirty seven. What are you reading?" I asked, trying to work on my social skills.

"*Dr. Zhivago*. It's Russian."

"You can read Russian?"

She laughed, "No, it's been translated into English."

My face turned red while looking at the floor, but then I suddenly realized, "I could read it then."

"You could. If you can read Cooper, you can read this, that's for sure. I'll loan it to you when I get finished, if you don't lose it," she said with a kidding grin.

"No, ma'am. I'll guard it with my life!"

"You don't have to do that, just remember where you put it."

"Sure will," I promised.

We had a pleasant conversation about books in general. She offered to make me a reading list. I accepted, and not wanting to keep her from her reading, I soon excused myself.

I was walking down the hall, looking at the floor as was my habit, and thinking to myself, "She's kind of pretty, for an older woman," and practically bumped into Karen.

"Hi, Bob."

Quickly glancing the halls for Butterbean, I said, "Hi, Karen."

"You," she said. "Are you going to be at the big Thuse this afternoon?"

I didn't know what a "Thuse" was but found out later that it was a pep rally and stood for "En-thuse-e-asm." I guessed it had something to do with football, because she was wearing a cheerleader's uniform.

She stood close. Gently reaching to hold my forearm, she put her face close to mine. I could see her sun-made freckles on clear skin and smelled the shampoo of her sandy-colored short hair that bounced when she walked.

Through wide, serious, light-brown eyes she said, "It's important that everyone attend, school spirit is so-o-o important for us all, Bob, and that means you too. OK?"

"OK."

She turned and ran down the hall a few measured steps, then spun to wave good-bye, and that made her white pleated skirt twirl up to reveal well-exercised legs that extended on up to the maroon panties that flashed. She quickly gave a vertical jump that made the rest of her precocious anatomy jiggle.

With one fist raised into the air she said, "Go Boaz Skip Jacks!"

She then twirled the opposite way to run the entire length of the hall. For the first time since this morning, Butterbean was not on my mind.

Searching for Mike, I found him leaning on the counter at the Texaco station. He was talking to Cecil and drinking an RC Cola. They were both looking down at an unfolded page that had been torn from a magazine.

"It's got thirty-two horsepower and they're coming out with a thirty-six horsepower," Mike was saying. He flashed me a crooked grin to keep his still slightly puffed lip from hurting and said, "You didn't die yet, huh?"

"No, seen the Piggotts?" I asked.

"Nope," Cecil said. "If I do, there's gonna' be a head thumpin', you can bet your sweet ass on it."

Clyde Piggott wasn't the only one with a prison record. Cecil had also done some time, for stealing tools from a service station in Sharpsburg that had fired him. Cecil said they owned him money and wouldn't pay, so he was trying to make things come out even. Someone witnessed him and another fellow carrying the tools away. That was that.

The picture on the page that was unfolded and lying on the counter before them was of an odd-looking car.

"What kinda car's that?" I asked.

"Germans make it, called a Volkswagen. There's a couple of them around Sharpsburg. I saw one the other day. Thinking maybe I'll get this kind of a car."

Cecil said, "You be wastin' your money, boy." He slowly walked out into the lift bay and began putting tools away.

"Cecil's not impressed," Mike said with a smile.

He folded the page, sticking it in his shirt pocket, while at the same time we heard the first bell, indicating that lunch would soon be over. It came from a round bell and hammer that was attached high on the outside of the school building.

On the way back to school Mike explained to me what a Thuse was, plus how we could sneak off before it started.

I asked him, "What's a borderline intelligence mean?"

Mike stopped and made a face. "A what?"

"The principal said I had a borderline intelligence."

"He told you that?"

"He wrote it on a paper about me."

Mike looked back toward the Texaco station. "I don't think it sounds too good."

"No sir, I don't either, and I think it means I'm dumb."

"You ask a lot of dumb questions and tell a lot of big lies, but I don't know about you being dumb."

"I don't tell lies!"

"What about your uncle killing that bear?"

"Uncle Lester did kill a bear, I swear! He's still got the teeth. I can show them to you. I can!"

He shook his head, put his hands into his pockets, and went on into the building.

I tried to read for the next couple of classes but mostly fumed at Mike. It was soon time for the classes to let out early for the Thuse that was being held in honor of a football game that would be played tomorrow after school.

Mike had it all worked out. He explained that we needed to sneak into the empty girl's dressing room beside the gymnasium, wait until the coast was clear, and then escape from the school using the exit door of the adjacent teacher's lounge. Except when we headed for the exit, I remembered my again-forgotten book. I wanted to go back for it.

"I'll meet you on the tracks. Don't take all day, and watch out for monitors," Mike said, as I hurried back.

I retraced my steps, retrieved the book that was forgotten on a desk, and was returning when it became apparent that the shortest distance would be to go out the far end door, skipping the gym all together. Then I would cut across the parking lot to go directly over the hill.

Ahead, down the hallway, a girl was sitting in a chair, wearing white and black saddle oxfords with green ankle socks below a pastel yellow dress. Under the dress was a bouncy crinoline slip that was mashed down by a briefcase positioned on her lap. It was open. She sat arranging its contents and wasn't aware of my approaching.

"Oh!" She put her hand on her chest, surprised and a little embarrassed. I recognized her as the assistant helping with the IQ test.

"Could I please see your exit pass, please?" she said, in a business-like manner.

"I was, uh, just released from the first aid room and don't have it," I said, beginning to learn what a monitor was.

She searched the briefcase and held up her identification, which was cut from a sheet of mimeographed paper. Her name was hand printed at the top.

"My name is Penny Sharpe. I am a hall monitor for special events, and the Thuse is a special event. I cannot allow you to exit from these premises."

She got up, laid her briefcase on the chair, and turned back to me, still displaying her credentials while standing with a straight back that made the large green bow, loosely hooked to the top of her head, tip backwards. She maintained her defiant look while pushing glasses back on her nose with a forefinger.

"I'm new around here and didn't know about this stuff, so I'm sorry," I said, turning to go.

She held up a hand. "Wait! I need your name for my report," she said and searched the briefcase to find a pad and pencil, then stood again ready to write. "Now what's your name?"

"Bob."

"Bob what?"

"Bob Boggs."

She seemed a little surprised. "Are you related to Butterbean Boggs?"

"Oh yeah, we're double cousins."

"You know I'm in the 9-5s and tutor him in algebra, don't you? He's in the 9-3s, you know? What class are you in?"

"9-4s." I was hoping not to be recognized.

"Oh? Well you know, you will have practically the same math as us, except we will be doing some calculus, and you will not. But you will have it in high school, so don't worry about it. It will not count against your getting into college, I'm sure."

She emphasized her remarks by shaking the pointed finger of her pencil hand in time with her words. "Mother went to the University of Louisville. What about you?"

"My grandpa went to, Cincinnati," I said, creeping slowly backwards, nodding in agreement.

She went on after considering what I had said, "You know that's probably a good school too, best of luck to you, but it takes more than luck. I, myself, study four hours every night at home and much longer on the weekends. This dedication will pay off in the long run. You know that, don't you?"

"Thank you." I smiled and cupped my hand into a small good-bye wave.

Bowing my head, I turned, walking fast toward the gymnasium, while she continued talking as though I was still standing close to her. I quickly escaped by the unguarded door that Mike told me to use in the first place. While exiting, a roar came from inside the gymnasium.

"Give me a *B*, everybody!" the cheerleaders said.

The students in unison shouted, "*B*!"

"Give me an *O*!"

"What took you so long?" Mike was tired of waiting.

"Monitor almost got me; got away from her. What's a calculus?"

He looked at me again with squinted eyes and said he thought it was some kind of math and hard to do. Then he looked at his watch that had a new twist-o-flex silver band.

"I'm going to time you. No questions for five minutes; now let's go see Kay."

At the country club we found Jerry Joe sitting by himself under a tree. He was enjoying a "brown cow," which was made by filling a paper cup with white milk, then adding two scoops of chocolate ice cream. He had bought it from the snack bar, using the specially designated caddie's window. Lower prices were charged at the caddie's window.

We three caught a ride upriver with an older caddy and piled out of his car in front of the Schultz Dairy sign. We walked to the house by the long front road, which was bordered on each side by square wire fencing attached to substantial wooden posts that swooped behind the occasional large tree. We continued around and into the pool area and found Kay in his chair. He was wearing a Cincinnati Redlegs baseball hat and a much-too-large white terry-cloth robe that had the sleeves rolled up many times. Sticking out from the opened bottom were his small, swollen feet.

"Where you all been? I been sitting waiting, and you three are out pissin' around. We got work to do. OK, let's take care of the important business first. Jerry Joe, go get four boxes of cards from the secret drawer."

Jerry Joe went through the kitchen door while Kay made vague general hints about something important that was about to take place but was not understood by anyone but himself.

Jerry Joe soon returned with several unopened decks of playing cards and four opened orange pops from Veada. He walked over to us carrying the bottles with one hand. The necks were wedged between his fingers. The other hand was wrapped around the card decks. Kay scooted to the stand that was sitting beside his chair and pecked the top with his finger.

"Open them," he said. We each did.

Jerry Joe opened a box for Kay. Kay paused and looked with an awkwardly stiff neck around the pool area to see if anyone was within ear range.

He tried to whisper, saying with dramatic formality, "I started a club many years ago, when me and Jerry Joe were just little kids. It's a secret organization. We use the code word 'club,' you see, in case we get overheard, but it's really a gang."

He looked at the three of us with a pinched face and serious expression. We were silent.

"It's time to add a couple new members, don't you think?" he said, looking over at Jerry Joe.

"Yeah, sure." Jerry Joe took a drink of pop.

Kay continued in a slow, serious manner, forgetting the attempt at whispering.

" Read about this gang name in *Gang Busters* funny books and decided to go ahead and use it myself. I made me and my friend Jobare a member one time, over in Switzerland, but he died. So now it will only be the four of us. So, does everyone see eye to eye? I can't even tell you the name until we all say yes."

He had everyone paying attention. We said yes in semi-unison.

Kay raised his hand like he was giving a blessing. "Take out the aces from your deck."

We followed the instructions.

"Now take out the ace of spades. Then keep it with you, in your pocket or somewhere, because this is the proof you belong to The

Black Ace Gang. Then if you get in a jam of any sort, the rest of us will do anything that needs done to help. No matter what kind of trouble it is, the other people will help you; forever. You have to say, 'I agree.'"

"I agree," we said in unison.

Jerry Joe grinned, not being able to tolerate seriousness for long, and held up his bottle. "Hear, Hear!" he said, imitating the toast he had seen in *The Crimson Pirate* movie.

We all held up our bottles and repeated, "Hear, Hear!" and it was done.

"You can't tell a soul about this, even if they torture you," Kay added.

We sat in the quiet, listening to the reclining dogs pant in the warm temperature of the enclosed area, a result of the heated pool.

"There are two black aces," Mike said.

"Well if someone shows the wrong ace, we'll know they're a fake, won't we!" Kay shot back.

"So we're not, The Black Ace of Spades Gang, then?"

"No! No! The Black Ace Gang, don't you understand anything?"

"OK, don't have a conniption fit, I was just asking," Mike said. It was settled.

Veada stuck her head out the door. "Don't go outside dressed that a-way. I'm not sittin' up all night with you. You know what the nurse said about you catchin' a cold."

"We're conductin' business here, go away!" Kay then added in a lowered tone, "I won't go out."

"Well," she nodded and disappeared.

"What's a gang do?" Curiosity had gotten the best of me.

Kay puckered his mouth and said, "They tell other people what to do. Instead of getting told what to do!"

Veda stuck her head out again. "You all want some iced cream?"

Three of us answered yes. Being outvoted, Kay reluctantly followed with his attire dragging behind like a royal robe. For the rest of our visit, he occasionally patted the black ace that was in the robe's vest pocket.

I made a decision to carry mine in my billfold's folding money section. Everyone seemed to feel a sense of accomplishment by the events, but we did not discuss the "gang" for the remainder of the afternoon.

"Just in case, because spies might be listening," Kay said.

"What time is it?" I asked after a time, suddenly thinking of a missed supper.

Jerry Joe decided to travel with me downriver . We hitchhiked and Mike stayed with Kay, presumably to make gang plans. The fellow that was nice enough to stop and give us a ride was going on to Sharpsburg, so Jerry Joe rode with him to help Gloria sell tickets at the rink.

After firmly shutting the old car's door, I walked between the Maplewood gate markers and cut across backyards to ease inside the house by using the side door under the carport.

I laid my library book on the kitchen counter to wash my hands in the sink, and then moved quickly to my seat. The family was already seated at the table and chatting. They were mostly just stalling to give me a few more minutes to arrive. I was not officially late, but close.

"What did you do in school today, Bob?"

"Nothin'."

"Nothing, dear."

"Nothing."

"Oh, come now, you had to have done something. I'm going to that school one of these days and see for myself if you don't tell me."

My two younger brothers were elbowing each other. Father gave them a look. They quit.

"Where did we come from? I know Fred's Creek, but before that?" I asked.

Mother's fork stopped halfway to her mouth. She gave me an odd look, "Before that, let me see, probably Virginia. Yes, Virginia.

"Before that. We're not from Italy, are we?"

"Lord no, we're not. What kind of a question is that? Probably England. Yes, I'm sure it was England. What's got you a wondering about things like that?"

I gave her the look that says, "you don't understand anything."

"That's what we did in school today," I answered, with fake patience.

"Oh, I see," she said, sounding surprised.

She went back to eating, while father sopped his brown bean juice by using a torn piece of cornbread. He smiled.

Day Five

"Honey, we're going up home Sunday, for church."

"Need to caddy."

"They're expecting us, all of us, so you be here with bells on, young man."

"Yes, ma'am." I started for the front door and school, getting away with a T-shirt, instead of wearing another of the new plaid shirts. Mother went into the front room. The telephone was ringing. She called my name.

"It's for you," she said, surprised.

"Hello."

"We're gonna have a club meeting. Bring the thing with you," Kay said.

"What thing?"

"We don't talk on the phone. You know, the bang bang."

"To school?"

"Yeah. Mike's not going. He's sick, he told his folks that. We'll pick you up," he hung up.

"Who was that? What did they want?" Mother asked, standing with her hands on her waist. I had received few phone calls. This was the first in the morning.

"Kay Schultz, you know him. He's wantin' to know about homework."

"Oh."

I went to the bedroom and stuffed the gun and holster, plus my library book, into a paper bag. Then added my Chuck Taylor All-Star Converse sneakers, along with a pair of shorts needed for gym class, and quickly headed out the front door, avoiding more questions. I gave the necessary waves at the bus stop and descended over the hill. Jerry Joe was missing from his couch. He was probably not back from Sharpsburg. Garvin was nowhere to be seen, so I walked the tracks alone.

Random pieces of coal had shaken from the passing trains since yesterday. I reached for a chunk here and there, tossing them at intervals to the hidden piles that Jerry Joe and Cecil had started beneath the round corrugated drains that were used to let rainwater run beneath the tracks before flowing on down into the river. They would eventually gather this coal in a cardboard box or burlap bag. It would be piled in front of the house against the row of cinderblocks that kept the chunks from rolling over into the river. It was free heat for winter.

I walked along, remembering when I was about five years old and traveling somewhere by car with my grandparents. I was in the back seat with Mattie, my best friend. Mattie lived upstairs at my grandparents' house in Fred's Creek. She slept in the room next to mine. We spent more time together than about anyone else in the family because of my being too young to help much with the work and her being too old. She was my great-grandmother. Her job much of the day was to keep an eye on me. We were more friends than anything. She left the discipline to others and was always on my side. We had secrets like friends do.

She sometimes told me stories of Joseph, her long-dead husband. How he brought her flowers and candy. So I brought her flowers, usually dandelions or violets from the yard, and gave her an occasional piece of the horehound candy that I was allowed to buy during trips with my grandparents to the feed store. She smiled, thanked me, and seemed to enjoy anything I carried to her. Even the "pretty" rocks I found in the garden.

We were riding in the car. Grandfather came to a rough railroad crossing that required him to stop and ease slowly across to prevent damage to the car. There were people walking beside the tracks with cardboard boxes that were held balanced on their shoulders by a hand. They sat the boxes down occasionally to bend over and add something.

Pointing out the window, I questioned Mattie, "What they doin'?"

"Pickin' coal," she said.

I remembered squatting and watching, fascinated, when the dump truck arrived. It raised the truck bed and slid a big pile of coal into our backyard after grandfather finished giving hand signals to exactly where he wanted it dumped.

"Why don't they get some in a truck like us?" I wondered.

"They can't afford the money for that, Bobby."

I looked over at her. "Are they poor?"

"Could be," she said.

I folded my arms and settled back against the seat, assessing my good fortune to have been born into such a wealthy family.

Up ahead behind the Texaco station, Garvin was sitting on the ground and leaning back against a stack of empty pop cases. He was looking down my way and sitting unusually still.

I went up the bank. "Hi," I said.

"You ever do any traveling, Rooster?" he asked.

"Been over to Ohio," I said, pointing out across the river.

Garvin frowned. "Those people are all crazy, don't go over there. Know how you can tell if a dog's from Ohio?"

"No."

"Pick up his tail and look; if there's a big O, it's from Ohio."

"They all got an O," I said laughing, but he only smiled. A sad look remained on his face in spite of the smile.

"Been all over, traveled about everywhere. Been over to Europe. Went and stood on the spot I lost this." He wiggled his arm's short stub. "You know what was there? Everywhere I went?"

"No."

"I was."

"What?" I said, not understanding.

"I could walk to the North Pole. When I got there, there I'd be. You can't run off and leave yourself. See?"

"Yeah," I answered, with a slight understanding. I put down my bag of stuff to pull an empty pop case from the stack and sat on it. Garvin reached inside an old tire that was leaned against the station wall and pulled out a pint bottle of whiskey that said "Kessler's, and below—"Smooth as Silk." He held the bottle between his knees, then removed the top, laid it on his knee, and took a slow drink.

"You ever do any dreaming?" he asked in a low tone.

"You mean sleepin' dreaming? Yeah I do."

"I dream a lot, Rooster. When I do, there are always two arms."

"Huh?"

"Well for instance, one dream I have, I'm at the country club at a big dance, wearing a tuxedo, kind of dancing and smiling at everyone. Shaking hands; making cleaver small talk. I always have two arms in the dream. Strange, don't you think?"

It was strange.

"It's even stranger because I never liked the club, didn't ever hang around there much. So what do you make of it?"

"You know Kay's dad, don't you?" I was trying to avoid answering. I had no answer.

"Yeah, his name's Kay too. We saw each other about every day when we were growing up. We were friends, like brothers through high school. Then he went East to college. I was going with him, but at the last minute the school needed one more spot for a kid who was a legacy. That means his father attended. They were required to take him, so you see with only one spot, Kay went."

"I was sent over to Edger College. It's not a bad place—takes rich kids, charges a huge tuition. It passes out just enough scholarships among smart kids to keep the alumni's academic achievements respectable. Then they hand out liberal arts degrees left and right."

"Well," I said. He might as well have been speaking Chinese to me.

"The problems started when I went to visit this girl I liked in her dorm room, late at night, when I wasn't suppose to. I will admit to being quite inebriated.

"Some girl spotted a man in the dorm and set off the alarm. I guess an impulse to help was what made the rest of the girls shove me down a laundry chute to the basement. The security guard found me there, passed out in a pile of dirty linen. The campus police were dragging me out when I regurgitated on their shoes. This added to my general disfavor."

He raised his eyebrows in a dignified manner that was meant to be funny, and it made me laugh out loud.

"Mrs. Schultz had the incident all smoothed over, and me another chance, when her husband, Booger—that's what most of us called him, Booger—started cussing and yelling at me. He tried to hit me with a lamp, so I smacked him. I left and never went back."

"Never?"

"Later on I stopped by and stayed for a while but not long. I still go see Veada. She and Della were the only ones besides Mrs. Schultz who ever took up for me. Well, the old bastard King Kay always seemed to like me for some reason. I don't exactly know why, because he never paid any of us too much attention. He spent most of his time figuring out how to make more money.

"But you see, Rooster that was a long time ago. I've had lots of time to give this whole thing considerable consideration. Weighing all sides and being empathic to everyone's situation. So after constant analysis over the years, I have come to an intensely enlightened decision on the matter. You know what it is?"

"What?"

"I decided—fuck 'em all."

I could not think of anything to say, so I mentioned school and stood.

Garvin said, "I like watching the river go by. Makes my nerves calm."

I agreed and then picked up my bag and walked off. From a distance I heard him yelling:

"Been from Main to Spain!

"Russia to Prussia!

"Been to a goat ropin' chicken pluckin' county fair!

"Shit in both oceans an seen buzzards fuck in midair!

"And I ain't never seen nothing like that old river out there!"

I walked along, thinking and laughing.

I stopped before entering the school, looked around to make sure no one was watching, and slipped the black ace from my billfold. I studied it, wondering what sort of consequences would come if my secret gang affiliation were discovered. If having the ace in my possession brought questions from anyone, "I found it along the road" would be my story. Carefully placing it back into my billfold, I headed in.

The idea of spending the day at school alone was not appealing. There was no alternative, so I deposited the bag in my locker and carried *The Deerslayer* on to homeroom, thinking that reading would help me get through the day.

"Where's Mike? Is he sick or something?" Susan asked, coming over and walking along beside me.

Her family owned the Chevrolet-Oldsmobile-Buick dealership in Sharpsburg. She was a cheerleader, and this morning was wearing a short sleeve white sweater. A chain with a small gold megaphone was hanging from around her neck. Her mother had been a cheerleader. Susan's family lived beside Karen, another cheerleader. Susan had bowed to the pressure and went through the motions of becoming a cheerleader. It was the path of least resistance. She complained to Mike about the pressure of her situation.

Susan had long, straight, brown hair. She was a little shorter and considerably thinner than her friend Karen, who was walking alongside her this morning and wearing a matching megaphone. She also wore a white sweater, but hers seemed to be at least one size too small. Karen's more voluptuous body was the type that fourteen-year-old boys have dreams about. They were both wearing scotch plaid pleated skirts that came to about four inches above their white knee socks and new, antiqued cordovan penny loafers.

I didn't know how to answer the question she had just asked me, so I made an attempt to look serious. "He's working on stuff I can't tell you about."

"What stuff?"

Looking around the hall to see if Karen was going to get me kicked again was mainly on my mind.

I said, "We can't talk here. Too many people listening; I'll tell him to see you."

She said, "OK" and looked puzzled.

I couldn't blame her, because I was puzzled also, curious to know what Mike and Kay were up to. The bell allowed me a merciful separation to homeroom.

"Bye, Bob!" the girls yelled in unison.

I sat beside Mortie again because the seats around him were always empty. I didn't know why. I had previously witnessed different girls in class slipping off a shoe to wiggle their toes in his direction. Mortie started cringing, making faces, and moving around in a most unnatural manner. Finally, he asked the teacher to be excused for the restroom. When he left, several in the class glanced at each other, giggling. On a second occasion he shut his eyes and hid his face under his folded arms on the desk, but eventually he peeked out at the foot, with the same results.

Something hit my arm. It was a note pitched by my Maplewood friend. She seemed always to be in the seat behind me. The teacher was looking away, so I reached down, and then read the note printed in a small neat hand: "Mort foot feend." What a foot fiend could be was a mystery to me, but by the looks of Mortie, it couldn't be good. I glanced over at him to see him looking my way with an odd smile, like he was proud of himself.

The homeroom teacher said loudly, "Bob, I want you to go with Mortie this morning and learn how to run the movie projector. In case he is absent someday. The class is in the audiovisual room; Mortie knows the way."

She held out her arm and waved between her fingers a written excuse for missing the first class and indicated for me to come and take it from her.

Mortie was following close behind as out the door we went. With this sudden move, I became a member of the audiovisual department. Mortie had no sense of proper distance. He walked beside me much too closely. Suddenly without warning he ran down the hall, plopped on his round belly, and slid on the waxed hallway, laughing.

"Come on, you slide," he coaxed.

"No."

"All right." He came running back to me and went sliding by in the opposite direction.

He returned to where I had stopped to wait on him and stood close, looking directly into my face. "They wiggle their toes at me."

I didn't answer. The brown hair over his entire head was the same length. This made the hair on top about average in length, but around his ears and down the back of his neck it was shaggy. It stuck in directions that had more to do with the way he had slept than with a comb. He had a faint unpleasant smell about him.

"I see the girls' feet. It's the same as they was naked."

"Naked?"

"You want to see a girl naked?" he asked.

I had considered the possibility. "Maybe."

"Me seein' girls feet is the same thing. See?"

I did not see. The thought to me was beyond belief, but deep down inside I could not help but feel that if it were true, he would be a lucky fellow. The chance of seeing a girl's foot was considerably greater than seeing the entirely nude person.

"What do you mean?" I asked.

He reached out and tapped my crotch with the back of his hand.

"Down here," he said.

"Don't do that. I'll hit you," I said, with a mean look.

"All right," he agreed, and nonchalantly walked ahead of me, on down the hallway. It was apparent that he had been threatened before.

We were the last to arrive at the audiovisual room. There were two male students attending from each class. All were seated when we walked into the room. The 9-5s representatives were sitting at the front. They were distinguishable by the slide rules, held in tan plastic cases and hanging from their belts, anticipating advanced mathematics.

I sat in the first available seat and was surprised again by Mortie when he walked to the front of the room. He nodded at a young male teacher who had been assigned to monitor the instructions. My jaw dropped when it became apparent that Mortie was the one showing this class how to use the equipment.

He knew everything there was to know about cameras, movie projectors, slide projectors, and reel-to-reel tape machines and had spent considerable time in every movie theater projection booth in Sharpsburg, both as an invited and uninvited guest. He was scornful of the outdated equipment that made up most of the school inventory but condescended to explain how it was used. He answered several questions without hesitation. For a few minutes, with brushed teeth, combed hair, and a clean shirt, he could have passed for a typical kid. Pointing to a specific projector on a shelf, he told us that the lamp was burnt out. He knew its wattage, the cheapest place to order a new one, and the procedure for replacement.

The class period passed with Mortie taking things apart and doing most of the talking, sometimes in a quite animated way. The more technical, the more animated he became. The teacher sat with his feet on the desk, reading his magazine for most of the period. The bell cleared the room at the end of the period. Mortie remained bent over a front table, cleaning the disassembled threading sprocket that he had removed from a projector.

"This pass here is only for one class period. We got to go now," I coaxed.

Rubbing the sprocket with his shirttail and periodically stopping to check for progress in removing the dirt, he raised to face me with a contemptuous look.

"One moment, please!" he said.

So I spent the next minutes strolling about the room, looking at the labeled metal containers that were holding film. They lined several racks built along the wall. They were mostly travelogues of other lands. He was finally satisfied with his work and consented to leave. Of course we were late. Walking down the hall, he again fumed about the school's inferior equipment while examining a handful of projector pieces that he had brought with him.

Not remembering what class we should now be attending bothered me more than Mortie. He had resumed his sliding practice when a teacher stepped from a classroom to witness him scooting by the doorway on his belly. Seeing there were two, he pointed and led us to the principal's office. The teacher told the secretary our story. Me showing the pass, now expired, did not help the situation. We were told to sit and wait for the principal to decide our fate.

For some unknown reason, Mortie considered this a good time to unroll his pants cuffs that were turned up several times to compensate for his large waist. They contained used flashbulbs, all broken. Mortie owned a flashbulb camera. The cuffs were also carrying assorted dirt, pebbles, lint, and wood shavings from somewhere. He made quite a mess, and when finished, sat with folded arms, ignoring my urgings to scoot the dirt back under his chair and out of sight. The principal walked out of his office.

"Clean that up, Mortie!"

"I'll need a broom."

The principal walked to a closet. He brought back a broom and held it out for Mortie. We watched Mortie push the mess back and forth slowly, and he finally formed some semblance of a pile.

"I'll require a dust pan."

That started the principal on a second trip to the closet. Mortie spread his legs and leaned over into a stiff-legged, comically awkward position to push most of the mess into the dustpan.

"I'll need a trash receptacle."

"Give me that!" the principal said.

He yanked the broom and pan from Mortie's hands, spilling some of the contents.

"Get in there, right now!" he yelled, while handing the broom and pan to the secretary. He shoved Mortie into his office.

The story was told. Mortie had been considered for expulsion the previous year. All of his clothes were stolen as a joke while he was in the shower after gym class. He walked across the gym floor and through the halls, wet and naked, to the principal's office to register a complaint. After the incident, he was permanently exempt from pranks. The principal, with the help of the football coach and teachers, announced that dire consequences would fall upon anyone ignoring the official order: "Do not mess with Mortie."

If you ever have reason to be involved with a group of people who are about to be whipped, try to always be the first. Don't sit and listen to the noise of your predecessor, because the anticipation is worse than the fact. Mortie walked from the office with the indignant self-righteous look of a person who obviously felt little pain. The principal motioned for me to be next.

He had in his hand a long, discolored wooden paddle with holes in the business end. They formed a cross. He was holding it purposely at my eye level so I would get a good look.

"You have not met the 'Board of Education,' have you? I will now introduce you to each other. Bend over the front of the desk, please," he said, with sarcastic formality, "and take everything from your back pockets. I do know all the tricks."

I laid my billfold on the desk, in a spot about where my nose would end up when bending over. I was fighting to suppress a shaking spell because I did not want to give him the satisfaction of seeing me shake.

The odd thing about a moment like this is the concentrated clarity of eyesight. It burns into your memory whatever the eyes happen to be staring at—the worn billfold, for instance: A cowboy galloping a horse was hand tooled onto the leather. The billfold was loop stitched around the edges with a strand of rawhide. The ace of spades was protruding slightly, and it became the object of my tunnel-vision fixation, a phenomenon that develops under pressure, when your mind darkens all things except what is exactly in front of you.

His first swing took my breath away. The next three hurt but not as much. I fought back tears and did a lot of swallowing during the following lecture about getting off on the wrong foot.

"You have been in this office almost every day, and if I see you again anytime soon, we will call your parents, and all of us will sit down and have a long chat. Do you understand me?"

"Yes, sir."

"Good, good! Now get to class and learn something!"

"Yes, sir."

Walking down the hall, carrying the billfold in my hand, I was still fighting the instinct to cry. Mortie was alongside, again much too close, and bragging that he got five "licks" versus my four. Mortie held the record for the most licks in a school year. He had been accused of fabricating trips to the office in order to pad the numbers. So for his licks to count, they now required verification by a third party. He was happy to have me for a witness. His year was getting off to a good start.

We stopped by my locker and checked the schedule card to see what class we should be attending. When putting the schedule card back into the locker, I absently touched my pistol's butt through the paper sack and stood looking into the locker. I slammed the door.

I said loudly, "Where did that damn book go this time?" Things were starting to get to me.

After finally arriving at the correct class and receiving our tardy mark, I found a seat away from Mortie. My bus stop friend rose from her seat and moved to the empty one behind mine. She handed *The Deerslayer* over my shoulder.

It was English class. The teacher stood leaning against the front of her dark oak desk, talking slowly, smiling, and looking from student to student as she spoke.

"Let's do one of our chants from last year to see who remembers. You all want to?" After a few halfhearted yes's she said, "Good!"

Her dress was pink with puffy short sleeves that had narrow white bands buttoned tightly around her flabby upper arms. When she started reciting and jerking her arms up and down like she was leading a choir, it made her heavy arms gyrate. A few students joined in.

"Is, be, am, are, was, were, been—have, has, had—do, does, did—may, can, might, could, must, shall, will—shoooould, woooould!" Smiling and still holding her arms high, she asked with dancing eyes, "What part of speech are they, class?" No one answered.

Mortie had taken from his pocket the projector parts and spread them out on his desk to intently study, occasionally scooting the pieces to form a new configuration, while picking his nose. He seemed unimpressed by the teacher's topic or method.

Physical education class was the last before lunchtime. Because I had forgotten my gym clothes in my locker, I was relieved when I found out that we were going to have an informal class today. The football coach, who was teaching the class, paid us little attention. The student trainers, under his direction and using the rollers filled with lime, began to make the line markings on the football field.

The first game of the year would be played after school today, a home game against one of the Sharpsburg schools.

We students milled around. Some, because there was nothing else to do, helped prepare the field. Finally, the coach blew his whistle and motioned us together. After nervously adjusted his baseball hat that had a maroon *B* on it, he called the roll quickly and began marking our attendance in the grade book that he had pulled from a hip pocket.

He called several names, then "Parsons."

"Here."

He looked in my general direction, not knowing which one had answered.

"Where you from, Parsons?" he asked in my general direction.

"Fred's Creek."

"What's your dad's name?"

"Tuffy," I said. Someone giggled.

"Your daddy's Tuffy Parsons?"

He was walking over to me now. I could see a rounded, red face, colored by the visible blood vessels running around in his ample nose and cheeks. He had the bulky undefined body of a football lineman.

I nodded. "Uh-huh."

"Did he ever box at the American Legion?"

I never personally saw him box, because mother put a stop to it when Tuffy was young, but Uncle Lester had told me the stories several times.

"Never lost a fight in his life" was always the last thing Uncle Lester said.

"Yeah," I told the coach, pride showing.

"You ought to come out for football. Ever play any football?"

"Some," I said, remembering Jerry Joe throwing me passes, "but we can't play intermurls."

He gave me an odd look and stood thinking. "Oh, you mean intramurals. No, the 1s don't play. They're afraid someone'll get hurt, I imagine, a good idea, but that can't keep you off the school team. Show up at practice Monday. We'll suit you up and see what you can do." He pointed at me with a serious look, "I'll be expecting you."

Someone yelled, "Coach." He finished calling the roll quickly and went back to pointing and yelling and sounding much like Kay.

I looked in the direction of the main road and thought about the football invitation, not totally opposed to the idea but more surprised than anything. A familiar black Buick slowed to a stop along Main Street. I took off running. Kay was in the front seat with Mike behind the wheel, sitting with his baby blue shirt collar turned up. His arm was casually dangling a cigarette out a driver's window that was positioned a little too high for him. He reached for a knob to turn down the loud rock-and-roll music. They were wearing matching pairs of black horn-rim sunglasses.

"Get in," Kay said.

"I'm gettin' in trouble. The principal's going to call my Mom," I tried to explain.

"Here," Mike said, handing Kay a folded piece of paper from his shirt pocket.

Kay passed it on to me with a dramatic flourish. I unfolded a well-worded doctor's excuse with today's date, written on Dr. Masters's letterhead. It included my name and an appointment time that would require my missing school for the afternoon.

"Pretty good job, huh? Take it to the homeroom teacher," Mike instructed.

"Then get your ass out here, quick!" Kay added. They didn't have to say it twice. I ran for the nearest entrance and went directly to my homeroom. The teacher had a free period.

"What are they going to do?" the teacher asked, reading the paper.

"Take x-rays."

"Of what?"

"My ears."

She looked at me while shrugging an agreement. I smiled and backed from the room quickly.

I now carried the library book crammed into my pants in the small of my back, like I did back in Fred's Creek, because the method would free both hands for carrying the rifle. It was a .22 single-shot, bolt-action Remington. I had become a good shot with the daily practice of walking one of several back paths to and from the Fred's

Creek school, hunting squirrel. The school had rules. All guns were to be leaned in a designated corner, unloaded, with the bolt open. They were not to be touched until the school day was over. They weren't.

The trip home from school would be slow and stealthy with periods of sitting in favorite places where the squirrel nests were plentiful. Finally, when I got home carrying squirrels by the tail, Grandmother would look them over and praise the success of the hunt. I would clean and take them to her, and she would wash and chop them into pieces, bone and all. They would then be dumped into boiling water and cooked until the meat separated from the bones. The bones would be removed. The remains were boiled to a thick stock that included the meat. This would be canned and then stored in the large pantry. It would be served about midwinter, usually with dumplings and a lot of pepper.

After cleaning the squirrels, I washed in a metal pan that was removed from where it hung by a rusty nail and placed on a wooden stand that grandfather had built in the backyard next to the well. Afterward I went into the house and removed the book from the back of my pants, where it had been riding comfortably, and inquired as the other men of the family did.

"What's for supper?"

The bell to start lunchtime rang while I walked down the hall daydreaming, and seeing the library ahead, I decided to duck in.

"Where's your book?" the librarian asked good-naturedly, causing me to quickly snatch it from behind. I held it up smiling.

This made her laugh. "OK, you have it, I give up. Bob, would you do me a favor and read something from your book for me?"

"What you want me to read?" This seemed a strange request, but I wanted to make her happy.

"Anywhere in your book would be fine. I just want to listen."

"Well."

I opened the *Deerslayer* to the first page, thinking she should hear it from the beginning, as opposed to the middle of the story.

"On the human imagination, events produce the effect of time. Thus, he who has traveled far and seen much is apt to fancy he has lived long; and the history that most abounds in important incidents soonest assumes the aspect of antiquity." I quit and looked up for a reaction.

"That's good. Do you know what it means?"

"I'm not sure."

"Just tell me what you think it might mean," she coached.

"The more you do, the older it makes you feel, and you always remember the quickest whatever part was more important to you."

"That's good, what you said; you also read very well."

I felt my face getting flushed and had no idea what her point was. We talked awhile longer about the book. She mentioned that she was glad to be done grading her share of the ninth-grade IQ tests.

While talking, I began imagining to myself that Kay was bouncing up and down, yelling because my trip was taking so long. I excused myself politely and ran for the car while replacing the book in my pants and jumped into the back seat beside a dozen black T-shirts with numbers that had been hand cut from orange felt and glued onto the backs. Oblong pieces of the same material were glued to the front and read Boaz Browns. They were hand lettered in black ink across the orange felt.

"The uniforms look good, don't they?" Kay asked. Before receiving an answer, he added, "Look at this."

He held up beside his head an automatic pistol for me to reach over the front seat and take from him. I looked at it carefully, checking first to see if it was loaded, then read the imprint on the barrel. It said "Savage Arms Co. Patented 1905."

Kay talked on, "It's got ten shots, and this extra clip here gives me ten more. That's twenty. It's a bigger size too, a thirty-two not twenty-two, so that beats yours. Where's yours?"

"Locker. I forgot it."

After Kay calmed down from my incompetence, Mike said, "We need Jerry Joe. He's probably at the club."

Mike made a U-turn through Stanley's and headed upriver.

I sighted the pistol at the floorboard. "Where'd you get this?"

"Market Street Hardware—got it awhile ago, when we picked up my uniforms. It's used, but that don't hurt nothin,' only cost twelve dollars and fifty cents, and I got two boxes a bullets right here." After a pause, Kay said in a casual, offhand way, "You know how to shoot it?"

I hadn't shot an automatic before but had inspected one or two. I pushed and pulled until the slide lock opened, then looked into the chamber. Further searching found the button that made the empty clip fall out into my lap.

Reading the small print on both sides of the safety switch, "Fire - Safe," I said, "Yeah sure, I can shoot it."

The plans were made. Go to the Caves and try out the new gun during our gang meeting, but first we pulled into the country club to locate Jerry Joe. I went searching, while Kay and Mike kept the Buick hidden in a residential area that started one street over from the clubhouse.

Jerry Joe was standing near the pro shop among some golfers. He saw me and came my way, motioning me to him by waving a well-worn, brown leather golf glove.

"Glad you're here- need you to caddy. Judge Black just called. He can't come today; they need a fourth and asked me if I'd play. So you caddy, and if you don't do me a good job, then I'm not gonna tip you," Jerry Joe said, excited about playing.

He laughed, put his arm around my shoulder, and started walking us to the first tee while I tried to explain about Mike and Kay.

"They don't need any money. We'll go see them when we get done, and, they give us any trouble, we'll tell their old man. That's who you're caddying for," he said.

We laughed at the situation while I adjusted the straps on the golf bags so they would fit my shoulders.

There is something about Jerry Joe that anyone who has played golf would remember. He was blessed with the "sweet swing," a beautifully unconscious and seemingly effortless motion. When the ball left the tee, it appeared to slow with a slight fade to the left, followed by a slight fade to the right. Then it seemed to open its eyes and quickly accelerate, sailing in a long perfect arc, hit and bounce, hit and bounce, and finish by rolling gracefully down the middle of the fairway.

While waiting for jobs, caddies would hit from the hill using an old driver and balls they had found. The person hitting the shortest distance would have to walk and retrieve all the balls. Jerry Joe drove with the older caddies, and he seldom walked.

Jerry Joe and Kay's father, called "Big Kay" when a differentiation was needed, were matched against Dr. Masters, and his partner today would be Susan's father.

Big Kay had the honors on the first tee. He walked up wearing a green Ban-lawn shirt, tan Bermuda shorts, and scuffed, white, wingtip golf shoes with long tongues flopping out over the laces. He was tall with a masculine charisma that seemed comfortable in an athletic contest, and outwardly during the competition, he had an easygoing physical presence that is common to men of privilege who spend their lives trying to be just one of the boys.

After high school, when his grandfather sent him East to attend Amherst College, he had played on the theme of being a backwoods boy. It disarmed most people. This image attracted a student attending the nearby girl's college. She had been introduced to him at one of the planned formal interschool functions. Later they saw each other informally.

Big Kay's grandfather, thinking it a waste of time when he himself was young, had not attended college. Big Kay's father did not have to attend either, but King Kay changed his mind with age. He developed plans for his grandson and orchestrated Big Kay's college acceptance by generous donations to charities and through contacts within the Eastern-banking establishment. The bankers knew him well. King Kay was their expert on the Sharpsburg area coal companies. This eventually led to the social contacts that allowed Big Kay and his average grades to be enrolled.

Big Kay's grandfather had owned percentages of and loaned money to the very same coal companies that he gave the advice about. He often played both ends against the middle to his own advantage, always remembering, "don't kill the goose." He gained quite a fortune.

Big Kay took a couple of practice swings, shook his shoulders to loosen up, and addressed the ball. Most business days he had the look of someone with heavy responsibilities weighing on his shoulders. Golf and the outdoors seemed to lift the burden, at least temporarily.

His grandfather had died at the beginning of his sophomore year in college, followed a few months later by the death of his mother and father, in an automobile accident; they drove over a steep bank and almost into the river while returning home from a party.

Suddenly Big Kay was in charge of an array of businesses that he could barely name; much less know how to run. The main business from a monetary standpoint was the Sharpsburg Savings and Loan. It was a seven-story landmark in downtown Sharpsburg that included a large apartment on the top floor. Big Kay stayed there a lot of the time nowadays when Kay was away. The old original Schultz family home in Sharpsburg, which sat on Market Street for many years, had been divided into office space and rented out by King Kay, mostly to lawyers.

Big Kay hit a nice shot down the fairway, then turned and smiled at the rest of us. Jerry Joe's shot was straight but not quite as far. We walked the fairway while Dr. Masters chased a shanked drive over in the rough. I followed with Big Kay's clubs on one shoulder. On the other was one of the loaner bags that were kept at the pro shop. Jerry Joe would use these clubs today. We waited for Dr. Masters's second shot.

"How's Della doing?" Big Kay asked.

Jerry Joe shrugged and grinned, "Oh, you know, about the same."

"Swell. I saw her helping at the Labor Day party, but we didn't get a chance to talk," Big Kay said.

They played golf, walking and talking.

"How are you doing?" Big Kay asked.

"OK." Jerry Joe looked around at intervals, grinning in my direction.

"Who's the big shot now?" I kidded him in a whisper. He made a motion like he was snapping his imaginary suspenders.

Later Big Kay asked, "What do you want to do when you get out of school, Jerry Joe?"

"Caddy, I guess."

"You can't caddy for the rest of your life. What else?"

"They say you got to finish high school. If not for that, I'd work on one of them riverboats. You got to be twenty-one too. That's what Cecil says," Jerry Joe said.

"You mean the ones that push the coal barges?"

"Yeah, those. You work thirty days, then you're off thirty days, and you get paid when you're off, just the same."

"Yes, but you see, you work four hours on and four hours off around the clock, unless you're docked, sometimes longer. Can you do that?" Big Kay asked.

"Any minute. You betcha I can."

"That deck gets icy in the wintertime, and you have to walk around the edge of the barges and not fall in. At night you'd be a cooked goose."

"I'd make it around OK. I sure would," Jerry Joe said, without hesitation.

"Well, maybe you can do it, but what's the matter with school?"

Jerry Joe looked at the ground, embarrassed. "I don't get there much," he said. Then he looked up with a hint of defiance. "I don't much like it either, everybody just sittin' and talkin'. I want to get up and go do somethin', you know?"

I thought Jerry Joe was in for a lecture but was surprised.

"I know what you mean. A bunch of people rattlin' on about stuff. I didn't care much about it either, but I had Granddad and Dad standing over me. They made me go. I did, but I didn't learn much, that's for sure. You don't have anyone making you. But Jerry Joe, you should go some."

"I'll be sixteen next spring and can quit legal."

"I tell you what, if you will go to school, and if you still think you want to work, come see me in the spring. We'll send you on a boat trip and see how you do. OK?"

"I ain't twenty-one."

"I'll talk real sweet and tickle them under the chin and change their minds," he said with a laugh. We all laughed. Jerry Joe was happy. I was impressed.

A black Buick was slowly rolling along the back gravel road near the railroad tracks, some distance away.

While pointing a putter in that direction, Big Kay said, "That looks like the car I keep out at the farm."

Susan's father spoke up. "I've sold six or seven just like that. You don't have the only one around—you're up." He and Big Kay had known each other since they were small children, and he was losing money on this golf game.

Jerry Joe and I exchanged a glance that Dr. Masters probably noticed, but he didn't say anything.

They hit tee shots and walked on. We stopped for Dr. Masters to take an extra stroke.

"You see Kay since he's been home?" Big Kay asked Jerry Joe as they continued strolling down the fairway, then stopped at the ball.

"'Bout every day. We went to the caves; Vernon took us."

"Good." A sad look came over his face. He looked off in the distance and absently thumped his club head on the turf.

Dr. Masters had walked over to where we were. He was listening and spoke for about the first time.

"You've made a heroic effort for Kay. I can assure you of that, Big Kay."

"Thanks, Tony," Big Kay said, addressing the ball. He dropped a seven iron shot onto the green, about twenty feet from the pin.

Jerry Joe's golf downfall was his short irons. He used a driver often and also putted on the practice green while waiting for work, but his short irons tended to be long. He went past the green. He and I hunted for the ball in the weeds over a hill.

I made a suggestion while we searched: "Tell him about the football team."

"Why?"

I didn't know exactly why, but it seemed like Big Kay should know. I was too shy to speak to him about it. Jerry Joe shrugged, said OK, and made a decent chop up and out of the weeds to save a stroke.

After playing on for a while, I poked Jerry Joe in the back, motioning toward Big Kay. He said, "You hear about Kay's football team, sir?"

Big Kay smiled. "Yeah, I have. I talk to him every morning on the phone, if I'm not out at the farm. What's that all about anyway?"

Jerry Joe was stumped, not knowing what to say next to him. He pointed back in my direction. "Tell him, Bob."

"He wants to play intramural games," I said, still not understanding the concept, but I could now pronounce it.

"Kay can't play football." He looked around with the "where did you come from?" look I often received.

I spoke up. "He's the coach. He's not playin'. Jerry Joe's on the team and me and Mike. He's got us uniforms too."

"Mike's on a football team?" Dr. Masters was surprised.

"Intramural." I was continuing in my hope that this would make things clearer.

Big Kay said, "I know he loves football. He talks about it all the time. We've been to a bunch of games over the years…He's getting worse now. We been expecting it, but I don't think this stuff would be so good. What do you think, Tony?"

"If he doesn't overdo it and it makes him happy, honestly, I don't see how it could hurt anything, him watching."

"They say we can't have a team." I tried again to explain the situation while shaking my head.

"Who says?" Big Kay asked me.

"The principal, our homeroom teacher, the coach, and everybody."

There was silence.

"Let me talk to Kay about it," Big Kay decided with a puckered brow. They played on.

Susan's father was always good for a few off-color jokes that tended to be dirtier than they were funny, but we all laughed. He was a fairly good golfer and played often. Today he carried Dr. Masters, who was a few years older than the other golfers and played below average and seldom. He was only here today because his wife insisted that he should try and play.

She was drawn to Sharpsburg for several reasons and was instrumental in his accepting the job at Sharpsburg Memorial. She liked the quiet social life that the town offered her family, so to make her happy, he played now and then. He did not hate playing but admittedly was not a social animal and would have been happier back at the hospital looking at x-rays, where he felt more at home.

Jerry Joe occasionally pared and then bogeyed two or three holes. Big Kay had won the club tournament several times over the years and kept them ahead.

After the first nine, everyone had something to drink, signed for by Big Kay. He seemed to get a little nostalgic when we started the back nine, talking to Jerry Joe between shots.

"Remember when you and Della lived at the farm? You and Kay raised hell. That contraption they built with the harness and those straps and wheels so he could learn to walk. You remember? You'd push him real fast, and he would laugh so loud. I loved that."

Jerry Joe shook his head in agreement and looked at the ground.

"You know I always appreciated that," Big Kay added.

"Me and Kay get along all right," Jerry Joe said with a grin.

"His mother and I, we were always glad you were around. She's had a hard time with Kay being, like he is. It about did her in. She's had health problems ever since, but it's been hard on both of us."

"She back East now?" Jerry Joe asked.

"Connecticut? Yes, she's up there quite a bit anymore, family business. But here last week she flew back out to California for some kind of treatment. She seems to like it out there. Kay talks to her on the phone."

The story was told. Kay's mother and father were both ecstatic when they discovered that she was pregnant. The unusual way the opportunity for the pregnancy presented itself still amazed them both.

For the next few weeks after his mother and father died in the car wreck, Big Kay had stayed out late, carousing in the Sharpsburg area, drinking too much, and generally trying to decide what to do next. His young lady friend from the girl's college called and told a secretary at the bank to relay the message that she would be at the Cincinnati train station at a designated time and for him to be there to meet her. This was a bold move for a young woman at that time. He showed up and was waiting when she got off the train. She talked him into going back to school. They went East on a train that same evening, after a dinner and a phone call to Vernon's father to come and get the car.

Things then may have gotten back to normal except for Pearl Harbor. A fraternity brother's father was a high-ranking officer in the Coast Guard. He talked Big Kay into joining along with his son. They both were soon in an abbreviated version of Officer Candidate School. By spring, even though Big Kay had an exemption from the service, he was wearing a uniform.

The Schultz Dairy was classified as agricultural and important to the good of the nation; therefore, its workers and owners were excluded from the draft.

The fraternity brother was sent to the territory of Alaska, ferrying supplies to outlying islands on an icebreaker. Big Kay was sent to work out of Plump Island Station, located at the end of Long Island, New York. He did rescue work when needed but mostly was patrolling for submarines on a converted fishing boat. It had been pressed into service and fitted with a .50-caliber machine gun, searchlights, depth-sounding equipment, and a catapult to toss depth charges at enemy subs if spotted.

After a two-week apprenticeship, he was turned out to patrol an area that included New London, Connecticut, and the town of Groton, which is situated across the Thames River from New London. Groton was the hometown of his now-steady girlfriend.

She was an adept sailor. In a short while the two of them began using surreptitious plans, with the help of his crew, so she could copy his sailing coordinates, plus times to meet that matched favorable tides. They created a number of rendezvous.

The sub chaser he commanded would travel in a wide circle. The two of them assured Kay's existence in the choppy waters of Long Island Sound, in the very sailboat that was now docked at the Boaz Country Club Marina.

A month or two later, after round-robin meetings with her doctor, Episcopalian priest, mother, and best friends, there was a well-planned, "spontaneous" wedding. Some of Big Kay's crew attended the wedding, while the rest waited on the boat at the river dock, not far from the Groton church. The wedding procession took Big Kay and his crew back to the sub chaser. She waved good-bye as he pulled away, going immediately back to work while wearing his dress uniform.

"She'll be back before long I guess. We try to go for a sail before they take the boat out of the water for the winter," Big Kay said, adjusting his grip on a practice swing and asking, "Who's up?"

The next hole was a short par five with only one sand trap, protecting to the left of an extra large green that could be reached with two very long straight shots. Most of the club's eagles were recorded on this hole. The green naturally sloped to the left. A ball placed to the right would sometimes roll downhill to the pin that was usually situated behind the sand trap. Big Kay executed this maneuver perfectly. Jerry Joe's second shot made the sand trap. The other two arched shots onto the green in three. Jerry Joe got too much ball out of the trap and was over the green again. Susan's father made a short putt to birdie the hole so he could get his ball out of Big Kay's putt line. Big Kay went by the cup on a long putt that would have been an eagle. His next, much shorter putt, gave him a birdie. Jerry Joe was back on the green and two-putted for a bogey. Dr. Masters two-putted for one of his few pars of the day.

Susan's father was talking to Dr. Masters while we waited for the foursome ahead of us to play out of driving range.

"Mike's OK, I like him, but when he comes in to wash cars in a long-sleeved white shirt, in eighty-degree weather, it just cracks me up, Tony."

Mike worked occasionally at his dealership, washing and parking new cars when they arrived. It was Susan's idea that her father should hire Mike. She would show up at the appropriate moment. They would walk to downtown Sharpsburg and enter the drugstore soda fountain for lunch. Mike held the door, allowing her to enter first.

Dr. Masters said, "Yeah, he's self-conscious about being skinny. I was that way at his age. His brother and sister take after their mother. They're big boned, you see. He'll grow out of it eventually. I hope."

They both laughed. Dr. Masters had wide shoulders but thin arms and legs. He was more concerned with Mike's lack of interest in school than anything else.

The story was told. Dr. Masters had taken Mike to a friend. They had been interns together. The friend decided to continue in psychiatry because he didn't like blood.

"Mike has a lot of anger from being compared to his older brother and sister. He seems to have interests that are not academic, such as automobiles and music," Dr Masters quoted his friend to Susan's father.

"Can't he get a degree in music?" Susan's father asked.

"I asked my buddy that very question, and he said he doubted it. Mike doesn't even want people to know he plays the piano. At this stage, he's just trying to define his manhood, and the piano doesn't fit in just yet. My buddy told me to hope for the best. I asked him, is that it? Just hope? My wife didn't care for his advice. She's talking about military school. I've been able to veto that, so far."

Dr. Masters continued to quote his friend. "He told me if she fights with him, she's going to lose. That they'll both lose. We should just be there for him and let him know it. Set parameters, such as he has to go to school. Mike's a good kid, but his judgment just hasn't fully developed yet."

Dr. Masters admitted that he considered this a scary conclusion, but he was doing his best to deal with Mike. His youngest was much different from the first two kids. They, like their mother, accomplished much by looking straight ahead and working hard.

"If he gets into any more trouble, she's not going to listen to my friend or me either one," he said with inevitability.

"I wasn't worth a damn till I hit thirty," Susan's father confessed, while they walked up to the tee to join the rest of us.

"You still ain't," Big Kay said, and we all laughed.

Big Kay asked Dr. Masters, "How's everyone adjusting to Sharpsburg, after Pittsburgh? You've been down here, what, two years or so now?"

"Starting our fourth," Dr. Masters said.

"You're kidding? It's been that long? We sure don't see each other very often. Put in some hours, don't we? Let's get together as soon as the wife gets back in town. OK?"

"Good idea, I'll tell my wife," Dr. Masters agreed.

"Swell," Big Kay said, and drove from the eighteenth tee.

Jerry Joe's clothing included the worn black brogans that he had long ago purchased at Gibson's Grocery. They were high-topped, coming up around the ankles, with copper rivets holding down the tie flaps. Most people called them clodhoppers. He was also wearing a T-shirt that could use some bleach. Still, from a distance he looked like he belonged on the golf course.

They walked down the eighteenth fairway, approaching the green that was located near the clubhouse, where you could sit and watch the golfers take their turn putting, from the informal summer dining area that extends out on a high-ceilinged porch, beneath overhead fans. Striped cloth awnings were attached to the outside of the large screened addition. A breeze was beginning to blow in from the river, and it made the awnings flap. They made a low muffled sound that was somehow pleasant.

Big Kay called the farm from the caddy shack in an attempt to get Kay to come to the club for dinner, but the nurse told him that Kay was asleep. Kay didn't like the club. Big Kay thought the farmhouse was too big and lonely, with no one around, but he would begin spending nights there now that Kay was back home.

Dr. Masters headed for the hospital to make his evening rounds. Susan's father headed for the bar to try and recover from his losses. Big Kay gave Jerry Joe all of the day's winnings: nine dollars. I made three dollars in tips, the most I had ever made

"I see Garvin's back in town, walking the tracks. You see him?" Big Kay asked Jerry Joe.

"He's got himself a new business. He's pickin' trash at the dump. Has a house full a copper wire and stuff," Jerry Joe said.

Big Kay shook his head. "Wish he wasn't so goddamn stubborn. You talk about someone who did well in school, made straight As without trying." He grinned. "That always pissed me off, pissed dad off too. Try and get him to come and see me if you can. I really need to tell him about something."

"Yes, sir, I will. Thank you," Jerry Joe said, counting his money.

"Swell," Big Kay said, and walked to the locker room for a shower. The burdened look was returning to his face.

Mike and Kay were nowhere to be found. Jerry Joe decided to stay at the club for the possibility of a drunksome later on. In the meantime, for extra money, he would wash and dry the golf clubs that the members had used today.

The club pro had watched our foursome play a couple of holes. He was explaining to Jerry Joe that he needed to use "less club" on his short iron shots and to swing down sharply to get more arch on the ball. Jerry Joe was washing a seven iron and nodding his head.

With nothing else to do, I went to the main road. I hitchhiked home instead of walking, to ensure I would arrive on time for supper.

The front door of the house was standing open, so I opened the storm door and went in.

Mother was standing in the rounded opening that separated the front room from the dining room. She often watched television from this spot so she could go back to the kitchen and check on food. Supper was almost ready. There were plates on the table. Father and my brothers glanced up from the TV and waved at me but said nothing.

She said, "Your friend Kay called twice for you; here's his number. Is it a long distance call?"

She handed me a torn piece of paper from the pocket of her apron.

"No." I didn't know.

I called Kay. He was upset that I didn't come back to the car with Jerry Joe. After he calmed down, he gave me rambling instructions to be ready early in the morning because he and Vernon would be by. At the end he added a few threats that I could be out of the gang if not ready when they arrived.

I assured him that I would be ready and hung up. I went to the kitchen and pulled the library book from my pants, flashed it in front of mother who was stirring something on the stove, and put it on the small table that was located beside the kitchen counter, where she could see it. This would head off questions about homework.

At the dining table she began asking how things went at school today.

While in the middle of trying to answer her without actually telling her about anything that happened, I suddenly blurted out, even to my own surprise, "Might play football."

"Football, that's dangerous. Read it in a magazine that a boy got his neck broke playing football. It's much too dangerous."

"I'll be careful, Mom. Dad, do you know the football coach at school?"

"Yeah, I met him one time," he said with a look that told me to not talk about this in front of your mother.

Day Six

It was Saturday morning and cool, a sign fall would soon arrive, and Mother fixed Cream of Wheat for breakfast. I was sitting outside with Father, waiting for "Badeye" to pick him up. Badeye was a childhood friend who was driving down today from Fred's Creek with his johnboat tied in the back of his Ford pickup. They were going "noodlin." That is, catching turtles along the muddy riverbanks by sticking a hand into holes and pulling the turtles out by the tail. Yes, occasionally they do back into the hole and any self-respecting noodler will have a few scars on his hands and a story to tell about each one.

Badeye was a logger by trade and was born with a milky eye that had earned him his nickname. He could make a tree fall in the exact spot marked, and anyone having problems with a tree went looking for Badeye. Most loggers have parts of their body missing. He was no exception, with the first two fingers of his left hand gone, caused by a drag chain snapping.

Father seemed in a good mood and was pulling on a pair of knee-high gum boots while sitting on the front steps. "You gonna play football, huh?" he said.

"Awh, I don't know. They asked me. You know the coach?"

"We boxed one time; at the VFW, before you was born. Those folks had a rule. If you got knocked down twice in one round, they'd stop the fight. They stopped the fight. He said he slipped and didn't much like it."

"Did he slip?"

"No. I tagged him good and square. He went down clean. To tell the truth, he surprised me by gettin' up a second time, most woulda stayed down. I offered to fight him again, but he wouldn't ever do it. He's gone around tellin' people different for years, but I just never paid him no mind."

"She don't much like you fightin', does she?"

"No, I'd a got my brains beat out before it was over, so she'd be right."

"You pretty much do what she says, don't you?" I said, casually stretching and yawning and looking away so I wouldn't appear to be too accusing.

He had been picking at a place on the palm of his hand with a pocketknife and stopped to look over at me. I thought maybe I had gone too far and he was getting upset.

He finally grinned. "You shoulda saw her when we were kids. She bossed me around like I was an ugly stepchild. I just didn't pay her much attention. Your Mom tries hard, harder then me or you either one, so you need to respect that, understand?"

"Well."

"If I tell you the reason, will you keep it between you and me? Won't tell her?"

"Nope."

He told me a man-to-man story. "I'd a been maybe three years older than you are now when it happened."

The story was told. Dad and Uncle Lester were "chopping" tobacco. That consists of hoeing the weeds from between the rows and loosening the dirt around the plants. Lester was having one of his days. Uncle Lester had a hole in his head. A round hole that was about the size of a half dollar, right in the middle of the back of his skull, and the piece of bone knocked loose was indented under the skin. If pressed with a finger, it would move. I was occasionally allowed to do this when I was young. He said a German did it with a hammer. The reason the German hit him was because Uncle Lester was howling at the moon while being held a prisoner of war during World War I.

Knowing Uncle Lester, he probably was not a model prisoner and was howling at the moon "cause I wanted to." On this day Lester continued to get upset about several different things. Father was getting fed up with whatever he was haranguing about. Sometimes when agitated Uncle Lester would inadvertently switch to speaking the German he had learned while being held.

Father was hoeing behind Uncle Lester and raised the hoe to come down hard, venting his frustrations on the weeds. At that same second Lester stepped backwards and Father's hoe came down on his heel. A chase ensued. Tuffy ended up in Sharpsburg.

"Your mother was goin' to high school."

If living in Fred's Creek back at that time, you went to high school away from home, much like college. She boarded at the YWCA with a few other rural students and found a ride home on the weekends if Grandfather could not come for her. She heard about Father's fight with Lester, tracked him down, and invited him to a YWCA dance.

The night of the dance, he was lying on the bed and looking at the ceiling of a small room that he and two other people about his age were renting together to save money and they were telling Father about their plans to rob a gas station and wanted him to go along.

"Thought about it, but I told them, 'I got a date,' and these two fellas got themselves arrested and sent on to prison. I've wondered what woulda happened if she hadn't come and asked me to that dance."

"Mom saved you?"

"I do think she did."

Badeye came turning into the driveway in his old pickup with the boat bouncing in the bed. I walked out to say hello and watched them drive away, thinking I probably wouldn't exist today if Father had decided not to attend that dance—a confusing thought for a fourteen-year-old.

Returning to the porch steps, chin in hand, I was thinking I should have gone on to the club and put my name on the list to caddy.

It was first come, first serve unless a golfer asked for you by name. Waiting around the house was costing me money, and they might not even show. A horn startled me. There they were.

They were all riding with Vernon in his faux police car. Kay rolled and then slid down from the front seat, wearing the helmet and blowing his whistle.

"Practice!"

The lot beside our house was for sale and still mostly in grass, so we decided to use it for practice. Kay barked orders with Mike centering the ball from between his legs and Jerry Joe passing to me as I ran out to catch.

Kay taught me the "buttonhook route:" run straight out, then suddenly reverse directions, running back toward the passer before the defense can recover. Even Mike began having fun.

At a distance, on a mound of dirt at a home construction site, squatted our 9-1s classmate, with her dress pulled down over her knees. She watched carefully with thin arms hugging ankles and a chin resting on her knees. She had two homemade dresses. They were both white with large flower patterns, and the dresses hung straight to just above her knees, like sacks, with long ties sewn to the sides that usually hung untied. Her high-topped, scuffed, brown shoes without socks were hand-me-downs, probably from an older brother.

"Who's that?" Kay said and pointed in her direction.

"Don't know," I mumbled.

Jerry Joe and Mike looked at each other with a grin.

My little brothers wanted to play. We let them rush the passer. But the oldest brother wanted to run with the ball. Kay told him to get lost, so he went into the house crying to mother.

She followed him back outside. "You're just playing, let him play too."

"We're practicing for a game, Mother. We're not playing." I made an attempt at explaining.

"Oh pooh, you let your little brother hold the ball for a few minutes. Don't be so selfish."

"This is important, Mother, please."

"Nothing is more important than your little brother."

I quit arguing. My brother snatched the ball from my hands and strutted around with it curled under his arm until she returned to the house. Then Kay waddled over to him. My brother was a little taller than Kay.

"Give me my ball back, kid, or I'm gonna break your neck!"

He handed Kay the ball and started running for the house screaming, "Mother!"

Jerry Joe picked Kay from the ground while he still held the ball. We quickly piled into the car where Vernon was sitting and eating a candy bar.

Kay sat holding the ball and said disgustedly, "Hit the road."

We left before anyone came out of the house, traveling upriver, trying to decide what to do next.

"We need to have a gang meeting," Kay decided. We pulled into the parking lot of Boaz Junior High and continued practice on the playground while Vernon made a U-turn in the empty lot and headed for Stanley's and a milkshake.

We practiced awhile, then slowed down, and finally just stood around talking more than practicing. We ended up lying on the well-trodden grass beneath the chestnut oak tree behind the gymnasium. Kay waddled back and forth in front of us, waving his arms and talking.

"We need to do somethin'. I think we ought to throw a smoke bomb in the teacher's lounge, and when they come runnin' out, we could pick 'em off one by one, with mine and Bob's guns. But Mikie here doesn't think so!"

"I'm afraid you'll hit somebody you shouldn't."

"Who—Susan? Mike's in lo-o-ove!"

"You can shoot some football players if you want, I don't give a damn, but you see, you can't hit the side of a barn. You'd come closer to shooting your foot off as anything. Besides, they'll see you doing it." Mike said.

"What do I care? What they gonna do to me? That nurse is sending out applications for a new job! Does that tell you something, genius? Hells bells, I'll be dead before they could even have a trial. If they did have one, I'd be famous and in magazines like that Dr. Shepard guy. I'd be signin' autographs like Otto Graham."

Personally I thought his plan was a bit too much and spoke up. "Maybe we could just kidnap the principal and hold him for a ransom till we can have a team. Awhile back, I read this story of Mark Twain's, where they did somethin' like that, but it didn't turn out so good." This suggestion received some consideration and was put on the list of possibilities.

"What do you think about everything, Jerry Joe?" Mike asked.

He was lying on his back, using the football for a pillow and chewing a blade of grass, with his arms folded and eyes shut. One clodhopper heel was resting on the other's toe. "I ain't got nothin' for none of them."

"I don't want any of you to go around sayin' stuff, so I'll just shoot some football players," Kay said.

"You see, that's still not going to get what we want. What the hell do we want anyway?" Mike said, looking at all of us, and then he asked Kay directly, "If they let us have a team, will that do it?"

"OK, yeah, but if we lose, I'm still gonna shoot somebody," he said.

Silently we all tried to think of a solution.

"We could threaten to blow somethin' up," Jerry Joe said.

"We could call somebody up and tell them that if they don't treat the 9-1s fair and square, we'll blow up the school," Kay said, liking the idea.

"What if they call our bluff?" Mike said.

Jerry Joe sat up. "Yeah, I know. How we gonna know how to blow somethin' up?"

"You get some dynamite and hook a fuse to it and then you just light it," I said. "It's not that hard. Uncle Lester blew the whole side of a hill off one time."

Mike held his hands out and shrugged in a disgusted manner. "Where are we going to get any dynamite?"

There are events in life that we look back upon and think, "I should have kept my mouth shut."

"Uncle Lester's got lotsa dynamite," I said.

We were soon headed for Fred's Creek to see Uncle Lester, of course. He was many things to me, but mostly he was an adult male who treated me as an equal most of the time, when I was anything but. By his actions he told me that I would be a man someday and that he had no doubt about it, even if I did. He listened to my harebrained ideas and had a few of his own. He was much gentler with me than he had been with Tuffy.

In Fred's Creek, the culture does not allow people to criticize their relatives, at least not where others can hear, so the relatives would brag on one another. The more they bragged the more they didn't really care for one another. Grandfather and Uncle Lester bragged on each other quite often. So when Grandfather told me once that Uncle Lester was "crazy as a June bug," it was some strong talk. Grandfather didn't tell me this where anyone could overhear, especially my grandmother. She was Uncle Lester's younger sister.

One of Uncle Lester's professions was "blaster." He learned from his father as a kid, and at twelve years of age he set charges to blast new roads. He had also worked for a time setting charges in coal mines. Later, during World War I when the Army learned of this talent, they put him to work turning quaint bridges all over Europe, some dating to the Middle Ages, into piles of rock.

If you wanted a water well dug, tree stump removed, or a hillside flattened for a road, you came looking for Lester. If he was not available, you talked to Tuffy. He had learned it all and had also been put to work by the Navy, blowing things up in World War II. So it was natural for Lester to have a shed on the hill behind his house where several cases of dynamite and many yards of fuse cord were stored. I had been along on blasting jobs and was allowed to prepare and light fuses or push the plunger when blasting caps were used.

The trip took awhile. We went to Sharpsburg and then turned onto the road that followed the Big Piney upriver. It rose into the ridges and hills. The steeper grades of the road had recently added a second lane uphill to allow the passing of slow, laboring trucks. This improvement had cut the traveling time considerably.

When reaching Fred's Creek, there was little indication that you had arrived. Sams was the only business except for the feed store. But the feed store sat out of sight, behind a house at the end of a twisting, unmarked gravel lane. Sams had a hand-painted sign that said "Truck Stop." There was little room for a large truck to pull in at the single gas pump, which was in front of the steep-roofed red brick building with wide garage doors. Built onto one side was a newer whitewashed cinder-block addition. The addition had a contrasting, almost-flat roof. This extended area contained the restaurant, grocery store, and general merchandizing wing of the establishment, and a half pint of whiskey could be purchased if you knew one of the Sams family members who ran the place.

As a child I could walk to Sams from my grandparent's house, buy candy, and say "put it on the bill," when given permission. My first memories of being away from the family took place at Sams.

On one of these early trips, I was standing eating a piece of licorice and daydreaming when a man came in carrying a thick sales book and wearing a tie. Ties were unusual in Fred's Creek. Even at this young age, I was aware that he wasn't from the area.

The standing joke by the patrons of Sams was that a person wearing a tie and driving a gray car would pull up and say, "I'm from the government and I'm here to help you." U.S. government vehicles were gray.

This always got a big laugh, so when the person wearing the tie walked in, I automatically looked out the window to check the color his car. It wasn't gray, so I relaxed. He wanted to sell something to the Sams family, but they were all working out in the service station area.

He asked me if my licorice was good and waited for them to finish and someone to come in. After a minute we both heard the screeching of tires, and an old dented Studebaker slid to a stop in front of the window. A man jumped out with a pair of baby shoes still swinging back and forth from where they were tied to the rear view mirror. He had on laced, knee-high logging boots and a red plaid Mackinaw with several diagonally sliced holes in the material of one front shoulder. A revolver stuck up out of the wide leather belt that was buckled around the outside of the coat. He came past the window and in the door and looked around, rubbing his beard stubble, ignoring the two of us, and yelling down the building in the direction of the service station area.

"Any you all seen Dickey Byrd lately?"

"No!" came the answer in unison from people out in the garage.

"Tell 'um I want to see him right damn now, if he's to come in here!"

"We will," came an answer. The salesman had inched behind the coal stove for protection. The big, agitated guy rubbed his short, blond hair and left.

Slamming the car door, he made his tires smoke and squeal, fishtailing first on the gravel and then on the road. Up the hill he went as fast as he had arrived. Things were quiet. We could hear the clock on the counter ticking. The salesman came out from hiding just as one of the Sams came into the store area.

"Shouldn't we call the police or something?" the salesman asked.

The Sams looked at him puzzled. "That was the deputy sheriff that was just in here. What you need him for?"

"Nothing."

Vernon was picking out candy at the Sams counter. The rest of us were sitting at one of the two tables and waiting for an order of french fries. We were lucky that it was the weekend; they only heated the grease in the deep fryer on Friday and Saturday, because during the week there was a lack of french-fry orders.

The place felt familiar to me, yet different. Not in a physical sense but more from a perspective that comes with absence from a place and then returning, carrying back with you the experiences from other places. Jerry Joe was like a cat that hunts familiar territory with quiet detached grace, but here in an unfamiliar place he was on alert and keeping watch. Kay had eaten New York strip at the Four Seasons, Chef Escoffier's Peach Melba in France, and now french fries at Sams. He was equally unimpressed with all three. His mind was concentrating on the logistics of obtaining the dynamite.

Mike was fascinated and quite taken with the place. His perspective of Boaz being as far out in the woods as you could get was changing. Vernon was keeping a close eye on Kay, in the event that he would need to rest or be given one of the shots riding in Vernon's pocket.

I felt a strange detachment when we left Sams, like it was different than it had once been. We rode slowly by the big white house of my first memories, where my grandparents lived; and a short distance later, at the top of the hill, I gave directions to turn at a level place where Uncle Lester parked his truck during bad weather, when negotiating the road back to his house was impossible. We went down the narrow, almost hidden dirt lane, which had a grass strip growing between the tire tracks. A few low tree branches brushed the sides of the slow-moving car as it went winding between two steep hills. The long lane arced back around behind Fred's Creek until it suddenly opened onto an area of gently sloping bottomland. About thirty oblong acres that were made up of mostly a pasture and hay field stood before us, surrounded by hills. At the far end was an old single-story black log house with a wide roofed front porch. Uncle Lester and Aunt Nellie lived there.

A stranger to the area would be confused in trying to understanding the social and economic structure of its residents because the houses in Fred's Creek appeared old and run down. They were for the most part. These houses had been lived in by three or four generations, usually descendants. It was considered in bad taste to add things to the house that would be deemed by neighbors as unnecessary. These new things would be scorned as attention-drawing opulence.

So most casual visitors would consider the people painfully poor, which was true in some cases. Most area residents were happy to be comfortably poor. One house would be the home of relatively wealthy people, and the next house would belong to a poor family. The difference between the two houses would be too subtle for a stranger to recognize.

The only hint of where the residence at the end of the lane before us would fit into this mix was the three oil wells sitting on the far side of the field with rotating arms, each pumping individual, arrhythmic beats. We drove the lane toward the house and saw Uncle Lester standing with his thin shoulders hunched forward over a high waist that his long legs created. He stood by the well in the front yard, where he had moved after leaving the porch to study the strange car approaching.

I explained to the rest, "Let me out first. Stay in the car a minute."

Uncle Lester wasn't the problem. Smokey was the problem. Lester had a dog that didn't bark. Uncle Lester had a theory as to why Smokey didn't bark: "He's a feared they might run off before they get close enough to bite off a hunk."

"It's Bobby! Nellie, it's Bobby!" Uncle Lester said.

A round Aunt Nellie came out the screen door, wiping her hands on an apron. She hugged me, and I tried not to be embarrassed. After the introductions and after Smokey finished putting each new visitor's scent into his memory bank, we sat on the front porch among clutter, each of us finding one of several available spots.

I sat by the leather harness that smelled of linseed, having been oiled for winter storage. The harness belonged to Woodrow, Uncle Lester's mule. Lester had a tractor but still used Woodrow for pulling logs along steep grades that no tractor could negotiate. He owned 537 acres. Across the hill it stretched to the back of my grandparents' big white house, which sat facing the main road in Fred's Creek.

Occasionally Uncle Lester and Badeye wandered the hills and discussed individual trees that were approaching time for cutting. Vague decisions on the optimum time for cutting were made, taking into account such things as if the tree was located on a ridge or in a valley, plus many other variables that would change the growth rate, such as whether it was on the sunny side of a hill or close to the stream.

These were serious discussions, and a final decision on an individual tree could take several years. The decision would also depend upon the prices that logs were bringing at a certain time.

"They don't eat nothin'," was Lester's motto; he wouldn't be rushed.

Aunt Nellie brought us each a glass of buttermilk. She kept it in sealed jugs that were enclosed in a wire cage and then lowered into the well water, which remained cold even in the hottest part of summer.

"Did you stop and see your Grandma?" Aunt Nellie asked.

She was technically a grandmother through Tuffy's adoption but deferred to my mother's mother because she was my closer blood relative.

When visiting Fred's Creek, it was a breach of social custom not to visit your closest relative first. She was a little uneasy until I said it was a business visit. Business visits take a slight precedent over social visits. She then became less apprehensive and went back into the house to her work, which usually had something to do with sweets or dairy products.

Aunt Nelly loved sweets and had sugar, both white and brown, hidden in tin boxes all through the house. Her craving was the result of a deprived childhood plus the Great Depression trauma of her generation, a period when Fred's Creek had only homemade molasses for sweetening. She soon came back outside to offer everyone a piece of blackberry pie. We all declined, but Vernon followed her back to the kitchen. They immediately became soul mates.

I had been trying to think of a business reason for us to be here, along with a way to get to the dynamite shed without detection.

"Kay here is in the milk-cow business. We thought he might be int'rested in your calf," I told Uncle Lester in a serious tone.

Aunt Nellie milked one cow, a brown Jersey named Trudy. She was about two-thirds the size of the ones at Schultz Dairy. Trudy had calved recently, and she gave about half the volume of milk that Kay's cows gave, but it was much richer in the cream that Aunt Nellie made into butter. It could be purchased at Sams, wrapped in wax paper. About a ten-minute trip would take you to my grandparents' house; it was a walk over the hill on a well-beaten trail with flat rocks imbedded as steps where needed.

I had made the trip over the hill many times, carrying to Aunt Nellie a bucket filled with Grandmother's homemade bread. I carried back with me the wrapped butter, and the bucket was filled almost full with milk. It had white cheesecloth draped over the top to keep out the dirt and insects. The dynamite shed was in that direction.

Before Uncle Lester eased his long legs over the fence to go after the calf, Jerry Joe said, "Want me to go and help you?"

"Come on, you won't hold me back all that much," Uncle Lester said, looking Jerry Joe up and down. Both smiling, they went to get the cow and calf for Kay to look over. Lester was older than both Aunt Nellie and my grandparents, but he was spry and walked with a long stride that country people use to cover ground quickly. Even Jerry Joe was stepping out to keep up. I told Mike and Kay to stay at the fence and do some talking. I casually walked off and went around to the back of the house.

I continued on behind the barn and up a path, pulled the hand-carved cedar peg that held the rusty door latch, and filled one of the burlap bags that was lying in a corner pile with dynamite sticks taken from the stack of wooden storage boxes. Carefully removing only a couple from each of the different boxes so it would be less noticeable, I lifted a heavy lid and removed a few blasting caps from the square metal box on a shelf and wrapped them gently in my red handkerchief, then stuffed them into a pocket.

I then decided against taking the large roll of electric wire and plunger used to set off the dynamite. It would be noticed missing and was too bulky to sneak to the car, so I unwound the easier-to-use and easier-to-carry fuse cord from one of the large reels attached to the wall and measured the feet by winding it around my shoe, then up to my hand, which I carefully held approximately three feet away. After counting several yards, I cut the fuse with a big rusty pair of scissors hanging from a nail.

Following my training to "make sure you got enough to get the job done. You can bring back what you don't use," I added a few more dynamite sticks and dropped in a roll of black cloth tape. I carried the bag along an uphill path and around to the car, opened the trunk by pulling the knotted rope sticking out of the hole in the trunk lid where a key would normally be inserted into a lock, and snuggled the sack beside the football and helmet to keep it from sliding. My trip went almost undetected. The only individual that saw me was Smokey. He was by my side all the time.

Smokey was a big dog, almost a hundred pounds, and was black close to the skin. His long hair had ends that turned to gray. Uncle Lester brought him home as a pup, from a trip to the town of Goshen, which was in Perth County and located on up the Big Piney River. Smokey was supposed to be part wolf. Most folks questioned this claim by the trader until one day when I was tagging along after Lester and Badeye on one of their walk-and-talk trips.

We were sitting on a high rock ledge that protruded out toward the small stream called Bone Marrow Branch, which ran down through the property and emptied into Fred's Creek. Uncle Lester was departing wisdom, such as, "they don't make trees like they use to."

Smokey was quite a ways down below and was getting a drink from where the low, slow-moving water was concentrated into one of several wide summer pools. Suddenly we saw him freeze, pin his ears, and slowly walk into the water until totally immersed, with nothing sticking above the waterline but his nostrils and eyes.

We sat quietly, watching his curious actions. Soon we saw what he was sensing. Three deer, all does, were walking in single file along the other side of the branch. As they slowly walked beside the water hole, Smokey carefully turned his body to remain facing them and kept his eyes pointed directly at the deer. The deer casually traveled on upstream without any awareness that Smokey was less than ten feet away. Everyone agreed afterwards that he was part wolf.

He had accompanied me over the hill on trips back to my grandparents' house but would stop at the edge of the woods and sit watching as I walked around the large garden and on to the back door. He would then travel back to Uncle Lester and Aunt Nellie.

Today Smokey and I walked back and stood beside Mike and Jerry Joe, listening to Kay and Uncle Lester discuss the calf, among other things. They seemed to be getting along quite well. Woodrow's curiosity had drawn him over to the wooden gate, and he hung his long head over to see what was going on, moving his big ears around, pointing them at whoever happened to be speaking at the moment. The calf was a heifer. Lester would have no trouble selling her based on the reputation of her mother. The talk turned from business to a more social discussion.

People with physical problems that lived around Fred's Creek often found a specialty, such as basket-making, sewing, or making quilts. Many older people thought that God took very personal interest in them and talked to them in a special way, and some told people what they thought the future might hold. Their intuition about the future was given consideration when making decisions. Lester and Nelly accepted Kay without question because he was with me.

Aunt Nellie came outside carrying her milking buckets. It was a little early to milk, but since Trudy was at the barn, she would go ahead and milk. She did the milking most of the time because the cow liked her. Nellie said that Lester talked too roughly to Trudy. She thought the cow gave less milk when he was around.

The group moved into the barn. Trudy and Aunt Nellie became the main attraction. The calf, which was muzzled to keep it from nursing the milk, was waiting for its share, which would be poured into a bucket with a rubber teat protruding from the side. The stainless bucket was hanging at an appropriate height on the wall. Even Smokey watched while she filled his personal pan with milk, followed by a second that quickly attracted several cats. I was aware of what was about to happen and watched the other kids' faces when the looks of surprise appeared. Kay turned and was about to head for the barn door, but Uncle Lester calmed him.

"She wouldn't hurt a fly," he said.

A six-foot blacksnake slowly curled down one of the cedar poles supporting the hayloft. "Jezebel" flicked a tongue that alerted her to the abnormal number of warm bodies present. She lived in the loft and kept the barn and surrounding area mouse and rat free in return for the splattering milk that Aunt Nellie was squirting directly into her open mouth from an expertly aimed teat.

When the show was over, I carried Aunt Nellie's buckets back to the house.

Mike, speaking almost for the first time, asked Uncle Lester, "Could I see your bear teeth?"

"You can. Go 'round to the porch and I'll fetch em," he answered.

The teeth and claws were rolling around in a Hav-A-Tampa cigar box that said, "2 for 9 cents." The gang was fascinated, examining the contents closely. Lester said he killed the bear along Bone Marrow Branch when he was thirteen. It weighed 370 pounds on the feed store scale.

The only time I ever saw Uncle Lester with tears in his eyes was caused by my asking questions about the bear.

I was six or seven. "Where are all the bears now?" I asked.

He told me that there weren't any more, at least not around Fred's Creek, because they had all been killed.

"You mean there's no bears for me to kill?" I asked.

The tears came to his eyes. He said quietly, "No, Bobby, reckon not."

Nellie cooked on a woodstove. She could go from zero to a full breakfast in twenty minutes without trying very hard. She quickly whipped up a plate of biscuits and called us to the table. It was considered bad manners not to eat while visiting relatives. The table had assorted jellies and preserves, including my favorite, persimmon, along with a big bowl of fresh butter.

Mike ate several biscuits. Jerry Joe and I watched him, smiling at each other when Aunt Nellie said, "Wish I had you around fur a while, put some meat on those bones, we would."

Mike held up a biscuit that was half eaten, laughing along with everyone. Kay had raspberry jelly on his face but managed to get most of the biscuit into his mouth. Pieces and crumbs fell down his front. Without comment he allowed Nellie, holding a wet dishcloth, to wipe his face and hands.

It takes a long time to leave Fred's Creek. We all inched slowly in the direction of the car. Kay pulled his gun from the seat to show Lester. It was admired. He asked Kay if he had seen my pistol. Kay informed him that he had shot it personally. Soon Kay began pushing on the loose bone floating in the hole of Uncle Lester's head while he bent over to accommodate Kay's height. Aunt Nellie was watching with her hands resting high on her round hips. The elbows were sticking out almost straight.

She said, "Lester, quit playin' with your head! You're gonna mash somethin' in there you might need!" but she was ignored.

Aunt Nellie shook her head with a disgusted look and began wiping flour from her arms with the homemade apron. Her gray hair was pulled back into a tight bun. She was several years younger then Lester, but his thick black head, which was cut by Nelly about twice a year, had only scattered gray hairs.

Soon we were waving to them from the car, slowly headed out the lane. I looked back, waving again at the two of them standing in the front yard. Some of Lester's many words of advice came to mind.

"If a man can't take a piss off'en his own front porch anytime he wants, it's time to move on." Smokey traveled along behind the car until we turned onto the main road. He sat watching us ride away, then turned back.

"Did you get it?" Kay asked.

"Yeah."

"Enough to blow up the school?"

"Don't know if it'll blow the whole school or not, but we can make a big hole."

"Let's stop and explode some," Kay said.

"Not here," I said.

Kay was riding beside me in the back seat. While still talking, he stretched out with his head on my lap, falling immediately into an exhausted sleep. Vernon negotiated the curves while holding a Mason jar of candied yams wedged between his legs. It was a parting gift from Aunt Nellie. We rode along, silent and full. Mike, by the front seat window, was peering out over the drop-offs beside the road, to see what could be seen down below. He was intrigued.

Stopping in Sharpsburg for gas, we debated about going to Pinky's Pool Hall for a while but decided to go on back to Boaz. While Vernon filled the car, Kay insisted on opening the trunk to look into the bag, just to see what the dynamite looked like.

"You all come stay at the farm tonight. We'll have a gang meeting to figure things out," Kay decided. "We'll shoot my new gun."

He was still hinting for me to show him how to load it, without admitting that he didn't know.

"Take me by the house. I'll ask," I said, doubting that I would be allowed. I had been to Mike's house overnight during the summer, but only after our mothers talked on the phone. We pulled into Maplewood.

I told them, "Let me go see," and went into the house.

Things did not feel normal. Nothing jumped out as the reason. My brothers were quietly standing in the otherwise empty kitchen with their hands in pockets.

"What you two doin'?" I asked.

"Nothin'," they said in unison.

Father came in from the front room. It dawned on me what was wrong. Mother wasn't home, and it would soon be time for supper. There was no smell and no noisy mess that normally went with the meal's preparation.

"Where's Mom?" I asked.

"Some kinda meetin' about bein' a real estate agent."

"Agent?"

"Sellin' houses. That guy that sold us this house is startin' his own business here in Boaz. Your mom is thinkin' about going to work for him, sellin' houses. Being that you kids are in school now." My youngest brother had just started first grade.

We stood looking at each other, not knowing what to do. This was an unusual situation for the Parsons family. The youngest brother was showing the most aptitude for the new situation.

"Stanley's," he said.

Father smiled while shrugging and wrinkling his forehead. We all headed out the door.

"Can I stay up to Kay's tonight?"

"We're goin' up home tomorrow, you know. Be here by seven in the mornin'."

"I'll be back."

"Call your mom later and clear things. We'll go eat, and then we got to pick her up. You hungry?"

"I can eat at Kay's," I said, happy.

With that, we were off easier than imagined and waved to Father while pulling away. My middle brother and Kay had been giving each other dirty looks because of the football incident. We were on our way to blow something up.

"Mother is traveling with the debate team; she's the sponsor or something. Dad'll be at the hospital, so I'll just call later," Mike said.

Jerry Joe quietly blew cigarette smoke. We all envied him because he was not obligated to ask anyone.

"She's gonna be sticking a hose up my ass," Kay complained. We pulled to the back of the house, and the nurse was waiting for Kay. The shots made him constipated, and he received an enema every day. He had slept most of the way back from Fred's Creek and seemed rested. He followed the nurse off to his room. Vernon went to check on his cows.

Kay's room was on the ground floor. It was attached to the library that displayed many leather-bound books. His grandfather had acquired the matching books in one large order, to emulate the libraries he had seen on his trips east. It was an attempted refining and civilizing touch. I wanted to inspect them sometime.

Kay's windowless bedroom was big, with two beds, and looked much like a hospital room. There were several machines on roller carts lining the wall, ready to monitor his different problems. A long, white porcelain cabinet that had many drawers was sitting against a second wall. Beside it, in a corner, was a wooden desk that held a ham radio station. There were postcards thumbtacked to the wall, showing the call letters of the other radio operators that Kay had exchanged addresses and call letters with over the years. The nurse told us to go on in as she came out the door. He was drinking something that did not look good. It was yellowish and milky.

"For my kidneys," he explained.

The nurse soon came back for a final check and left with the empty glass. Kay wiped at his mouth with one of the bed blankets that was handy, and then peeked out the door to watch as she exited the opposite end of the library.

He shut the door and turned to the rest of us. "OK, what are we gonna explode?"

"I thought the school," Mike said.

Kay was excited and waved his arms. "We gotta practice on something first."

"If someone hears, it'll be evidence against us," Mike pointed out.

"You sure you can make it go off?" Kay gave me his questioning look.

"I did it before."

We were silent. Everyone was thinking.

Finally Mike said, "OK, here's what, we get the boat and go out where nobody sees us. Then we'll blow something up, and then we go to the school, sneak up the hill, maybe somewhere around the swimming hole. We'll put it ready to go, somewhere inside."

"How we gonna get in?" I asked.

"He can get you in anywhere," Jerry Joe said, grinning and looking at Mike.

Vernon was at the barns. One of his favorite cows was due to calve, so he was not going to be happy about leaving to take the helm of the sailboat. Vernon had become efficient over the years, taking Kay and others for slow motoring cruises that traveled up and down the river.

Kay, being an expert at getting people to do what he wanted, had a remedy for Vernon's reluctance, a bottle of schnapps. It was obtained by first getting a key to the liquor cabinet; the key was hidden in the back of Kay's bottom dresser drawer. Then he walked through the library and on into a big room, with the rest of us following.

The large, almost-square room had a ceiling that reached to the top of the second story. It was decorated with a formal fleur-de-lis pattern that was on maroon and gold wallpaper. Thick, dark wooden doors with round, ornate pulls stood closed at the main entrance. They were seldom used except for parties. There had been relatively few parties recently. Situated directly across the room from this formal entrance was a wide fireplace that was big enough for a person of Kay's size to walk into with room to spare. The fireplace was complete with a wide, carved wooden mantel.

An elk's head, centered high over the fireplace, was mounted in a dramatic pose. It protruded from a large carved plaque, looking down. Its big neck lowered the head and turned it to one side, and the eyes were wild like it was about to charge. It was a trophy from one of the hunting trips that Kay's great-grandfather had taken out West when he was a young man.

We left by a door on the opposite side of this room. The new room held side-by-side pool tables, one for snooker and the other for pocket pool. Jerry Joe unlocked and reached into a large leaded-glass liquor cabinet at the far end of the room and found what he was looking for. I looked around at the many photographs that were framed and lining the wall.

"Who's that?" I asked Kay while we waited, pointing to a large picture.

"My great-granddad. That other fellow is Roosevelt. Teddy Roosevelt. It's a Republican politics meeting. He was president, you know."

"He's a Republican?" I asked, surprised.

"You never saw a Republican?" Mike asked, shaking his head in his continuing wonderment of my ignorance.

"I saw Eisenhower, and he's a Republican. Uncle Lester and me went and watched him talk out the back of a train when he came past Sharpsburg once," I said.

"Are you a Republican?" I asked Mike.

"No, Kay is. Don't get him started."

Kay was too excited about the dynamite to get started. We headed on our way.

When I was younger, Uncle Lester told me that Eisenhower was coming to town to campaign. He explained that Eisenhower was a Republican. Uncle Lester confided to me that he had never looked at a Republican up close, so we went to Sharpsburg to see what one looked like. On the way home he decided that Eisenhower looked almost the same as normal people and explained to me that he was now confident that he could point one out when he saw one.

Vernon decided the cow would probably wait until tomorrow when his eyes rested on the schnapps bottle. We drove back a narrow road to a comfortable-looking old brick house that was in good repair. It was sitting on a high knoll, pointing toward and overlooking the river.

Vernon, Herky, and Veada lived here. It was one of the older Schultz homes and many years ago was used during the summer. The bigger one, the one they now lived in on the farm, was built by the Schultz family around 1900. Vernon's father ran the dairy for years and had died recently, replaced by one of his assistants.

Herky argued with Vernon about the use of their car, but Herky finally agreed that Vernon could continue using it. He gave in more to Kay's wishes than Vernon's and also agreed he would look in on the cow.

Veada told us all to be careful, and speaking to Vernon said, "Don't keep him out late."

Kay had a dark knit toboggan cap pulled over his ears to disguise himself for our secret trip. When Veada questioned him, he told her, in a civil manner, that he felt fine.

Veada spent nights at the big house. She used the extra bed in Kay's room, with a phone close by to reach the nurse in her apartment if needed. Veada was closer to a mother and confidant for Kay than anyone. She knew everything about the Schultz family for generations, good, bad, or otherwise, and had told Kay most of it in long question-and-answer sessions late at night when he could not sleep because of the acute attacks of pain that he had lived with most of his life. If people were aware of how much Kay knew about his family, himself, and others connected to his family, they would be surprised.

The story was told. Kay's mother loved him very much and had considerable contact by telephone, even from Europe. Her life was one long trip, either arriving or departing. She spent her time on no particular schedule, in California, New York, Connecticut, and the South of France, where they owned a cozy, remote farmhouse. She took detours as the mood struck. Having a need for exploring new places, she appeared to be continually searching for something, but she never seemed to know exactly what.

Her holiday time was reserved for Boaz. The house took on a festive mood with a big, bright Christmas tree, accompanied by parties that included the Boaz "social A-list," plus Big Kay's business and political friends from all over. She kept in touch with her astrologist, was on a lifelong diet, and became deeply depressed when she was around Kay for long.

We arrived at the marina. Mike and I carried the dynamite bag and fuse cord. We all boarded the classic, wooden-hulled sailboat, which shined with much brass and bright work. It was painted two toned: navy blue from the keel and up out of the water to the dark "old gold" stripe that was painted about ten inches wide and circled the boat just below the five square portholes on each side. From the stripe on up, across the deck and including the mast, the boat was painted navy white. The sloop measured twenty-nine feet at the waterline. Kay's grandfather on his mother's side had bought it in the mid-thirties, and he willed it to his daughter.

After she became pregnant and they married, Big Kay was transferred to the North Carolina Outer Banks. He had actually happened upon and rescued some Germans adrift in a life raft after they had experienced mechanical trouble with their submarine and abandoned ship. They were amazed that his name was Schultz and amazed further that someone named Schultz would have to look up German words in a translation dictionary.

Big Kay finagled a week's leave and returned to Sharpsburg to be present at certain business proceedings that could only be conducted by the owner. Kay's mother insisted on meeting him there in spite of being eight months pregnant. Vernon's father, using government gasoline ration tickets that were supposed to be for the milk trucks, drove an automobile to Connecticut and delivered her back over the objections of her doctor and family. The trip must have caused something to happen because within hours after arriving at the farm, she went into premature labor.

The same family doctor that had delivered Big Kay was called. Veada, along with Della, assisted in the delivery. Kay weighed less than four pounds and did not cry. He moved little and lay breathing laboriously.

There was still in use a little discussed but age-old solution for this situation. The father was handed a pillow by the doctor and left in the room alone with the infant, to smother the life before him in order to save it from what was assumed to be prolonged unnecessary suffering.

Big Kay sat and cried. He could not bring himself to do what was expected. He told his wife of the situation after she woke and then asked her advice. She said they must do everything possible for their child, so they did. The doctor and Big Kay bundled Little Kay into blankets. With the automobile heater turned to high, they drove him to a Cincinnati hospital, after the doctor called ahead, telling the newborn unit to be ready.

One night in Kay's bedroom when he was complaining to Veada that his parents did not want him around, she sat quietly for a while, thinking, and then told him this story.

He said, "I see."

He quit complaining so much and never mentioned it to her again.

Kay's mother had a long recovery from a birth that had several complications. It included depression, and when the war was over, in an attempt to brighten her up, Big Kay and she sailed the boat down the East Coast, stopping here and there. He showed her where he was stationed in North Carolina during the war. They continued on around Florida and stopped in New Orleans before navigating up the

Mississippi. Then forking into the Ohio, they ended their pleasant cruse at Boaz by dropping anchor and rowing a rubber dinghy to the bank. Walking hand in hand up the hill, they ended their journey at the big house.

Vernon, over the years, had become proficient with the boat. Not with sailing— he knew nothing about sailing—but he could maneuver the boat with the help of the forty-five horsepower diesel engine that was hidden in her belly. Even this was not easy, because she drafted almost five feet of water. After being pulled from a sandbar or two, he learned to stick to the main dredged commercial channels and with time became fairly knowledgeable about the stretch of river that ran from Boaz to Sharpsburg.

Kay was sitting in a low-slung deck chair on the foredeck with the blanket Vernon had put over his legs. He pointed and yelled back at Vernon, giving orders and directions. Jerry Joe and I were having a contest to see who could hang out over the water the farthest by holding a stay wire with one hand while holding the opposite arm and leg away from the boat and out into the air. Mike was at the stern trying to talk Vernon into letting him take the helm.

Kay had me load his pistol. I showed him the safety.

"Shoot it," he said, from his chair.

I fired one round, at a sharp angle to the water so it wouldn't ricochet. Kay laughed but did not get up to shoot, because he had learned not to move around on the boat. I handed it to him butt first. He carefully engaged the safety, following my instructions, and pushed it back into the pocket of his jacket.

We headed for the caves, where the water was deep, and glided up against the huge flat boulder, bouncing when one of the rubber finders hanging over the side of the boat made contact against the rock face.

"OK, now I want to see you dumb bunnies blow somethin' up!" Kay said.

He rose and by sliding on his behind and holding onto various things, he slowly and carefully negotiated the deck back to where the rest of us stood down in the cockpit. I dug around in the dynamite bag and began working in light that was changing to dusk. Vernon showed Mike the switch for the running lights. While Mike kept an eye on things, Vernon went below for a handheld spotlight. Together they hooked it directly to the engine battery. It would be ready when needed.

I decided one stick would do, guessing at about a minute's length on the slow-burning fuse cord that I had chosen, and began connecting everything together like I had been taught. Then I gave directions that we needed to cruise upriver to the end of the boulder. With the fuse lit by Mike's Zippo lighter, Jerry Joe threw the dynamite up against the steep mud bank, which was plentiful because of the low river that existed in late summer.

Dynamite doesn't necessarily make a loud bang. You mostly feel the vibration of a low rumble when it ignites. The noise made was not impressive, but the raining down of refined clumps of black river mud was. In seconds the boat and everyone on deck became dotted with the sticking ooze. Kay loved it. He laughed his high, cackling laugh, that started him coughing, and immediately he held up his arms—a habit developed to help clear his lungs—and started laughing again. The rest of us stood for a moment, looking at each other speckled with mud; then we began laughing along with Kay. Vernon was grinning from ear to ear and wiping mud from one eye while looking around for witnesses to see what kind of trouble he might be in. He took a healthy drink of his schnapps and turned downriver, increasing the engine to almost full speed.

"Let's head for the school. This mud stuff makes good camouflage!" Kay said.

We traveled quite a distance, occasionally giggling but not talking much.

"You have to stay on the boat, Kay," Mike finally said.

"If I don't go, nobody goes! And that's that."

"You too big for the bag?" Jerry Joe asked.

"I can fit."

Jerry Joe went below to reappear with an old, wrinkled Coast Guard sea bag that Jerry Joe had used in previous years to carry Kay around. It had a carrying strap on the side and came up around Kay's neck when he stood inside. Jerry Joe carried it hanging under his arm like a golf bag. They practiced a minute; the procedure seemed to still work.

Finally ahead, a large oak tree leaned out over the water with the roots on the riverside exposed. Swimmers used these roots as steps for climbing up the bank after swinging out and dropping into the water from a long, knotted rope tied high on a limb. This swimming hole was a bone of contention between the school and students. Sneaking down for a swim would draw the investigating principal and teachers, who often caught the swimmers.

Mother had a rule against swimming in the river. The reason other than drowning was polio. It was one of her parental fears. She was convinced that the creeks and rivers had germs and were a source of polio, and she had agonized over taking her children for polio shots because she had read in a magazine that the shots themselves might in some cases actually cause polio. We received the shots. She closely watched for any suspicious changes in her children. Of course there was still the no-swimming rule.

The water was deep in close to the tree. We could maneuver up to the roots, but Kay was too awkward to hand across the distance.

"I'll swing across," he said.

"How are you going to swing across?" Mike asked, mildly exasperated.

"Tie this damn bag to that rope. I'll swing across, you know, like Tarzan."

"Tarzan?"

"Quit yappin', we don't have all night, chucklehead! Jerry Joe goes over there, where he can catch the bag, and then Vernon takes us up to that rope. Do I have to do everything myself?"

It took three swings to get him where Jerry Joe could snatch the bag. On the first swing he was trying to yell like Tarzan. The last, he was cussing our incompetence. I carried the dynamite bag, and Mike, the roll of fuse. We made it up the hill, all except Vernon who stayed with the tied boat. We walked the often-used path that wound through the browning field corn that had yet to be picked, and continued across the railroad tracks and up the hill to the back of the school yard. Jerry Joe was still carrying Kay.

It was almost dark. Mike and Jerry Joe smoked. We all stooped except for Kay, who was looking off to the school, trying to spot things that might cause us trouble.

"Look out for enemies," Kay said.

"Who's the enemy?" I asked.

Kay pushed the bag down from around himself and dug into his pocket to awkwardly pull the newly loaded gun and waved it around with both hands. "Anybody who's not one of us."

In a line across the schoolyard, with Jerry Joe still carrying Kay, we crept to the window outside the coach's office. The office used some of the space under the bleachers. Mike borrowed my pocketknife and slid a blade between the sashes to push open a latch.

It was now almost dark. We had forgotten a flashlight, but our eyes adjusted to the darkening conditions. Mike and I squirmed into the office. Jerry Joe stuffed Kay headfirst, bag and all, to us and we lowered him to the floor. Jerry Joe handed the dynamite bag and fuse on through, then quickly slipped himself in and pulled the window shut.

Kay wiggled from his bag and dragged it behind himself. Mike turned the knob, and we felt our way out the office door and along the walls. Finally we were standing in the middle of the basketball floor.

Kay said, "Now what?"

"Wait here, Mortie showed me something," Mike said.

He felt his way up the bleachers to turn a switch in the projection booth. It brought to life the stage lights hidden in the floor. They were on a rheostat and could be lowered for dramatic effect. Mike turned the knob to low.

"People are gonna see, you idiot!" Kay said.

Mike bounced down the stairs nonchalantly. "The lights are on all the time in here when the janitors clean. If it wasn't Saturday, they'd all be on."

He patted Kay on the head.

Kay swatted at Mike's arm with a hand. "I got a gun and know how to use it, Bub."

Jerry Joe hopped onto the stage and started walking like a goose, back and forth in the light. Mike followed by climbing the side steps onto the stage, pretending to talk into a microphone.

He said, "Give me a *B*."

We answered, "*B*!"

"Give me an *O*."

"*O!*"

"Give me another *O*."

"*O!*"

"Give me an *M*."

"*M!*"

"What you got?"

"BOOM!"

In the meantime Kay was crawling up the steps to the stage, still dragging his bag. We were all laughing.

Mike waved him over to say, "Look, here comes a ventriloquist's dummy. Maybe we can make him talk. What's your name, young man?" He held the imaginary microphone where Kay could speak.

"Charlie McCarthy," Kay said.

"What you doing here tonight, Charlie?"

"I came here to get all these bastards that laugh and say I'm a freak, and I ought to be in a circus. I'm here to blow 'um all to hell, and another thing, if I can't have a football team, they ain't gonna have one either!"

"All right, all right, and what about you, 'King of the River Rats' Culpepper? What you got to tell these nice folks?" Mike coaxed.

"It just ain't gonna be their day," Jerry Joe said in a slow deadpan voice.

Mike quickly stepped to me. "OK, OK, here's a hillbilly from Fred's Creek. Now it's your turn to tell 'um."

"Don't like 'um tellin' round I'm stupid or beatin' my ass with a board or kickin' me in the stomach. Don't like it one damn bit."

"And finally folks, this skinny, little dago from Pittsburgh is here to tell you all to get in line and wait your turn to kiss my ass."

We all laughed while randomly walking about the stage. Finally Kay plopped to his behind on the stage floor beside one of the lights and motioned us to him. He fished in his bib-overalls pocket, held up his ace of spades, and with a flourish, placed it on the floor in front of him. We formed a circle sitting on the floor and produced our cards, placing them near Kay's on the floor.

"Before long, they're going to put me in my room to stay. Don't let 'um. Get me this." He dug around and then showed each of us his gun. "Get me this so they can't keep me there. I am not going to die stretched out in that stinking bed. I figured that out a long time ago," he said.

Quietly, with some difficulty he shoved the safety off, and using both hands, pointed the gun to his forehead. "I'm not gonna let them do all that crap to me anymore. Do you understand?"

We all nodded. There was tension in the air. We sat quiet. Kay finally lowered the gun.

He said, after a few seconds, trying to resume the job at hand, "So where are we gonna explode it?"

He had a pained look on his face. We could that see he was getting tired.

I reached over, pushing the safety back on, and said, "Let's hide it in my locker and find a place during school. Where's a good place to put it? I don't know."

"Maybe in the boiler room. I been down there and know where they keep the keys hid," Mike said. "We can crawl under the floor here." He moved his arm to indicate the basketball floor: "There's room to put it down there."

"And blow it up when there havin' a Thuse," Kay said.

"Can't, Susan might get hurt," Mike said.

"We'll blow it up during football practice then," Kay said, regaining his cheer.

We all agreed that this might work.

Kay said, "Go get Vernon, I need a shot."

"We could take us a shit on a teacher's desk or somethin'," Jerry Joe said.

"That'd tip them off that somebody's been in here," Mike said. "But I like the idea, maybe later."

We put the sack of dynamite and fuse in my locker. I opened it while Mike held his Zippo. Then carefully removing the blasting caps from my pocket, still wrapped in the red bandanna, I gently laid them in a back corner. At Kay's urging, I removed my revolver and holster from the locker.

"In case we need it," he said.

We went out the window. Jerry Joe headed for the boat to go back to the marina and bring the car for Kay. Kay, along with Mike and me, strolled on the sidewalk and traveled around to the front of the school building, trying not to look suspicious. Kay refused to ride in the bag even though he was at the end of his spurt of energy. He had me bring it with us because it had his father's name stenciled on the side. He thought it would be evidence against us if we left it. I dropped my pistol into the bag for concealment.

In the light of Stanley's, we were a muddy mess. While sitting in a booth picking the mud off, I looked up to see a familiar vehicle driving by. It was a two-toned Packard with a white bottom and red top, and it was carrying the Parsons family. Mr. And Mrs. Parsons were up front and two of the three Parsons children were leaning out the back window jabbing the air with fingers, pointing out the missing family member who was sitting inside Stanley's. I bolted out the door, still carrying the bag, then slowed to walk casually to the stopped car.

"What you doing here?" I said.

Mother was upset. "Look at you. Where did all that mud come from? You look terrible, and out here in public too. What are you doing, Bob? Why aren't you home?"

"Dad said I could go up to Kay's." I pointed to the other gang members, now headed out our way.

"This ain't Kay's house. You were going to call," Father said.

"We went frog-giggin' and forgot."

Father laughed. "Ain't no frogs at Stanley's either. That your frog bag?"

My brothers laughed at his joke, still proud they were the first to spot me.

"Yeah, we got a boat down on the river, just now walked up here for a Coke."

Mother said, "It's too late in the evening to be drinking Cokes, you won't be able to sleep well. Do you know how dangerous it is out on that river at night? Sometimes, Bob, I worry that you don't have good sense."

Kay adjusted the knit cap that kept creeping down over his eyes.

He started talking. "Hello, Mr. and Mrs. Parsons, nice to see you. This whole misunderstanding is entirely my fault. I was in such

154

a hurry to go out on the boat, I told Robert here not to take the time to call you, even though he said he must. So please blame me for this whole rotten mess." He dramatically patted his chest to emphasize the point.

Mother, not knowing what to make of him, did not have an answer.

"Bags not full. Did you get any frogs?" Father asked.

"Nah, heard some, but they were skittish, hard to sneak in on. Did you catch any turtles this mornin'?"

"Couple small ones. Badeye took um on with him."

"Never mind that. Bob, you get yourself in this car right this minute," Mother said.

"Mike here was gonna drive me on home, stay the night, and go with us to Fred's Creek in the mornin', to church,'" I said, off the top of my head.

The culture of Fred's Creek was to try and get new people to attend church, even if it meant going out of your way.

"Do you drive? Are you old enough?" Mother asked him.

"Oh yes, because I was sick, rheumatics fever. The teachers thought it best to hold me back in school. I recovered nicely. Vernon went for the car because Kay's sick." Kay gave a small cough. "We are going to my house so I can get clean clothes, then we were coming on to your house. Yes, ma'am," Mike answered, dripping sincerity.

Mother, basking in all the politeness and civility, said, "OK then, do that." She looked at me and said with an edge to her voice, "Don't take all night, Bob."

"Yes, ma'am." We waved as they pulled around and into a place to order.

When Vernon arrived, we headed Kay toward bed. Veada and the nurse were waiting. They both complained about the mud.

"Men get dirty sometimes, it can't be helped," Kay said condescendingly.

We tried talking Vernon out of his car while Kay was being worked on, but he would not budge. He feared Herky's wrath but said it was OK for me to store the sea bag with my revolver in his trunk for safekeeping. Kay had returned and motioned for us to follow him to his bedroom.

155

"Take my car," he said, so we did, after searching in the same drawer where he had hidden his gun.

The drawer also hid keys to everything on the farm. Soon, Jerry Joe, Mike, and myself were motoring downriver in the shiny, new Buick.

We stopped at Mike's house. He washed off the mud and changed clothes, adding fresh oil on his hair. We then paused to leave a note for his father, who had earlier left a note for Mike.

He was at the hospital on an emergency call. Dr. Masters had learned his skills during World War II in a field surgery unit and had returned to the Army when Korea called. Local accidents in which bones were broken required his presence most of the time. Mike's mother had yet to return from her trip with the high school debate team. Jerry Joe took a shower, changing into an expensive lime green golf shirt that Mike found after searching his father's bedroom. We were off.

"We go in, pretend to go to bed, sneak out the window," I said.

"I'll be waitin' here," Jerry Joe said, and stretched out in the backseat to light a cigarette from the electric lighter conveniently located in the car door by the ashtray. Mike parked the car facing down the grade, pointing back out to the gates of Maplewood.

"Hello, Mother, what are you doing?" I asked.

She was sitting at the dining room table with papers and books spread out before her.

"Trying to learn something. You have to take a test to get a real estate license. If I decided to sell houses." She glanced to the front room where father and my brothers were watching TV. "If I decide to," she repeated.

" It gives all the different interest tables in this book. Do you two know that only about five dollars of our first house payment went to pay off the house loan? The rest goes to the Sharpsburg Savings and Loan in interest. No wonder they got that big building in the middle of town. Wonder what else they spend all that money on?"

"Swimming pools, big cars," Mike said with a little, crooked grin.

"Lester said he'd give us the money, but you wouldn't hear of it," Father said, from around the corner.

"You know Dad would get upset, me taking money from Lester."

"It's your mom's money too. We'd pay Lester back to make your dad happy. Pay the interest money too. That shoulda suited everybody."

"I know, Tuffy, I know. You two stink like cigarette smoke."

"Oh, that's Vernon. He smokes like a fiend, but I can't ask him not to; it would be impolite. Me and Mike just hate the way it makes us smell," I said.

"That's true," Mike added, looking concerned.

"Mike and I, dear, it's Mike and I. Go wash up. I'll get you all some milk. Where's your pajamas, Mike?"

"I forgot to bring them."

"No problem; you can wear a pair of Bob's. Now you two run along, and get that mud off of yourself, Bob," she said.

"Oh, Mike, your mother tells me you play the piano," she added, as we were about to leave the room. "That's wonderful!"

" Bob, she also told me that you could take lessons on any musical instrument, for free. All you have to do is sign up for it at school. Don't you think you would like to do something like that? After all, your grandfather plays the piano. Well, some."

"Yeah, I'd like to play the drums."

"Oh no! Not the drums. I read in a magazine not too long ago about Gene Kruppa. He's a famous drummer and a fine-looking man. Playing the drums made him start taking drugs. It has ruined his life. No, not the drums, Bob. What other instrument do you like?"

"I'll think on it."

We headed into my bedroom. Mike whispered, "Pajamas?" I shrugged and shook my head, not answering.

Mother made several trips in and out of the bedroom. My brothers tried to hang around, but I shooed them away to the bedroom they shared. Things settled down because Mother's plan was to be at Fred's Creek by ten o'clock in the morning for church. She wanted everyone to have plenty of sleep.

I entertained Mike with some of my treasures, including a long, round soapstone that Uncle Lester's grandfather had found along

Bone Marrow Branch. It looked oddly like a penis and was worn on the sides where it had been used for many years to sharpen knives.

"I like Fred's Creek," Mike said. "Might move up there and live someday. Down by the creek someplace."

"We'll look for a place tomorrow," I answered seriously, and we waited for everyone to go to sleep.

When everything was quiet, we went out the window. Mike put the car in neutral, and Jerry Joe and I shoved it to the Maplewood gate. All that could be heard was the crunch of the new gravel. This avoided the suspicious noise of an engine starting in front of the house. We piled in and pulled onto the main road.

"Pinky's or the skating rink?" Mike asked.

"Let's go to Pinky's first, 'cause Gloria don't get too happy if we go there, then leave," Jerry Joe suggested.

"If you leave," Mike said.

"Yeah, may be." He was embarrassed.

Pinky's was a man's place, run by a man named Pinky, who previously had been a horseracing jockey. He entertained customers with stories about making money, women, and getting hurt. The last included showing scars of his different spills. He was short, of course, but had gained weight over the years by sitting behind the counter drinking beer. He had gained a lot of weight and was now round. He wore, all of the time, a snap-brimmed hat to cover his bald-head.

"Only take it off for one thing, and it ain't sleepin'," he often said.

Pinky owned the pool hall, located across Market Street from the Lucky Strike bowling alley and skating rink. In the summer, with the door propped open, the pool players could hear Sammy across the street, playing the organ for the skaters. Pinky lived by himself on the second floor of his establishment, except for the occasional live-in girlfriend, who never lasted long.

He possessed a great ability in knowing the people who came through the door, mostly in self-defense, because of the gambling activity that went on nightly in a second-floor room. When we entered, he knew Jerry Joe was a Culpepper, Mike was Dr. Masters's kid, and even though my presence had been limited, he knew I was Tuffy Parsons's son.

When I was a small child, I had gone to Pinky's with Father and Uncle Lester, when we were on trips for supplies. They stopped for a beer and sometimes shot a game of pool before heading back to Fred's Creek. Pinky liked kids and gave me a soft drink and sort of babysat while they played. After one trip, when we returned to Fred's Creek, my mother asked where all we had been. Father named off the stores we had visited, skipping the Pinky's visit. In the meantime, I found behind a door the notched hickory stick used for measuring. I got down on the floor, pretending to hit pool balls, while holding the stick in the appropriate position.

Mother, Grandmother, and Great-Grandmother Mattie started laughing and called Father back into the room.

"You're not suppose to tell!" he said to me, and laughed along.

He was caught red-handed. This was a much-told story over the years. I liked to go to Pinky's. It made me feel like a man, and as long as you acted that way, they treated you like one. Taking all the kidding was the first thing to learn.

"You boys out on the prowl tonight, are you? We better lock up the women I guess, just to be safe." Pinky laughed good-naturedly. "What'll it be, men?"

"Draft and a bag of chips," Jerry Joe said.

Mike and I mumbled, "Same."

We took our glass mugs of beer and sat on the chairs that lined the wall. They were positioned up on a long narrow platform that looked down on the line of pool tables. I would have preferred an orange drink, but it would have been embarrassing to order anything but beer, so I sipped without making a face and ate the chips. Pinky knew we were not old enough to drink beer but was tolerant about serving minors and watched things closely.

The culture of the pool hall consisted of the old men and kids sitting in the elevated chairs. The players stood around the tables. The table next to the front door and food counter was for the best players in Sharpsburg, or the ones who played for the highest stakes and thought they were good. Pinky sat on the only stool in the place, behind the counter and next to a black gas grill. He had a refrigerator and shelves of the accoutrements needed for making the chili that was constantly on a low burner, even in summer. It included two kinds of beans, spaghetti, and sometimes chopped celery.

He could also make, among other things, fried baloney sandwiches. Cooking time was about twenty seconds. They were made by slicing a piece of baloney from a roll, then cutting nicks in four places around the edge so the piece would not swell in the middle. It was quickly blackened on both sides and slapped between two pieces of white bread. The sandwich would be plopped before you on wax paper, along with an open jar of mustard that had a short, wide butter knife protruding.

There was a brass foot rail across the bottom of the counter and matching spittoons at each end. Several other mismatched spittoons were scattered randomly around the hall. They were often spit at and were hit maybe half the time. A fellow named Motherload cleaned the place and lived in the basement. He had appeared one day, years before, and asked Pinky if he had any work. Pinky showed him how to brush the felt covering the pool tables and had to come back and take the brush away "before he brushed clean through to the slate."

The long, white porcelain urinal against the wall in the back restroom could accommodate four good-sized men standing shoulder to shoulder, without touching of course. No one envied Motherload his cleaning job, and no one kidded him more than a little, because he was high-strung, and when agitated, would lose his temper. He was tall and weighed at least 350 pounds, so he mostly went about his business of sweeping, taking drinks upstairs to the men playing cards, and cleaning up what needed cleaning. Unless Pinky had someone causing trouble; then he would yell, "Motherload!"

Everyone else moved out of the way.

We sat watching for the people at the last pool table, in the back of the building, to quit playing. When they quit, we walked back to inspect pool cues taken from one of the racks lining the wall. After finding sticks that were reasonably straight, Jerry Joe yelled "time" to Pinky. He waved and looked at the clock to mark down when we began. You paid for playing by the amount of time the tables were used.

Mike and Jerry Joe were both better than me from playing on the tables at Kay's house. I was getting beat and stood leaning on my stick, scanning the room, when a shaking spell suddenly felt eminent. My eyes had locked onto Lonny and Clyde Piggott entering the front door. They casually took seats without buying anything and whispered to each other. They were looking our way. I explained the situation to the others after turning my back to the Piggotts.

"What we gonna do?" I asked.

"Nothin'," Jerry Joe said, and took his turn at the table. Mike looked at me, and we were worried. "They probably won't do nothin' in here," Jerry Joe explained.

The Piggotts sat and watched players at the other tables and began ignoring us. I started feeling better and finally made a shot. We were playing "cutthroat," one of the few games that three people can play. Finally, they sank all my balls, causing my elimination.

I was hungry and decided to venture to the counter for another bag of potato chips by moving along the tables on the opposite side of the building from where the Piggotts were sitting.

I ordered the chips. "How's Tuffy doin'?" Pinky asked.

"Doin' OK."

"Hear he's workin' at a chemical plant. He like it?"

I had never before wondered if he liked it or not and made a note to ask him. "Yeah, says it's OK."

Starting back, feeling good that Pinky knew me, I automatically glanced across at the Piggotts. They were not in the seats, but were walking to the back of the pool hall. Jerry Joe was stretched across the table, getting ready to make a shot. Mike was watching intently, while absently chalking his cue stick. Neither saw them coming.

All self-respecting pool halls, and for that matter anywhere men hang out, have a back door for unobserved entrance and exit; whether the patrons need to sneak or not, it is part of the allure. Pinky's was no exception. The Piggotts each reached to a wall rack and pulled down a pool cue while still walking, not taking their eyes off Jerry Joe. Clyde drew his stick back and closed quickly on Jerry Joe.

Still a couple of tables away, I suddenly heard myself yell, "Jerry Joe, watch out!"

All it did was cause Jerry Joe to look in my direction about the time Clyde came around with a full swing, using the butt of the cue. It caught him across the eye. Lonny was behind Clyde, swinging at the air and hitting nothing. They both dropped the sticks and ran out the back door. By instinct, not logic, Mike and I went out the door, chasing them up the alley.

Two things came to my mind while running behind them. One, I could run faster than both of them and was closing ground rapidly. Two, what was going to happen if they were caught? I slowed to a stop.

Mike caught me and said, "Let's go see about Jerry Joe. We'll get those bastards later."

"OK."

We went back. Motherload was furiously at work, cleaning the felt of the pool table where Jerry Joe had bled. Jerry Joe was sitting in a chair holding to his eye a counter rag that Pinky had given him to stop the blood, which had run down onto the green golf shirt

The patrons were discussing the wound. "You know, you got more blood in your head than anywhere else in your body?"

"You do?" another answered.

"Yep, but you see, it hurts less because you got less nerves in your head."

"You do?"

"Yep, he'll be needin' stitches."

"I'd say so," another added.

Jerry Joe slowly got up and walked out the front door, heading across the street to the skating rink, still pressing the cloth against his head. Mike and I trailed behind.

"Let's go see Gloria," he said.

Gloria was not happy. There was a mandatory rest period of five minutes every hour, during which the skating floor was emptied. People stood talking and eating. Gloria was talking to her friend Linda and glanced over to see Jerry Joe.

She skated quickly to us. "What happened?"

"We was fightin'," I said.

She looked at the eye and then went after a first aid kit that was in the office. Sammy, the manager, returned with her. Sammy had on a loud plaid coat and bow tie that he wore on stage while playing organ music. His hair was suspiciously black and combed from the back of the head forward, to cover the baldness. Then it swept to one side and was held in place by oil. Jerry Joe had confided to me that

Sammy went to Della's to get his hair dyed. He smelled bad and squinted at Jerry Joe through thick glasses. Sammy told Gloria that in his opinion, Jerry Joe should go to the hospital.

"Come on, we're goin'," she said.

Jerry Joe shook his head, still pressing the rag. "I'm OK now."

"We're goin' to the hospital if I have to drag your ignorant ass all the way there by your hair!" she said, and slapped his arm.

She went to get her street shoes. I told our story to Linda, about how we chased the Piggotts but were unable to catch them. We stood around until Gloria got back.

She waved her arm and said, "Come on."

We all walked into the hospital. Mike said, "wait here," and asked the person at the front desk to call Dr. Masters.

"He's had an emergency operation that lasted forever, so he's probably asleep in the doctor's quarters by now. Why do you need him?" the lady asked.

"I'm his son and need to see him. We'll go up. I know where he is." Mike motioned for us to follow down a corridor.

We went up a flight of stairs and into what looked like an apartment. Mike went through one of several closed doors off of the main sitting room, and was soon back with Dr. Masters, who was wearing stained white operating clothes. It was obvious that he had been asleep. He immediately saw Jerry Joe and motioned where he wanted him to sit. He turned on a table lamp to carefully examine the wound in silence, then walked us down the hall to an operating room and put nine closely placed stitches into the eyebrow.

"You're going to have a beaut of a shiner. Maybe a scar, not a big one, but you got a hard head and it should be OK," Dr. Masters said.

The hard head crack made us all laugh. Mike explained that Jerry Joe fell while diving into the pool at Kay's house. Mike said he was the only one awake to drive the car, so it was an emergency. Dr. Masters seemed to buy the explanation, or at least was not making it an issue. A nurse came and took Jerry Joe, with Gloria following, to wash and put salve on the finished operation. We went back to the hospital apartment. Dr. Masters began making coffee in the kitchen area.

"You two want something?" he asked.

"No, we're fine," Mike said.

There was a long pause. I blurted out, not being able to contain my curiosity, "You from Italy?"

"My parents are, but I was born in Pittsburgh," he told me. "Their name is Masttero, but the name was written Masters on the immigration papers, so they went by Masters because they didn't know any better. I was born Anthony Michael Masters. I didn't know any better either." He laughed, and looked at me while pointing to Mike, "Mike here say's he's changing his when he gets old enough, aren't you Mike?'"

"How old you have to be?" I asked.

"I'm not real sure you have to be any certain age, but I'll find out. Mike, it's illegal for you to be driving without a license, you know that. No matter what your name is. I can't leave here just this minute, till I get this patient stabilized, so you be careful going back and don't speed. That's what got this guy I'm working on all busted up."

"I was wanting to go with Bob up to Fred's Creek, to look around in the morning. His parents have invited me, and they're going too, so is it OK? I'll get Vernon up to drive us over to his house."

"They really would like for him to go," I added.

"Be back early; your mother's coming home tomorrow afternoon."

"I will."

We started out the door. Behind us, Dr Masters said, "That shirt Jerry Joe has on looks familiar."

"It's yours. I loaned it to him."

"Your mother bought it. I always hated that thing and it's way too big. Tell 'um to keep it."

We turned with everyone grinning and parted ways. Jerry Joe went back to the rink with Gloria. She refused to let him out of her sight.

We drove to my house but killed the car engine before we got there and coasted quietly to a stop in front of the house. We slipped into the bedroom by using the window and lay on our backs in the bed with our clothes on. Arms folded across our chests, looking at the dark ceiling, we discussed the day's events and eventually drifted to sleep.

Day Seven

"Bob, wake up! You slept in your clothes. Why didn't you put on your pajamas, right here in front of you? I wish to heaven I knew what makes you act like this." Mother was talking.

I could hear her through my sound sleep, and then opened my eyes to Sunday morning and a family trip to Fred's Creek. Mike was already awake, looking her way, wondering the same as I, "Why is she going on about something so obviously unimportant as pajamas?"

We washed and dressed in the clothes that Mother laid out. She gave Mike one of my white shirts because his was wrinkled. In her opinion it was not suitable for church. We traded so he could wear the long sleeves. After pancakes, we were off, but not before an argument.

"No, you two are riding with us, and that's final. It'd be silly to drive two cars when we can all go in one, with gasoline up to twenty-five cents a gallon and all. Now get in the car," Mother said and pointed to the Packard. Father was sitting behind the wheel.

I dropped my head and said to Mike, "Come on."

We each got into an opposite side, using the back doors. My middle brother was now sitting between us and began whining that he was supposed to sit by a window. My youngest brother was up front on his knees, leaning back over the seat, making faces at all three of us.

My middle brother began climbing over me to be by the window. "Move your butt over," I said, and shoved him back to the middle.

"Mom, Bob said butt to me," he said, leaning over the front seat to tattle.

"It's the Lord's Day Bob, don't say butt," Mother explained quietly over her shoulder.

"Yes, ma'am." I gave my brother a look that said she would not be around to protect him all the time. He quieted down.

We rode downriver toward Sharpsburg and turned up beside the Big Piney. Mother had us in a position to begin her questions. We had no escape.

"Well, Mike, what church do you go to?"

"Catholic."

This drew silence because grandfather was convinced that the Catholic Church was trying to take over the world with a secret organization called the Knights of Columbus. Then the Pope would run things, "wearin' those robes 'round." He didn't care for the robes either. I made a mental note to ask Mike not to say Catholic in front of Grandfather. None of us wanted him to, because of the sermon that followed.

Convinced that the Holy Gospel Church was the one Jesus established in the Sermon on the Mount, Grandfather was jealous of the Catholics because they number in the millions of course, while his church numbered about fifty on a Sunday with good weather.

"Where's your family from, Mike?" she continued her investigation.

He seemed to take her questions tolerantly. "We're from Pittsburgh, but Dad's family came over from Italy, Northern Italy. Place called Como."

"Like Perry Como," I explained.

"He doesn't look, well, Italian," she said. She had seen his picture in the paper.

"Yeah, they're from northern Italy. Lots a blond-headed people around there. My black hair came from Mom."

"Where's she from?"

"I think from around Sharpsburg somewhere. She said her family drowned in a flood, so then she was an orphan and was raised by the nuns and met Dad at Duquesne College. That's in Pittsburgh too. She taught school and he went to med school."

"Well it's nice when the woman of the house can work and bring home additional income. You must be proud of her, Michael."

"Yeah, sure," Mike said, looking over at me and shrugging. He moved his hands back and forth to silently ask, "What is she talking about?" I shook my head and had no answer.

Mike and his parents had been to Italy. They had visited Como the previous summer. We had discussed his family history. Mike's grandfather, when about fifteen, started digging graves, many graves, because of the smallpox epidemic that killed his parents and most of the rest of the family. He, for some unexplained reason, was immune. Mike's grandmother recovered after she became infected and to this day had some scarring that resembled acne. Both grandparents considered this a small price to pay compared to the surrounding devastation.

With nothing left, in mourning and despondent, Mike's grandparents decided to leave Como. They were able to sneak through the quarantine and walked and caught rides to Genova, where they were promptly swindled. They lost their small amount of money when they bought fake tickets on a ship to America. They then walked and caught rides to Rome, where they worked three years and saved money to buy real tickets. This time they both carefully checked for authenticity before the tickets were purchased.

In New York, with a misspelled name and a pregnant wife, he got a job digging ditches and worked for a while. Then for a slight increase in pay, he accepted a new job digging ditches. A representative from the city of Pittsburgh offered him the job. He bundled his pregnant wife and went by train to a town he called "Pissburg" and began digging drainage ditches along the Monongahela and Allegheny rivers, where they merge to form the Ohio. Mike's father was born soon after. He became the light of their life and was followed by several siblings. He grew up influenced by the stories his parents told and wanted to become a doctor and save lives.

"You know what a 'dago' is?" Mike had asked me one day.

167

"Can't say that I do."

"It's a name people call Italians. It all started when the workday ended, and it was time for them to go home. Grandpa and his buddies spoke poor English and would say, 'day go,' to mean quitting time. It stuck. They call us dagos."

Mike's father was making preparations to specialize in the field of infectious disease medicine when the United States' involvement in World War II became a reality. He was asked to join the Army as a trauma surgeon. He said he would be glad to help. Mrs. Masters was left with three children, including Mike, the newborn youngest. Mike's father landed in Italy with the Allied invasion. He amputated arms and legs at Anzio among other places.

Mike's grandfather had explained to a young Mike in Italian, which Mike understood but could not speak very well, "I buried whole bodies, your papa buried only parts of bodies, now maybe you won't have to bury anything. We Masttero are making progress."

After the war Mike's father stayed in the field of trauma surgery because he found he was good at it. When asked, he went to Korea and buried more body parts.

Mother asked Mike how he liked school and if he had a girlfriend. My brothers both made faces at the suggestion.

Tuffy finally looked at Mother, smiled, and said, "Leave the boy alone."

"I'm just trying to be friendly, Tuffy."

"I know."

We finally arrived at Fred's Creek, turning down over the hill opposite the boardinghouse, and drove the lane that ended at the Sacred Gospel Church's gravel parking lot. It was a plain, oblong wooden lapboard building, sitting on an incline and leveled by rock pilings. It stood without spires or crosses. They were considered "graven images." It was looked upon as only a building. The members were the church. Anywhere they assembled was considered holy ground.

"Whether it be in this building or in the middle of the road," as Grandfather pointed out frequently.

I had made the groundhog colony that burrowed into the dirt beneath the building miserable by hiding in the weeds with my rifle, waiting for them to stick a nose from one of the holes.

We were early, and Mother joined a group of women who were standing and talking. Tuffy sat in the car while my brothers began running randomly with a group of young boys. Their yelling increased in volume when they passed the group of young girls who were also standing and talking.

I motioned for Mike to follow me down the hill to Fred's Creek. We stood by the place where new church members were baptized by wading out into the creek.

"You want you a place 'round here?" I asked.

"Yeah, I want to build a log cabin like your uncle's."

"OK, I'll help you."

"OK."

The black walnut trees are the last to leaf out in the spring and the first to lose their leaves in the fall. These finger-sized leaves were floating downstream at a moderate speed. I pointed out to Mike the place not too far on downstream where the clear Fred's Creek water empties into the Big Piney's murkier water.

"That's a good place to fish right down there. They found Joseph sittin' dead, up on the sandbank over there," I said.

"Who's Joseph?"

The story was told. Joseph was married to my great-grandmother Mattie. They found him punctured with several shotgun pellets. The wounds were not all that bad, but one had clipped an artery in his neck. People figured that if he was drunk, as he tended to be often, he probably was oblivious to the wound's severity and sat and hemorrhaged to death. They found him nestled back into the sandbank, sitting in blood. Beside him was an almost-empty whiskey bottle. He seemed to be staring at the river, with a half-rolled cigarette on his lap and a live, upset but unhurt chicken buttoned inside his coat.

The previous night, before they found him, up across the main road and over the hill, the guinea hens were making noise in the chicken coop behind Lester's house. Lester was a young man and had already killed his bear. He heard the noise and rose from bed.

Quietly reaching for his shotgun sitting against the wall, he went out of the back door. From the porch he could make out the small red glow of a cigarette at a distance, down the path behind the chicken coop, just over the hill from the outhouse.

He came up slowly and fired once at the cigarette. It dropped to the ground. Lester's father was standing behind him by this time and holding his own shotgun. He put his hand on Lester's shoulder.

"Go to bed, we kin go find that chicken thief tomorrow mornin'," he said, so they did. But all they found at the next light was a homemade cigarette butt, and near it was a blood trail that seemed to head over the hill to Fred's Creek.

Mike and I walked back to the church building while I finished the story. Mother was standing at the entrance, motioning us to hurry because church was about to start.

"If you talk in church, I will make you come and sit with us. Do you understand?" she threatened.

"Yes, ma'am," I said, agreeing quickly in order for us to sit on the back row and not with the family. I waved and smiled at several people already seated, including Mary Berry, who was my age. Her family owned the feed store that was off the main road, not far down the hill from Sams. The hymns began. It was four-part harmony and sung a cappella. I sang the bass line and was having trouble hitting the low notes. Mike sang the melody quite well. Everyone looked around when the noisy front door announced Aunt Nellie coming in late. She walked down the aisle to sit by Grandmother.

I knew Uncle Lester was outside in the truck because he never came in the building. I think there were two reasons. One, he was claustrophobic about being in a room with a group of people due to the confinement he endured when a prisoner of war. He slept near the front door, sitting in a rocking chair positioned so he could look out a window. And two, he said he was having a fight with God. I asked him about it.

He said, "It's 'tween the two of us, Bobby, you stay out of it." I said I would and asked no more questions.

The singing stopped. Grandfather walked carefully to the well-oiled pedestal pulpit, which was sitting on a low platform. Both were built with his own hands. He had learned to work with wood when as a kid he decided one day to leave Fred's Creek and go to Cincinnati. He asked at doors for a job till someone said they could use him. He had been working for several hours before he learned that the largest casket maker in the Midwest was now his employer.

For a time he worked making the wooden caskets and discovered that he had a knack for cutting and fitting wood, but in the end he became homesick and returned to Fred's Creek. He wanted to come back to take care of some unfinished business and to see his mother, Mattie, and sister Nellie, who were both living behind and working in the rooming house. After Joseph's death, Lester's mother had walked up Bone Marrow Branch to their cabin and insisted that the family come and work at the rooming house.

Lester's father had had the idea of building the rooming house in anticipation of a growth in population and many visitors. His reasoning was that because of the oil and natural gas deposits being discovered in the area, new people would be coming to Fred's Creek for exploration that made the rooming house seem needed.

Grandfather was a small man, just over five feet tall, with flashing green eyes and a head that was bald and large. He had a demeanor that commanded respect. His most distinguishing physical features were his forearms and hands. They were large and powerfully developed from long hours of nailing with a carpenter's hammer and sawing boards with one of his many handsaws. He had two great loves in life, the Bible and hunting. Both were passions. He would disappear into the woods with a firearm at every opportunity after his family obligations were met. This was followed by late-night studying, when he would sit at his desk hunched over one of the many ancient books acquired from a variety of sources, reading the thoughts of obscure fundamentalist scholars and their opinion on some finer point of the Bible.

I saw him vanish once. It happened when I was a small kid. After following him down the driveway of the rooming house and across the main road, he told me to return home and to watch out for automobiles on the way back. He took steps down a path that went in the direction of Fred's Creek. I glanced at the road for cars only a second, then looked back to say good-bye, but he had disappeared in that instant. I scanned the trees intently but didn't see him again until later in the evening when he returned from hunting. He had blended into the land so quickly that he was impossible for me to see. I am sure the animals had the same problem.

Grandfather spoke quietly from the pulpit this morning, mentioning by name the sick and shut-ins. He asked the congregation to include these individuals in their private prayers. Then in the same low voice he announced the monthly business meeting, to be held Tuesday evening, normally attended only by the deacons and elders.

Everyone has a person they try to emulate. Grandfather's hero was from the Bible. He was Paul the Apostle. The Lord spoke to Paul on the road to Damascus and blinded him for doing bad things to Christians. Then God gave him his sight back and filled him with the Holy Ghost. Paul, with this new spirit, became a most outspoken Christian defender and suffered great punishment. Grandfather was not blinded but felt he was filled with the same "will of God." He was suddenly saved and his life changed, in an emotionally similar encounter.

In his teen years, when the circumstances of his father, Joseph's, death and the story of how Lester had killed him became clear, he was outraged. He, his mother, and sister were now living in the small building behind the rooming house owned by Lester's family. He realized suddenly one day that he was taking charity by eating meals at the rooming house's large table. He immediately signed on to help guide a raft of timbered logs that were being readied to float down the Big Piney. After several stops, the group floated into Cincinnati and sold the logs. When the others started home, he stayed.

When he eventually returned to Fred's Creek, he wore a large black overcoat that almost touched the ground and a matching snap-brimmed hat. In one pocket was a purchased gun that he fully intended to use on Lester the first time he laid eyes on him. In the other pocket he had a pint of whiskey.

After reuniting with his mother and hearing the news that his sister was about to marry Lester, Grandfather excused himself by saying he needed to go for a walk. He went over the hill to where Fred's Creek emptied into the Big Piney and sat on the sandbank and drank from the bottle.

It was winter and snow was on the ground. Grandfather sat with the gun in one hand and the whiskey in the other. He stared at the water that was flowing by out in the middle of the stream; it was moving too fast to freeze like the ice closer to the bank. He had been traveling and was tired, and gulping the whiskey put him to sleep.

Grandfather was not a self-righteous man. He would tell a story about himself and his own shortcomings before telling one on others and was prone to tell often the ones that impressed him most, so what happened next had been heard by many.

He awoke shivering and heard what he thought were angels singing. He was startled, thinking he might be dead. He also thought that hearing hymns being sung might be a good sign, and maybe he was in heaven. Slowly he stood and stomped both feet to get the feeling back into his legs. He walked toward the sound of the singing.

Looking ahead, he saw something white and bright sitting on a wide, flat Sycamore branch that was extending out over the reflecting water. It was brightly lighted by the clear sky and full moon of February. The moonlight also reflected from the snow and gave everything the appearance of eerie daylight.

He took another step. The white body sitting in the tree moved and looked down directly at Grandfather, with large staring eyes. He felt a warm glow on his face as if standing by a fire. The warmth moved slowly down his body. The object of Grandfather's attention continued to sit on the limb, gazing at him. After a time that seemed to stand still, it looked away. Then it spread wings and flew effortlessly, without a sound, down the Big Piney while Grandfather stood watching. When it flew out of sight, his hearing returned and again he recognized the singing.

"Shall we gather at the river, the beautiful river of life," the voices sang.

Grandfather, several years after the event, found a book with a picture of the flying form. He purchased the book and now kept it on his bookshelf over the desk where he studied his "lessons," occasionally taking the book out to show others.

It was an owl. A snowy owl, large, white, and indigenous to the Far North, but it was known to travel south in search of food on rare occasions when driven by exceptionally harsh winters.

That winter's night, still drunk and walking with difficulty but convinced that the Holy Ghost had come into his soul, he staggered up the hill. He followed the sounds floating down from the rooming house, where a group of Fred's Creek residents were using the big sitting room for hymn singing and Bible reading.

He staggered up the steps and entered. Everyone looked his way. Walking unsteadily, he came forward to tell them of his great experience. He tripped over a chair that was sitting in his path, fell forward, and the pistol he still absently clutched in his hand flew out ahead of him as he tried to catch himself. It slid noisily on the wooden floor and stopped against the leg of the large coal stove, that the group sat facing in a semicircle. The people looked around. Most thought to themselves, "just like his father."

Mattie got up from her chair, picked up the gun, and took it to a large closet in the hall. She slid it under a pile of towels, then came back with a pillow and blanket and propped his sleeping head, and then covered him where he lay on the floor. Returning to her seat, Mattie began singing and the rest joined in. Her face spread with a smile, one of the few times that she had smiled in ages. Mattie was happy that her boy was back home.

The next day Lester came to see Grandfather, and they talked.

"Was going to kill you last night, but God sent the Holy Ghost into me, so now I can't," Grandfather stated formally.

Lester was even thinner then normal, looking much like a skeleton, and was prone to long pauses when his eyes would not completely focus and he would sit slack jawed. But this morning he was concentrating on Grandfather with all of his ability.

"So whatcha gonna do now?" Lester finally asked.

"Gonna build a church in Jesus Christ's name."

"Where you gonna build it?" Lester asked.

"Down by the crick."

"We got lumber for that. What we don't have we'll hook up the saw and cut, if you don't mind me a helpin'," Lester said.

"Look a here, you can help the Lord if you want to, but I ain't takin' nothin' from you ever again, you understand?"

"Understood." Lester offered his hand. Grandfather took it. In time they constructed the church building, down over the hill below the cemetery.

It sits there today, overlooking Fred's Creek.

Grandfather was today making a point from the pulpit about the triumvirate "God in heaven, Jesus sufferin' on the cross, and the Holy Spirit descending in the form of a dove.

"You see, there would be three distinct and absolute different bein's. God, the all powerful in heaven, allowed his own son, who was down here on earth and hangin' on the cross, to die for all us poor souls. There's nothin' to reprahzent the third part, the Holy Spirit, except for that dove. There's nothin' in our mind to think on when describin' the Holy Spirit. Words don't seem to work here, you see, you jest open your heart and it flows in. You can only feel it. It fills your whole body. When it comes, it'd be a calm true feelin'. You will know without a doubt when that happens," he added, with a knowing grin.

Church was over after a long prayer that mentioned the sick by name. We started walking up the hill toward my grandparents' house, knowing Mother would stay and talk a long time. I wanted to show Mike around before everyone else came up the hill.

We walked by the graveyard.

Mike asked, "Is Joseph buried in there?"

"Yeah, you want to see him?'

"Yeah."

We weaved our way over to a place I knew well, avoiding a number of other graves. We looked at the wide stone marker that had two names. It had been added to after Mattie died. It said "Joseph Spencer" over one grave and "Mattie Spencer" over the other.

After a while Mike asked, "Who's that back there?"

There were seven headstones, identical except for names. They stood in a row and each had the number seven carved into the rounded top portion of the thin, oblong stones. At a young age, I thought the seven meant that there were seven graves, but that was a coincidence; it meant the Ohio Seventh Regiment.

175

I said, "They all got killed in the war."

"What war?" Mike asked.

"The Civil War."

"Are they Yankees or Confederate?" Mike asked.

"Yankees."

Mattie explained to me that her grandmother told her the people around Fred's Creek didn't care much about the Civil War, one way or the other. But the Yankees "paid 'um money fur fightin', so they took it."

A dozen or so had taken their rifles and walked to Sharpsburg, then traveled by boat upriver to Marietta, Ohio, and joined the Union Army. They could earn two to three hundred dollars as an enlistment bonus, paid for by more affluent citizens who did not want their sons drafted for the war. This was quite legal at the time. The father of one of the enlistees went along and sewed the bonus money into his coat, then came back to Fred's Creek and distributed it to the families. Land was selling for twenty-five cents an acre, so it was a lot of money.

Soon after enlisting, the Fred's Creek men were sent to what was then Virginia, along the Cheat River, and were killed in an ill-conceived plan by McClellan, their leader. He sent them to a spot in a valley that was hard to defend but after suffering severe causalities, they still managed to turn the Rebels in full retreat. But McClellan failed to act and did not send the needed reinforcements. Most of the Rebels escaped. Lincoln promoted McClellan to commanding general of the Union Army but removed him after more battles were lost because of his continuing reluctance to engage the enemy.

While telling Mike this story, I wandered around in the adjacent weeds, picking late-blooming goldenrods, and placed the bunch on Mattie's grave, without comment.

Mike was still asking questions while we walked back to the gravel road going uphill. We saw my cousin Paul standing ahead, at what I knew to be his father's grave. His father's body was not buried in the graveyard, but Grandfather thought it appropriate to put up a marker anyway. Paul's father was my mother's younger brother, and he was also named Paul. He had been missing in action since the Korean War. His remains had not been returned.

"Hi, Paul," I said.

"Hi."

"Came up to church, huh?" I asked. He now lived with his mother in Sharpsburg. They had arrived for Sunday dinner and church, much like the Parsons family. Paul was younger than I was. He looked at me from the corner of his moist eyes. "I'm a going over there someday and kill me a bunch a Chinamen," he said.

"I'll go help you," I said.

"Me too," Mike said, not knowing why but wanting to help.

The three of us walked up the hill.

"You livin' in Sharpsburg now?" I said, trying to get his mind off his father.

"Yeah, Mama says there's nothin' for her to do up here."

"Women, sometimes you just got to go along with 'um a bit." I was repeating a phrase that I had heard used in male groups when things were inevitable.

"I guess maybe," he said without conviction.

He took off running to catch my middle brother, who was closer to him in age. They would be having a rock-throwing contest soon. Grandfather was the Fred's Creek all-time-champion rock thrower and gave a kind of quick sling from about belt high. He was deadly accurate from many hours of practicing as a kid when he hunted game with rocks because there was no money for ammunition. Grandfather could still put a dent in a pie pan at twenty yards, almost every time. Before the day was over, he would be coaxed into demonstrating and then would give an impromptu lesson on the choice of proper throwing rocks.

Uncle Lester had driven Aunt Nellie to the rooming house and was sitting in his truck. It was an old International, dark green with rusted spots scattered around randomly that gave the inadvertent appearance of camouflage. We approached and passed the time of day with him. Mike pulled the magazine page from his back pocket, and unfolding it, showed Uncle Lester the picture of the Volkswagen.

"I've seen these things before, in Sharpsburg, didn't have 'um when I'z over there playin' with the krauts," Uncle Lester said, while spreading the page out on his steering wheel.

"They any good?" Mike asked.

"Don't have much good to say about those people, they 'bout starved me to death. But if the Germans make these, they'll run good. I'll tell you that much. They'll make things that run good, yes sirree."

We talked randomly till he said he had to get back home "and do a few thangs." He would be back later for "Nellie and a bite a cream."

There would be homemade ice cream after the meal, turned by Tuffy and the other men, taking turns cranking the wheel on a large enclosed cylinder immersed in a wooden tub of ice. The ice would be occasionally sprinkled with rock salt to make the contents freeze faster. Everyone, young and old, would comment on the quality of today's batch that was to have diced peaches, soaked in sugar water, mixed into the cream and vanilla. It would be compared to the many past batches.

Adding a person at each corner could expand the main table that normally seated twelve. The youngest kids were seated at a table in the large kitchen. The kitchen table was sitting on wooden blocks that raised it to a proper height for the cooks to stand and prepare food. Removing the blocks lowered the table to a height for children to sit. This was one of Grandfather's many "inventions."

They always set Lester a place at the main table for these big family dinners, but I never saw him in the house except when Mattie died. Before the funeral they put her open casket in the sitting room, where people could come by and pay their respects. Lester came in and stood and looked at her, then went back outside. Someone, if there were a big crowd like today, would end up sitting at Lester's place to eat. It was usually a guest such as Mike. Everyone would agree that if Lester came by, they would get him a plate and squeeze him in.

"There's plenty a room," Grandfather would say to unanimous agreement.

Everyone at the table except for Mike was related, at least by marriage, and knew each other well. It created an environment where a small, seemingly random act could have a deep personal meaning.

Grandmother was a head taller than Grandfather, strong and graceful, and came around the table with a large bowl of the dried green beans. She put a big pile on my plate without comment and smiled, then politely asked Mike if he would like some, and he said yes.

When I was young, Great-Grandmother Mattie would sit on the front porch with a bowl of freshly picked Kentucky pole beans on her lap, snapping and stringing and putting the finished product into a second bowl. While in the yard, I would spread sheets of newspaper. Grandfather considered reading the newspaper important. He bought one at every opportunity, so we always had a stack. I would then search and find rocks to hold down the edges of the newspaper, carefully picking my spot for maximum sunlight. I spread the beans on the paper to be sun dried. Later they would be strung with a needle and thread and hung in the pantry for winter use. Mattie bragged on my excellent eyesight when I threaded the coarse black twine into the eye of the needle that she used for stringing. In the wintertime we sat at the supper table eating "shuckbeans" and discussing how good they tasted. So today when Grandmother put the beans on my plate, several older people observed the act and knew the meaning.

Mike and I finished a big meal, but the others sat unhurried, talking casually, so we excused ourselves and went around a corner into the sitting room, or parlor as some people called it. This room had a large, brown floor-model radio that I had listened to a great deal. A sofa, with matching wooden-framed chairs, was positioned where a coal stove sat in the winter. Against the wall was a rack that stored wooden folding chairs. Beside the rack was a large black piano.

It said "Peerless" on the milky, framed glass front of the tall top. This top protruded a short distance out over the yellowed keyboard. There was a slot for pennies. A penny was supposed to signal the internal mechanism to play a song, but the rollers were long gone. It now could only be played manually and was uniformly out of tune in a flat minor direction.

The piano had a checkered past. Grandfather purchased it from a house that he had contracted to tear down. The house was in Sharpsburg, not far from where Della peddled her whiskey, and was reported to have contained at some point in time a "house of ill repute." Although everyone knew the story of where the piano came from, it was not discussed in mixed company, but giggled about in the kitchen. Grandfather paid the owner twenty dollars, then assembled Tuffy, Lester, Badeye, Paul, Grandmother, and a couple of the Sams to move it from his big flatbed truck and into the parlor, along with the ornate stool.

It is difficult to describe Grandfather's piano-playing ability, but every song he played sounded exactly like the one just finished. He would announce a title and then bounce around from chord to chord. The style sounded like a combination of ragtime and bluegrass, if such a thing is at all possible on a piano. I have never heard it duplicated. He had such a good time playing that everyone smiled and listened when he was in the mood to play. All agreed that the piano's presence in Fred's Creek was a good thing.

"Look at this thing," Mike said.

He sat on the stool that was draped with a large silk shawl. It had been sent to Grandmother by Tuffy, from the South Pacific, and it matched the other two that my Mother and Aunt Nellie received in the same package.

Mike tinkled the high register keys and smiled. "Can I play it?"

"Sure."

I had heard him play at his house. He played some popular songs, but others were unrecognizable to me. Today he started pounding out the Fats Domino hit "I Found My Thrill on Blueberry Hill." Shaking his head up and down to keep time caused the hair to fall over his ears. I thought it was great and moved around, keeping time. Mother quickly appeared at the open doorway leading from the dining area. She was looking wide-eyed. Grandmother was standing behind her with the heel of a hand over her mouth. Her fingers were cupped over and covering her nose and trying to conceal a laugh. Soon everyone was in the room.

Technically, it was the Lord's Day. This sort of thing was not supposed to be done, but Mike was a guest and obviously knew no better. The culture of Fred's Creek says, "never make a guest feel embarrassed about actions they do out of ignorance." No one said anything. After a while, Grandfather walked to stand at the piano beside Mike. When he finished, everyone applauded.

Grandfather said, "You know this'n?"

He reached over and began pounding out one of his many identical tunes. Mike moved the stool to give Grandfather a place to stand and after watching the elementary fingering and with a couple missteps, Mike was soon playing along on the upper keys. This impressed Grandfather.

They played several of Grandfather's tunes. Mike seemed to know them all. They finally quit and stood together and bowed to a round of applause.

Someone said, "Let's start the cream."

Everyone slowly scattered to the porches and yard.

Grandfather put his hand on Mike's shoulder and said as they walked from the room, "This boy is almost as good as me." Mike was combing his hair.

Mother and Grandmother began helping the other women clear the table. They burst out laughing and laughed again each time they made eye contact.

This parlor is the location of my first memory in life. I can remember my second birthday and have the proof in the form of a picture. I was standing in front of the floor-model radio, beside a birthday cake that was sitting on the silk shawl covering the piano stool. There was a stranger with a big box camera mounted on a tripod. Pictures were taken.

Moments before the picture, I had been outside behind a large water maple that was located down the drive from the house. I was squatted, watching ants crawl a designated path among the roots. Mother was yelling for me to come for the pictures and was saying to Grandmother and Mattie that she hoped I wasn't all dirty. The tree blocked her view. I remained still, feeling glee because they could not find me. After a while they came to the tree in their searching and discovered my hiding place.

"Didn't you hear me call for you, Bobby?" Mother asked.

"No."

"I really do think we need to have his hearing checked, just in case," she told Mattie, while walking to the picture session holding my hand. Great-Grandmother Mattie held my other hand and mildly agreed.

Today Mike and I strolled outside and around the house, past the holding pen located on the downhill side of the sloping land that ran away from the house. The area residents who were sending animals to the Sharpsburg Stockyard to sell would bring them to this pen, and after arrangements were made, a truck, sometimes Grandfather's, would back up to the loading chute and transport them as a group. The pen had originally been built with split locust posts, but time had grown trees, mostly hackberry, along the fencerows. Now the rusted barbed wire was hooked or had grown into the trees.

"Come on up the hill and I'll show you the singin' tree," I said.

"You got a tree that sings?"

"Lester says the wind blows into the hollow parts and makes the sound."

"You ever hear it?" Mike asked.

"I heard, but it sounds like real low moanin' to me."

We could look back down after a short climb up the path to see the people standing in the side and backyards of the house, with cars and trucks parked randomly on the grass. Following a lesser-used path took us to a knoll that opened out flat. There was a stand of sweet gum trees. In the middle, with limbs shading enough ground to create its own clearing, stood a chestnut oak that eight good-sized people would have trouble reaching around and touching hands.

"When one a Grandpa's beehives swarm, they come here. He climbs up and scrapes them in a box and takes them back to their hive."

"Why do they come here?"

"Lester says the bees can hear the tree singin', even when we can't."

One of several lower limbs dipped down far enough for us to jump and grab and wiggle up onto. We walked up the limb's incline with our hands and feet to a lower fork.

"Uncle Lester knows about trees, and he says this'n is at least three or maybe four hundred years old. The Indians used to talk to dead relatives, right here."

Lester's great-grandmother was Cherokee. She had told Lester that the Native Americans would bring ornamental bags, each containing a few small bones and hair of an ancestor, and they hung them in the branches. When the wind blew and the bags moved, they could then ask questions about things that were troubling them. The dead ancestors would answer by giving the appropriate feeling to the person asking the question. The feeling would help decide the proper actions that should be taken. This religious ceremony was practiced before Lester's great-grandmother's time. She was only telling stories that she had heard from older relatives.

"Can you ask it questions?" Mike asked.

"Tried a few times, but I guess I don't have enough Indian in me, 'cause it never said anything back."

"I'll ask you one then. You think we should let Kay shoot the football players?"

"I don't know."

"They need shot, like the Commies," Mike said.

"And the Chinamen," I said.

"And the Japs and Germans," Mike said.

"And those Rebels."

"I kinda liked the Confederates," Mike said

"Yeah, me too, but Mattie said they shot first." I gave Mike a serious look.

"Well, maybe that bunch shoulda been shot."

"We could just tie them up, like Gene Autry and Hopalong Cassidy," I said.

Mike laughed. "And leave them for the sheriff."

I laughed too, now seeing that it was not such a great suggestion and said, "I think Hopalong is a queer because of those clothes he wears."

"Yeah, and he never loses his hat either."

"No, he don't," I answered, carefully considering Mike's insight but could draw no conclusion from the hat. "Well, we'll just blow the Goddamn place up then."

"All right," Mike agreed.

I looked off into the far trees and locked eyes, well one eye, with something peeking from behind a tree. I smiled and pointed and said, "Smokey." He trotted to the bottom of our tree and sat looking up.

Mike, impressed, grinned as we climbed down. "Not a lot gets by him, does it?"

"Nope."

Smokey walked behind us down the hill to the edge of the trees. We said good-bye. He turned and headed back up the hill, where he would have a better vantage point to keep watch.

I pointed down to the animal paddock that we had passed earlier, where Grandmother was now throwing hay over the fence to several of the calves waiting for a ride to Sharpsburg. She loved animals and took care of the chickens and anything else that needed feeding. When walking out the back door she would scatter a handful of chicken feed from the pocket of her apron. The chickens followed her like she was their mother, and she sort of was, because of her turning the eggs under the heat of an incubating lightbulb. She removed the eggshells when they made their first attempt to escape from the eggs. Grandmother would pluck and cook the grown chickens, but someone else had to do the killing. She refused.

"You know what happened to Grandpa's gun that Mattie hid in the closet?"

Mike looked interested. "No, what?"

I told him that after Grandfather was filled with the Holy Ghost, he helped wherever he could. When the weather started warming, he dug holes for the paddock we were now standing beside. The locust posts were to be delivered from across the hill by Lester, for springtime setting. When they arrived, everyone pitched in, setting the posts and stringing the barbed wire. With the addition of a gatepost, it was in use. Time passed and the church building was erected. One day a few years later, Grandfather and Mattie were sitting on the front porch.

"Mama, whatever happened to that gun I brung from Cincinnati?"

"Put it away. Tell you where it's at someday."

Grandfather nodded his head in agreement.

Years later, when Mattie was dying she told him, "Pitched that gun you asked about in one o' those holes you dug out to the side for that fence, but I swear I can't remember which one it is."

Grandfather started chuckling, and then laughing. Mattie, lying in bed, quietly laughed, and everyone in the room laughed along.

He said, "I'm not gonna dig 'um all up to find it."

"Suit yourself," she answered.

There was a smile and a tear on everyone's face.

Standing there we could hear the calves over the fence, loudly crunching the dry hay. We moved on down to join Grandmother for the walk to the house.

"You and your friend better come on and get some cream 'fore it's eat up. Nellie tol' me you was over to see her yesterday. Why didn't you come by here?"

"I wanted to, but I'z ridin' with other people, and they was on business and in a big hurry. I'm sorry," I said and looked at the ground.

"Well, don't you be gettin' too big for your britches, young man. You come on by next time."

"Yes, ma'am."

We arrived at the house, and Mother gave us each a bowl of ice cream. We sat on the steps of the wide back porch that was used for clothes washing in warm weather. We ate and watched the kids scream and run.

Grandmother sat beside us on the steps. "How is it?" she asked.

"Real good," I said, and Mike nodded in agreement.

"Good as the strawberry that time?" she teased. I laughed.

Grandmother had once mixed the required amount of sugar into the cream, and unknown to her, Nellie had added the required amount of sugar into the strawberries. The two combined in the ice-cream maker doubled the normal sugar amount. Everyone bragged on it as being the best they ever made.

"You got any ticks?" she asked. She pulled my head to her, and using her fingers, she expertly searched in my hair. "Guess not," she finally said, and gently sat me back. I continued eating all the while.

Grandmother was as rock solid as Grandfather was flighty. I think she was entertained by whatever strange idea he would have next. When young, I picked an apple from a pile where Lester was squeezing cider. After a bite, I glanced at the apple to see part of a worm wiggling and realized that I had just swallowed the missing part and went running to Grandmother, upset with the situation.

"Oh child, it's just apple, with a little skin stretched 'round the outside. It don't mean a thing," she casually explained.

Grandmother could lift a fifty-pound bag of chicken feed from the bed of the truck and flip it over her shoulder. She would walk to the storage shed with her free hand cocked at the wrist in a most gracefully feminine way. Even while carrying the burden, she seemed light on her feet. Her straight black hair was pulled to a tight bun, as was the common practice of Fred's Creek women of her age. It was in sharp contrast to my mother's dark hair, which was cut short and hung to just past the bottom of her earlobes; it was shaped by a home-permanent curl that fluffed the hair from the sides of her face.

A bucket sitting beside Grandmother contained the scraps from today's cooking: coffee grounds, eggshells, carrot tops, potato peels, and assorted biodegradable bits.

She said, "Bobby, you and your friend take this up to the pile fur me. Will you?"

"Yes ma'am."

I traded the empty bowls for the bucket. We walked to the muck pile that would become fertilizer for the garden next spring. It was behind the shed that Mattie, Aunt Nellie, and Grandfather had once lived in. The shed was now full of odds and ends. There was a bench that Grandfather had attached to the back of the shed, and it was shielded from the house. We jumped up and stood on it, after dumping the bucket's contents.

"Did you see that blond girl? I said hi to her in church."

"Yeah," Mike answered.

"She pulled her pants down and showed me herself once back here."

Mike looked over and gave a small, crooked grin. "She did?"

I nodded my head.

Mary Berry had blond hair; it was closer to white, with white eyelashes and eyebrows. She had fine, white hair on her arms and legs that was no thicker than normal, but the light color made it more visible. This was particularly so in the summertime when she had a tan.

She wore her hair in large, round, manufactured curls that moved up and down when she walked. Even when not in school, she wore frilly dresses, with thin, white ankle socks and strapped patent-leather shoes. We were the same age and had spent time together, mostly because we lived close. She would talk me into attending her pretend tea parties. When we were older, I had kidded her about the slips she wore that made her skirts bounce.

"What you keep under there that makes your clothes stick out?" I teased.

We both laughed usually, but one day, soon after she heard that my family was moving to Boaz, she turned and looked at me, not laughing.

"If you want to look, I'll show you."

"Huh?"

"You heard me, Bobby. Do you or don't you?"

"OK."

We walked casually and quietly behind the shed where Mike and I were now. She pulled up the skirt and held it with her arms. Then she pushed the white panties down to her knees and stood back straight and slowly turned completely around with the panties hindering her movement. She kept her eyes turned to the sky.

My first thought was, "Somebody cut her pee-pee off." Then I decided that maybe that's the way girls were. I started thinking of the time that Smokey was put into a cattle truck with a female dog in heat. A fellow had brought her to Lester's house, in hope that she would have Smokey's puppies. She growled and they almost fought. He finally mounted her, and they soon became hooked together. Both stood patiently in an awkward position, until they finally separated. I wondered if Mary and I would get stuck like that. It didn't look pleasant.

She finished turning and arranged her clothes back to normal.

We both stood quietly looking at the ground and finally she said, "Well?"

Not knowing what was expected of me, I looked up and said, "Thank you."

Smiling and blinking nervously, she said, "You're welcome."

That was it. We never spoke of whatever it was that had happened, ever again.

"You ever seen Susan?" I asked Mike.

"Yeah, well some, but we never did it."

I was now fairly confident of what "it" was.

Mike looked over, shook his head, and gave a little laugh, "My Grandpa told me he and Grandma lived together, sleeping in the same bed, for over three years before they did it."

"Why?"

"They wanted to come to America and be married here by a priest, to show proper respect for each other, so they waited."

"That'd be pretty hard, I guess, right beside each other?" I said.

"I don't think that me and Susan could do that. The only thing that ever got her saying no was when she heard I was going to change my name."

"She doesn't like your Italian name?"

That wasn't it. Her name was Susan Miller. She had several sweaters and other clothes that were monogrammed and was happy that both their names started with an *M*. After they were married, she considered it a bonus that she would still be able to wear her monogrammed clothes. When Susan learned from Mike that her new last name would be Masttero, she realized that it also started with an *M*, and she was happy again. The new name would be just fine.

There was always lurking in the minds of Fred's Creek people the thought of traffic accidents while traveling to and from Sharpsburg. The road had been improved in recent years and now had passing lanes and a tunnel through a major hill to cut the traveling time considerably. School buses made the daily trip for high school students. The bus often stopped along the road for nonstudents from the Fred's Creek area and took them on to Sharpsburg, for doctors' appointments, shopping, and sometimes just to ride. Grandmother was concerned and still considered the trip dangerous. We left in time to be back in Boaz by late afternoon so we would not be traveling after dark.

Aunt Nellie was the same way.

"Let's go 'fore she starts frettin'," Tuffy said, after listening to Nellie give him the exact time that it would be dark.

Mother had found out that I was in Fred's Creek the day before without her knowledge. She seemed amazed at the thought. All the explanations I could think of did not help. I sat quietly while she passionately explained an array of things to me. She finally calmed down.

Back in Boaz, Mother said it was too late for her to start supper but offered everyone some of the food that she had carried home.

"You have school in the morning, Bob. Be back at this house early. A good night's sleep will make you learn better," she said.

Mike and I eased to the Buick as she talked. We got in with her following and continuing to talk.

"Yes, ma'am," we both said several times.

Mike pulled slowly into the street after carefully looking both ways, twice, to show the still-watching Mother how safe he was. The car gained speed and passed the pillars of Maplewood. We crossed the main road and turned onto the pitted dirt road that went over the hill. We were looking for Jerry Joe.

He was sitting on one of several cross sections of trees scattered about in front of Garvin's house. He was holding a beer and listening to Cecil and Garvin argue about something that would be unclear to anyone but them. The two of them were more than a little drunk. The ground pit had a still-glowing fire, where they had roasted hot dogs for their traditional Sunday afternoon party.

"Welcome to the palace. Want a beer?" Jerry Joe asked.

I shook my head no. Mike fished one from a galvanized bucket. The ice that Cecil had stolen from the Texaco was melted. The Texaco station, by tradition, was closed on Sunday.

We inspected Jerry Joe's eye after waving hello to the others. It was a sight to behold, swollen about halfway shut and already turning a deep shade of red. We could see the careful stitches in the eyebrow. Mike and I were both instantly struck with a case of envy. We each imagined owning the scar, caused by a poolroom fight. It would be, in our opinion, a dashing badge of honor for the rest of our lives.

"How's it feelin'?"

"Sore, but I'm see'n OK."

Garvin and Cecil were sitting in folding lawn chairs with a larger cross section of tree between them. Garvin had found the chairs at the Boaz dump, but they had no webbing, so both sat on several odd lengths of two-by-four that were placed across the bottom to make a seat. Some of the boards had rusty nails protruding and were pointed down for safety. Cecil had cut and tied pieces of old automobile inner tube around the backs of the chairs, to lean against. There was a two-thirds empty bottle of bourbon and another of rum sitting on the table, along with open ketchup and mustard bottles, attracting flies. The remains of half an onion was diced and scattered on the wood surface, with an open pocketknife lying beside the unchopped half. The loaf of white bread, used to wrap around the hot dogs, was sitting on the edge. Several of the unused slices had fallen from the opening to the ground.

Garvin was talking. "It's good to be in a country where we can live off the fat of the land and just sit in the yard and enjoy the day. There are a lot of people who can't."

Garvin's house made Cecil's look good. Garvin piled the coal he carried home from along the tracks in the front room, mingled with scavenged copper wire and tubing. He slept on a door, covered by old blankets. The door was propped on four steel cartons that were made for carrying the Schultz Dairy milk bottles. The "bed" was positioned beside a small coal stove. Both were sitting in the middle of the room. The bathroom in his house had no commode. Some of the floor around where the commode used to be was missing because when winter came and the coal ran low, he would pry loose pieces of his house, or other uninhabited houses in the row, to use as firewood.

As a last resort he would stay with Cecil. Finally, he would walk the tracks to Sharpsburg and stay with Della until she caught him stealing more whiskey then she allowed. She would then make him leave, usually as the weather started warming for spring. He was ready for a change of scenery by then anyway and sometimes would leave town for several months.

Garvin received a disability check from the Army that arrived on the first of each month, sent to the Boaz post office and addressed "general delivery." A man he had attended grade school with handed it to him, and they would exchange pleasantries. Sometimes he collected several, if he had been traveling. He would go to the Texaco station and cash the check. Then he drank until the money was gone, usually a while before the next check came. To get by until another check arrived, he would borrow from Cecil and sometimes steal the returnable empty gallon milk jugs from porches in town. He sold them at Gibson's Grocery for the fifteen cents deposit.

He was talking now, mostly grandiose plans of how to make money. He often talked of starting a junkyard, or "scrapyard," as he insisted it be called. When there was considerable alcohol in his veins, he talked even more than usual. Some of the things he said were crazy. Some were philosophical.

"See those people over there?" He pointed to the river while holding a flowered drinking glass that was supposed to be a promotional giveaway at the Texaco station. Cecil had carried it home.

"See those people over there?" he said again. "Those people are a bunch of goat fuckers!" He had a general dislike for Ohio people. "I have it on good authority that that place across this very river, right here in front of you, is the land of the many goat lovin' fuckers! Stay away at all costs! Especially if you look anything remotely like a goat!" Everyone laughed.

It was funny even if Jerry Joe and I had heard it before.

He rambled on and landed on another favorite subject, hell. "Most people think hell will be a dark, hot, terrible place that is isolated from everything else, where everything you see and touch causes excruciating pain, or something like that.

"I think not! Hell will run along right beside heaven, with a fence dividing the two. You can go right up to the fence and look over into heaven anytime you please. You can watch all those healthy people who aren't growing old or wanting for anything. For hell to be hell, you will have to know what heaven is like."

"In heaven you can go barefoot and not get any cockleburs in your feet. In hell they're scattered everywhere, see? You must be able to see heaven for hell to be at its worst. Do you see what I mean?"

He looked around. Cecil was resting his chin on his chest with his eyes shut. Mike and Jerry Joe were talking about where to put the dynamite in school for the best results. I was staring at Garvin. That made him laugh.

"I knew it! I knew it! You, my young friend, are one of the cursed ones."

"Me?" I said.

"Yes, because you see, you have a glimmer of understanding. It will haunt you for life. This world is not a good place for understanders.

"A great family of nonunderstanders raised me. I know them well. They skate along untouched by the world. They ride high overhead in the airplanes that drop the big bombs. They drink coffee and have cookies and gossip, being ever so careful not to interrupt each other, because that would be frowned upon as impolite. They never witness the blood and broken bones that they have caused on the ground!"

He had moved to the edge of his seat and was pointing his finger at me and said, "Except."

He sat back with a smug look on his face. "Except, that every so often it happens to them or someone close to them. Then they are shocked. 'How can this happen to me,' they implore? 'How can this happen to us,' they say, as they look around to the others? 'We are immune from these terrible things! How dare they! Do you see what I mean, Rooster?"

"Been fishin'?" I asked, but he ignored me.

"Mother Schultz, the woman who raised me, was the kindest, most loving woman ever to live. She was killed suddenly one day because of her bully drunken husband. He just drove off a cliff. If ever there were a way that goodness or kindness would protect a person, she would be the one.

"If you are in fact a sweet, kind person, or if you only have the great high opinion of yourself that you are the embodiment of all of this world's goodness, in either case, it protects you from nothing. When the time for terrible things comes, you're on your own!"

We sat quietly. I could hear Mike and Jerry Joe whispering and laughing.

"You ever hear of Kay?" Garvin asked, in a low reserved voice.

"Yeah, see him about ever day."

"Not that Kay, his great-grandfather, King Kay."

"Saw his picture up at the house. Had a real old army uniform on."

"Yeah, that's him." Garvin laughed and shook his head. "Let me tell you about what he did one time when I was so young I was still pissin' the bed. You ever hear about the battle of Blaine Mountain?"

"Yes, I have. My Grandpa was there, and my Uncle too."

"I'll be damned, really?" Garvin said.

"It's true."

He sat to the front of his chair again with a serious face and began telling what happened, with me occasionally adding information that I had heard over the years.

"Your family coal miners?" he asked.

"My daddy's daddy got killed in one, but the real reason my family was around up there was because they was good friends of that policeman that got killed in Goshen."

"That started it all right," Garvin said.

The story was told. In the 1920s the miners were unhappy with the wages. Kids as young as twelve were going into the mines before daylight and coming out after dark, working for fifty cents a day. The owners decided to cut the wages because of a downturn in coal prices. They had a revolt on their hands.

King Kay told the New York interests that he would handle the problem. When the miners did not soon back down from the strike, phone calls were made, and thugs were sent from the streets of Chicago to force them back to work.

People in the area thought the Goshen policeman was as a fair and decent man. When he was pressed to take action against the strikers, he said publicly that he thought the men had a right to strike if they felt they were being wronged.

A few days after, in the middle of the day, he was gunned down. Shot from a moving car while crossing the street. Neither the state police nor any other law enforcement agency came to investigate. His funeral drew a large crowd. Soon miners from all around came flooding into Goshen. They formed an army of several thousand men. The uniform was a red bandanna, tied around their necks.

They streamed to Blaine Mountain. Those with military experience trained the rest. After several days, they sent a kid back to town with a written message, "No coal will leave this mountain." Police from everywhere were summoned to help. It was a standoff.

King Kay, fearing that if things continued to drag on he would be humiliated in front of the New York people that he pandered to, went by train to Washington, D.C., and called in big-coal political favors on a large scale. The United States Army was sent with machine guns and bayonets. In addition to this, the mine owners hired those who were expert in the field to assemble dynamite bombs, and paid still others to drop the bombs by hand from open-cockpit airplanes and onto the people defending Blaine Mountain.

"They killed people, captured the rest, and charged them with treason and anything else that came to mind," Garvin said. "Some were ten years old."

"Grandpa and Uncle Lester didn't work in the mines, so they just went on home, but I'll tell you somethin', people up there don't listen to nothin' the government has to say. You can bet on that," I said.

Grandfather still had his red bandanna in the desk drawer. He was too young for World War I and too old for World War II. It always bothered him that he didn't get a chance to participate in either. Blaine Mountain had been his war.

"We gave 'um a little somethin' to think on," he would say, and then he would smile and look off to a distant hilltop. He was proud to be one of that large gang the papers had dubbed "the rednecks" because of the red bandannas the rest of them wore along side of grandfather.

Garvin sat smiling. "Wouldn't bet against anything you're saying there, young Rooster, that old King Kay you saw hanging on the wall might as well have shot those men himself. His boy 'Booger' was the only thing close to a daddy I ever saw!"

"Booger?"

"Picked his nose a lot, so we called him Booger."

I made a mental note to be sure that no one was around when I was picking mine. We sat watching the coals in the pit turn gray. Cecil's head jerked from his chest. He rubbed his face and lit a cigarette, using a wooden kitchen match taken from the stack lying on the tree table. He pointed the still-smoking match up the rough road. It was Vernon's Ford that was creeping down the hill.

We sat watching without comment as the car slowly, almost walking over the pitted road, came to a stop. Vernon got out grinning from ear to ear. His three-day beard never seemed to get much longer or shorter. He opened the passenger's door. Kay slid on his belly down off the seat and held on until his feet touched the ground, then turned to us while straightening Herky's black cowboy hat back to the center of his head. He then adjusted my gun and holster, which he was wearing like a bandolier over his shoulder. The holster rode in the middle of the chest over his jacket that said "'Browns" on the back.

"I knew we'd catch all these damn car thieves down here. It's a good thing Herky's not here with a warrant, or all's you jugheads would be to jail!"

"Shut up, you little twerp!" Garvin said.

"You shut up, big twerp! I own these houses, you know. I'll get you arrested for that too! We're gonna straighten some things out around here."

He walked over to Jerry Joe and looked at his eye. "Heard about this. I knew someone was gonna kick your big dumb ass someday."

Kay looked around, trying to find a place to sit, and finally plopped on the ground in a small patch of grass close to the pit. Vernon eyed the remaining hot dogs, and after asking Cecil's permission, he went about roasting one while Kay continued to hint.

"Big things are gonna happen around this town, here before long."

"What kind of things?" Garvin asked.

"Can't talk about it."

"Why not? You talk about everything else. Still telling people that you caught more fish than I did that time?" Garvin asked.

"I did catch more fish! I caught seven and you caught five, so that's more."

"But one of mine was bigger than all of yours put together," Garvin answered.

"Don't make a difference. It's the number that counts. Vernon, you remember?"

Vernon bobbed his head in a noncommittal fashion. He was concentrating on the distance he should hold the stick-impaled hot dog from the coals in order to get a nicely browned snack.

Garvin grinned and looked down at Kay. "I shoulda used you for fish bait, that's about how big you are. Can you swim?"

"I can swim better than you. I could use you for fish bait, but you'd swim around in a circle, and probably get dizzy and drown!"

Garvin could not contain the laughter. We all laughed. Kay was proud of himself.

"You know your grandmama found me floating in the bulrushes, don't you? Just like Moses," Garvin said.

"Yeah, yeah, I heard it all before. You're a river rat orphan, and she took pity on you. That's what happened, on down the river. Veada told me all about it."

Mike glanced over with interest in his face. "Mom was an orphan from around here somewhere. She thinks so anyway. She remembers she had a brother. She sneaked into the orphanage records and found out her real last name was Parker."

"She was?" Garvin asked, looking directly at Mike.

Cecil pulled himself up and frowned. "You tol' me you had a sister once, Garvin."

"Get yourself another drink and quit talking so much!" Garvin said. This seemed like a good idea to Cecil, so he did.

"Have you ever been to New York City, young man?" Garvin directed the question to Mike.

"Yes I have. My sister's up there."

"What's she doing?" Garvin asked.

"She's teaching school while her husband finishes medical school. We went to visit her a couple of times."

"Well, my sister lives up there too, so how can she be your mother?"

Mike shrugged. "Guess not."

Cecil poured water from a Mason jar into the glass with bourbon and stirred the drink with a finger, frowning, but added nothing.

"Anyway the nuns told Mom her brother died, so that's that," Mike said.

"My sister and your sister, both in New York. I guess they probably know each other by now and hang around together, don't you think?" Garvin said. They both laughed.

"I kinda doubt that," Mike said, grinning more than normal.

"Me too," said Jerry Joe. He was absently running his finger along his stitches.

It was quiet for a while.

"You were in the Army?" Mike asked Garvin.

"Yep, landed at Normandy."

"What was it like there?"

"Don't really remember too much about it, because I was only there about fifteen seconds."

Garvin didn't often talk about the event, but he seemed to want Mike to know what happened. He told us the story in a subdued tone, unlike his normal demeanor. You could hear a pin drop.

The story was told. They were bouncing over rough seas in a landing craft; people were getting sick from the turbulence. He could hear crying and mumbled prayers being said by several other soldiers. He could smell involuntary bowel movement. The boat slammed to a stop, and the big guy behind him lurched with the sudden impact. They banged helmets. The large front of the landing craft dropped outward like a hideaway bed, quickly descending. He followed the people in front and walked into water that was about chest deep and held his M1 rifle over his head like he had been taught.

Suddenly, it seemed as if someone had snatched the rifle from his hands. He went underwater and twisted to plant his feet. Then he pushed the heavy pack and himself back upright in the water. He saw an arm bouncing beside him in the water and instinctively reached to grab it. He stood there in shock, holding the arm, wondering what he should do next. A medic who had yet to walk vary far into the water grabbed the straps of his pack, and with the help of the Navy personnel that were running the landing craft, dragged him back into the boat. The medic applied a tourniquet and gave him a shot for pain.

Garvin said he lay there with his eyes open and had the feeling of floating in the air and began itching all over. He could clearly hear himself being talked about. "We're not allowed to take people back. That's direct orders."

The medic answered, "I got to go, so if you want to throw him overboard, you're going to have to do it by yourself."

The medic walked into the water and headed for land. They took Garvin back to the troop ship. After another argument, he was strapped, arm and all, into a basket that was hooked to a large crane and speedily lifted and then swung to the bow of the ship. He was hurried below and into the sick bay, with a minimum number of soldiers waiting to go ashore witnessing the event. That was there intent.

Garvin went back to the States on the same ship as it traveled to load more soldiers and supplies. The ship's personnel got to know him. When he insisted on seeing his arm, it was brought it to him from the freezer where somebody, for some reason, had put it. He pulled his high school ring from a finger, and with help, put it on a finger that was still attached to his body. They had a ceremony and buried the arm at sea. Garvin watched from a wheelchair on deck. His stub had been operated on enough to keep it stable until they reached stateside.

We all sat quietly, looking at the coals and glancing at the worn ring on Garvin's finger.

Mike, after a while, got up and stretched. "Need to get this damn car back to Kay's house, so guess I better go," he said as he threw up a hand and walked toward the Buick.

"I'll just walk home," I said after him.

Kay was about to fall asleep and said in a low voice, "I use' to itch too when they gave me a shot. It was fun scratchin', but I don't itch much anymore." He looked over toward Mike and said, "Wait up!" then rolled to his stomach and stood awkwardly.

"I got some serious research work to do back at the house," Kay said, and began waddling after Mike, who stood waiting and then boosted Kay into the passenger seat. Up the hill they went.

"He's in bad shape," I said. Everyone nodded in agreement.

"We two were going to go into business one time, but the government stepped in and stopped us," Garvin said.

He had suddenly returned to his old animated self and began explaining the business plan that he and Kay had came up with.

"You ever see those furry cowboy vests that kids wear? They're black-and-white pinto designed? They dye them to look about like the cows up at the farm?"

I knew what he meant. I had one, along with a red cowboy hat and a holster with a cap pistol. My brothers fought over the outfit nowadays. I considered myself too old to be bothered. I answered his question by nodding yes.

"I got news for you, they're made from cat fur, believe it or not. Did you know that?"

I stopped shaking my head yes and moved it from side to side.

The concocted story was told. In the new business, they were going to catch stray cats and keep them in one of these empty houses and in cages on one side of the room. On the other side of the room they were going to catch and keep river rats, real river rats. After a short time they would all breed. They would then feed the rats to the cats till the cats were big enough to skin, and they'd sell the pelts. The remains of the cats were to be fed back to the rats, to make them grow and breed more so they could be fed to the younger cats, to make more fur.

Vernon looked unhappy as he chewed on his third hot dog because at the farm there were several cats that he took care of. He did not like this kind of talk, even if he knew it was just Garvin making stuff up.

"So," I said, not knowing any better, "you were gonna feed the rats to the cats, then feed the cats to the rats, then feed the rats back to the cats?"

"Yes, that's it! You see the beauty? No overhead. Pure profit!"

He started laughing and pounding his knee. The short stump of his already-buried arm involuntarily jerked up and down inside the knotted sleeve of the old khaki work shirt.

"The government, just a while back, stepped in to make it against the law to skin cats for the hide, so now they got to raise them in China or someplace like that. You know they eat cats in China? Rats too. Don't really know what they feed the cats over there, maybe fish or something. Too bad, though; another million-dollar idea right down the drain."

I excused myself and started up the hill. With the hot dogs gone, Vernon saw it as a good chance to leave and said to me, "I'll ride you up."

Jerry Joe told me he was going to caddy early tomorrow but would stop by school to see what we were doing. Cecil was snoring and Garvin sat drinking and staring blankly, first at the coals, then slowly he turned and looked out in the direction of the river.

When I got home, Father was sitting on the grass in the side yard and smoking a cigar someone at Fred's Creek gave him. He didn't normally smoke but occasionally puffed a cigar. It wasn't allowed in the house.

We sat and listened to the crickets. "Lots of crickets chirpin' means it'll be a nice day tomorrow," I said.

He was blowing smoke rings. A large, slow one, then a smaller, faster one went cleanly through the middle. "That's what they say."

"You ever kill anybody in the war?"

He sat quietly for a long time. "We blew some people up."

"Did Uncle Lester and Grandpa blow anybody up on Blaine Mountain?"

Father lay back in the grass and blew the rings straight up.

"Lester sent a big boulder bouncing down the hill, scared every U.S. marshal in the countryside. He told me them marshals were grouped up together like a flock a sheep. He's sure a crazy old fart. He's lucky he's not in prison," Father said, and looked around to see if Mother was within earshot.

"He scared the hell out of them?" I asked.

"That's what they say."

I sat for a while. Then I lay back on the grass and crossed my legs like his and asked, "What was Joseph like?"

"You mean Mattie's Joseph?'"

"Yeah"

He turned and looked at me and shook his head. "Don't reckon I ever been 'round a body who asks more questions than you."

"Sorry."

Father leaned over and said confidently, "He was so lazy, wouldn't take a swat at a snake if it was about to swallow him whole is what they say. He was around way before my time, just heard some stuff. Had women and kids spread over six counties and half of Ohio. People told me that."

Father told the story. Joseph went away often. He left Mattie and the two kids in a dirt-floor shack, high on Bone Marrow Branch, where Joseph and Mattie had first met. Mattie and the kids lived on turnips and what Grandfather, who was one of the kids, could kill throwing rocks. Joseph would be gone for a while, and then he would suddenly return. She would be glad to see him and take him back. Then he would leave again.

Women, father told me, seemed to love Joseph. An elderly woman came by the rooming house to ask about him years after he had died. Everyone was glad that Mattie didn't hear the woman when she was asking.

"Way people talk, he coulda been elected president if just women did the votin'. The best thing that ever happened to Mattie was when Lester's family took them in to feed. They were about to starve to death, with or without Joseph." He glanced toward the house to make sure he was not being overheard.

"Mattie showed me a picture of him a few different times. I think he was in another picture that I saw up at Kay's house," I confided. "Workin' cuttin' ice."

"Could be, I reckon," Father shrugged. "If he walked up here right now, I wouldn't know him from Adam's cat."

We lay there in silence, and soon went into the house. Mother was studying her real estate agent books. We joined my brothers to watch *The Show of Shows* with Sid Caesar and Imogene Coca.

"There's blackberry and peach pie on the counter, if anybody's hungry!" Mother said from the dining room.

"OK," we answered in unison.

Day Eight

It was Monday morning, and I was daydreaming into the bathroom mirror while brushing my teeth. Thinking of the days ahead when going to school would not demand the time it does, and I would be allowed to do with my life whatever struck my fancy. The idea of a job replacing school didn't occur to me.

Father was still home and sitting at the breakfast table. "My section shut down for adjustments," he said. "Goin' in after while. Eat, and I'll carry you to school on the way."

"Really could use the car today, Tuffy, but of course your getting to work is more important. What about tomorrow?" Mother hinted.

"John's drivin' tomorrow, so you can have it then. Probably be home early today too, just got paperwork till we get our section back on line."

"OK."

I ate breakfast, with Mother putting an unwanted second helping of scrambled eggs onto my plate. Without comment I added some ketchup and quickly finished them all to avoid a dispute. We walked outside; my brothers ran ahead and were bouncing in the backseat of the car. I climbed into the front seat passenger side, holding *The Deerslayer* where mother would notice, trying to ward off any last-minute homework questions. She waved good-bye. We slowly pulled away and soon stopped to drop my brothers at the grade school that was close enough to the house for them to walk. They normally did.

The two of us rode along. "How you like your job?" I asked.

He glanced over with a surprised expression. We continued riding quietly and finally he said, "It's a good job, make good money, don't do much, just sit and listen to the big wheels whinin' bout stuff."

"Do you like it?"

We rode in silence for a while longer; then he told me about the job. After returning from World War II, Father helped Uncle Lester with his work and did the heavy lifting around the old place, plus some blasting. Drank beer with Badeye and helped him cut trees. Even helped Grandfather build and tear down buildings when he was needed as extra help. Father was content.

Mother had three kids. We were living in the rooming house. For some time, because of a lack of area visitors, the rooming house had had no one in residence except the family members.

Mother told Father, "I want you to get a real job."

He did not understand why she was not happy and tried to decipher what a "real job" would be, and also where he could find one. Working in the coal mines was out of the question because of his father's death. In addition, years earlier Great-Grandmother Mattie had two brothers who had died on the same day. Their deaths were caused by a coal mine cave-in, and all the male members of my family had promised Mattie that they would never set foot inside a coal mine. When I was a young kid, I also promised her this, among other things. It is the only promise I have never broken.

Late one night, Mother and Father were having one of their many discussions along these lines. Mother was saying that he should fill out an application for the new chemical plant being built in Sharpsburg. The suggestion sparked in his memory an address that was exchanged in California, before heading home from the war.

The person at this address had been Father's commanding officer during the war. The military group he served with began the war divided into a number of "teams" of about twenty men each. Near the end of the war, they had lost a number of the original group. Those who were not dead, wounded, or missing knew each other like brothers. Even though the commanding officer was older, he had a close common bond with the entire unit.

The same chemical company that this commanding officer returned to after the war, as a high-ranking executive, was now building the plant in Sharpsburg. Father found the address in a trunk, stuck among old Navy papers. Mother wrote the letter, and the returning mail contained a plane ticket to Wilmington, Delaware, the company's headquarters.

There was no way for Father to get out of going. With Lester driving and Mother riding along, they took him to the Cincinnati airport and waved good-bye. After a warm reunion with his commander and a battery of tests, Father spent over a year flying back and forth to Wilmington. He was enrolled in a company-sponsored school and was drawing a paycheck.

The high school diploma requirement was waived when he passed an equivalency test. Whether he liked it or not, Father now had a framed diploma for accomplishments in math and chemistry and a production supervisor's job in the section of the plant that was developing a new, synthetic non-stick coating that could withstand high temperatures.

"Your mom thinks movin' here to Boaz gives you kids more things to do with yourself. Don't tell 'er this, but if I was doin' it, I woulda stayed in Fred's Creek. But then I ain't the only one 'round nowadays."

"We gonna stay here?" I asked.

"They been wantin' to promote me and send us to Texas, but I said no."

"Why?" I asked, thinking of the cowboys, and that maybe I could be one.

"Texas is an OK enough place, but it ain't home. This is home and we need to stay here."

"Why?" I asked again.

"'Cause someone needs to look after things 'round here and that'd be our job."

"Mine too?"

"I'd say so."

We rode along in silence, with me looking out the window at the passing houses with a sudden feeling of ownership.

My mind wandered.

I asked, "They called you'll 'frogmen' durin' the war, didn't they? Why?"

"We wore swim trunks and these funny-lookin' rubber flippers and a mask. We looked like a frog." He grinned.

"You blow things up?"

He did a U-turn around Stanley's, pulling to a stop in front of the school.

"We blew some stuff up. Swam in with a pack on our backs and set a chemical timer by breakin' this little glass bottle attached. Then we had thirty minutes to get the hell outta there before it blew up. It don't take no genius. 'Brains are a drawback,' we were told."

The story was told. At the close of the war, his group was planning to swim into Japan itself. Air tanks to breath underwater were heavy and only used to set explosives in deep water. They normally just strapped on a pack of explosives and held their breath or swam in an unobserved low profile at the top of the water, with nothing but a knife to defend themselves. They sometimes shaved all of their body hair, then covered their body with Vaseline, because the enemy sent electric shock waves through the water, and this grease coating helped keep them from being electrocuted.

The plan was to blow up a major submarine base or at least to close the channel that they and other boats used to get in and out of the Japanese port. A study of the plan revealed an obvious omission: how the frogmen were to escape from Japan. They were expendable and would be on their own. Two weeks before the mission was to be executed, while they practiced, the H-Bomb was dropped. The mission was scrapped.

I was thinking about the story when I pushed the car door shut and headed for the school building, stopping to wave good-bye to Father, then continuing in to my locker.

Mike was standing, waiting. "You smell that? Is it what I think it is?" he asked, when I was close.

It was the distinctive odor that dynamite emits when closed in a poorly ventilated place and is not able to "breathe" properly.

"Yeah, we got to move it out in the air someplace, soon. If you see Jerry Joe, have him get it. Here's the combination," I said.

I borrowed a pencil to write it on a piece of paper while we walked in the direction of homeroom, obeying the first bell.

Mike took the paper and said, "There were some football players that came by the locker looking for you earlier. You know why?"

"No, was it Butterbean?" My stomach was getting queasy.

"No, it was a couple of the others. Said they'd find you later and left. You don't know why?"

I was stumped. "No."

"Bob Parsons, you are to report to the library the first period this morning," the homeroom teacher said.

She handed me an excuse slip as soon as we walked into the homeroom, and she was about to add something more when she suddenly became busy refereeing a shoving match between Mortie and another student, who was also built like a Sumo wrestler. They were now wrestling and banging against desks in the back of the homeroom. The disagreement was over who was going to sit in which seat.

Mortie's opponent in the disagreement was known as "Umpteen." Umpteen Hendershot, because when asked how much he weighed, he would answer, "Umpteen pounds."

He habitually squinted one eye and had a devilish crooked smile on his face and a bad habit of pushing people out of his way. That's what had happened to Mortie. Umpteen combed his hair in a high oiled arch, with a finger wave added, and another student touching his hair was a declaration of war.

His father operated a bulldozer and Umpteen was friends with Homer, the small guy who wanted to be a truck driver and wore the Peterbilt belt buckle. Their mutual love of large engines somehow made them buddies.

I left the room unnoticed while both sides pleaded their case. My Maplewood classmate pushed her way in and stood directly between the two round bodies. She stood in silence with her arms folded and looked first at one of the wrestlers, and then she flipped her head quickly to look at the other, while the teacher mediated.

This seemed to me a good chance to do something with the dynamite. I walked the hall trying to think of a plan and heard a familiar, "Hi, Bob!"

"Hi, Karen."

"I heard the good news. Congratulations!" she said.

I said, "Thanks," wondering what she was talking about.

"We can really use you, Bob. I mean, losing the first game of the year, it's so-o-o horrible! Butterbean told me the good news. You know that the coach confides in him? He said you're a really good football player, so it'll be great having you on our team. How come you didn't tell me about this, Bob?"

She walked closer now and grasped my upper arm with both hands. Then lacing her fingers together while holding it, she gently pulled and pushed my arm in a playful manner, keeping time with her voice,

"When mother was a cheerleader, the Skipjacks never lost a game all year!"

Her eyes were now becoming moist with emotion.

"Skipjacks aren't losers, Bob! We're going to practice cheers twice as hard, and you practice football twice as hard. OK?" she said.

"OK."

It had not crossed my mind to ask anyone about who had won the game played on Friday. I was dwelling on the fact that she thought me to be some kind of great football player, when in fact I would have been hard-pressed to explain what caused a first down. I was stumped and thinking to myself, "Where did this come from?"

"Butterbean said he would do everything possible to help you in practice. Isn't that great?" she said.

She slowly squeezed my arm and leaned deliberately close and turned, casually grazing her breasts, first one then the other, against my arm.

"I'll help you any way I can too, Bob. Welcome." She pulled me hard against her and into my ear whispered, "Go Boaz."

With large, serious eyes and in one fluid motion, she released me and backed away doing one of her patented jump and twirls, sending her skirt bouncing, and ran down the hall backwards. She jumped to a stop, waved, and walked into the principal's office. I had a sudden idea of what might be in store. Butterbean was planning a killing. It was going to be mine.

I continued to the library, thinking over the new development and carrying my book. The librarian looked up and motioned me to her with a smile.

I asked, "You want to see me?"

"Well, I'm glad to see you of course, but the principal and the people from the high school that were giving the test you took? Want you to take it over," she said.

I was crestfallen. What else could happen?

"I didn't cheat or nothin'," I said.

Then I reconsidered the reason. "It says I'm dumb, don't it?"

She stood and pulled out one of the two chairs that were at the table adjacent to her desk, "No, Bob, no. Sit here and calm down, nothing's wrong. You look scared to death. Nothing's wrong, I promise."

"How come I gotta take it over then?"

"You're not the only one. Someone else is going to take it too. I'll be the one here giving it, so just take you a deep breath. You see it's not a bad thing. You did well on the test. So well, they want you to take it again just to double-check, that's all. When Penny arrives, we'll start."

"She did too good too?"

"Not exactly; she did average, so they want her to take it again too."

"Average?"

"It's complicated. I'm not supposed to be discussing these things, so don't say anything or I'll be the one in trouble, not you."

I sat for a few minutes thinking things over while she read her instructions about the test.

I asked, "So you mean I'm not dumb?"

"No, Bob, you're not dumb. Whatever would make you think that?"

"I don't know." It seemed obvious.

"Penny's not dumb either; she's only eight points below average. So that's not a low score, see, but don't say a word, please?"

"Won't—I promise."

Penny came in slowly, with red eyes, and carrying her briefcase. She had been crying. The librarian gave her a pep talk and said the test people thought we were, "an aberration." This did not sound good.

"I need to be helping with the locker searches this morning. As a school monitor, it is my duty to be there to help!" Penny said, frustrated.

"What's a locker search?" I asked.

"Making sure people don't have contraband in their locker. Last year we found a bottle of beer, a stolen sweater, and one other year they found the missing March of Dimes money, still in the collection jar. Caught him red-handed, they did. I am needed to help turn the combinations, because only the monitors are trusted with the list of combinations. You see?" Penny was trying to explain to both of us.

I considered what she said and was positive that dynamite would be looked upon as contraband. My skin became clammy. I felt a shaking spell trying to start. We began the test.

It looked about the same as last time. I nervously read and answered, trying to figure a way to get to my locker before the monitors. It seemed unfair that other people should be allowed in my locker. Penny sat staring at her test, absently running her hands in her hair, causing it to point in unusual directions.

I stood and heard myself say, "May I be excused?"

"You look ill, Bob. Do you have a nervous stomach?"

"Yes, I do."

"These tests put too much undue pressure on adolescents, in my opinion. I do not like them," she declared. "I'll stop the time, not supposed to, but I will. Go ahead."

I left the room quickly, with her thinking that it was one emergency and me knowing it was another. A group was assembled at the principal's office door; all were students except for the principal. They each had clipboards, and the principal was gesturing and pointing randomly. I ducked behind the recessed entrance leading to a restroom and carefully peeked, guessing they were the monitors, and at any second they would begin to open lockers.

They headed as a group to the opposite stairway and away from me and walked to about where my wall locker door was in a line among many others. They stopped and talked again. Then they all headed up the stairs, with Karen bringing up the rear, studying her clipboard. When they rounded the landing, continuing their trip to the second floor, I took off running and slid to a stop in front of my locker.

I turned the combination with shaking hands. It did not open. I tried again, turning the knob much slower after taking a deep breath, and finally pulled out the bag and fuse. I pushed into my pocket the blasting caps that were still wrapped in the red bandanna. Then I felt for my pistol. I couldn't find it and remembered that Kay had it. Shutting the door quietly, I ran for the nearest exit that took me out onto the playground and upriver from the Texaco station.

Walking slowly behind the building, scanning the playground, I jumped when I heard a sudden loud tapping sound above and behind my head. Turning quickly, I saw a teacher pecking the inside glass of one of her large classroom windows. The rest of the class was laughing and pointing in my direction. I smiled, waved, and walked slowly away. The teacher began trying to raise the window. I took off running, around the gymnasium, then ran across the parking lot and headed for the Texaco station.

I decided to hide the evidence behind the station where it could be found later. I ran to and ducked behind the station, looking around for a convenient, secure place.

"What you doing there, young Rooster?" someone said.

The sudden voice made me jump again. This time I came close to yelling. It was Garvin, sitting quietly up against the station's back wall and looking out beyond, to the river.

"I need to keep some stuff here till later," I mumbled.

He got up and came over. "Hell, I'll keep it for you, safe as can be. What you got there that's so damn important?"

I made a quick decision. "Dynamite. I do some blastin' work, got a job after school and need a place to keep it."

Garvin studied me for a second, then held out his arm for the bag. I handed it over. He set it down and fought the opening for a look.

"You're not kidding, are you?" He stood looking, and then squeezed the bag back shut. "I'll stick it right behind this oil drum. Nobody will bother it."

I laid the fuse on top.

"OK, thanks," I said, relieved. "Got to get back, takin' a test."

"Does Mike know about this?" Garvin asked.

"Yeah, he knows."

Garvin paused while thinking seriously and said, "You know, I think you're working too hard in school. Every time I see you you're hurrying to school. Now you're worrying about tests. It's just not healthy. You know that, Rooster? You need to develop some outside interests. Studying isn't everything."

"I will, but I need to go right now, so thanks," I said.

I took off at full speed, ran the steps, and opened the library door, out of breath.

"Bob, what's wrong? You're sweating and breathing so hard, we better get you to the first aid room!" the librarian said.

"No, please, I'm OK, believe me. Just need a second."

"You sure?" The teacher looked a little less concerned.

Penny sat looking at me, blank faced.

"Well, sit down and try then, but if you feel bad, you shouldn't be taking this test. These results are going to follow you the rest of your life," she said.

Penny's face developed an anguished look. She said to me for no apparent reason, "I think I'm going to join the Army. Lots of women do that nowadays, you know."

"Yes, they do," I answered. I didn't know.

Things relaxed a little. I began trying to figure out answers again. We had breaks and the librarian questioned me about *The Deerslayer.*

I explained, "Didn't have much time to read this weekend, ma'am."

At school and in class seemed to be the only time I could read without being interrupted.

Penny was still upset about the test and complained to the librarian, "When you take a test, the teacher tells you what chapters it will cover, so you outline the chapters and then read them over again and underline the important sentences. Then take the test. They said we couldn't study for this test because it's over everything. That is just not fair, and as far as I'm concerned, it should be illegal!"

The librarian was sympathetic. "Penny, I am so sorry that you feel that way, but sometimes things are just not fair. Do the best you can and forget about it."

"You don't understand. I have to be accepted into college!"

"You will, Penny. I guarantee that you will get into college, so stop worrying, please."

"Well, I better."

The promise by the teacher seemed to calm her some. The librarian made an additional suggestion that Penny should go to the restroom and freshen up, hoping she would comb the hair that she had been absently rearranging.

The bell rang and study-hall classes came and went. They avoided the front table where Penny and I sat. Finally, lunchtime arrived. I hurried on my way to deal with the dynamite and walked out of the library door, into the hall, and saw several football players casually leaning against the wall. They stopped talking when they saw me, as though they were waiting for me, and they were.

"Butterbean wants to see you," one said.

"OK, I'll see him after awhile."

"No, he wants you in the cafeteria, now."

They formed around me with their hands still in their pockets and herded me down the hall. I could tell by the look on their faces that protesting would do little good and thought about making a run for it, but the halls were crowded. They would catch me as I tried to push past the other students, so I decided to bide my time.

"You a football player, huh?" one of the group said. I found out later that he was the coach's son and team quarterback. I did not answer him. "What position you play?" he pressed.

"I catch it."

"What do you mean catch, passes? The football?"

"Yeah."

"So you're an end, offensive?"

"Yes."

He smiled a genuine smile and said, "Great, we need someone who can catch a football!"

He held out his hand and introduced himself and was followed by the rest, some bashfully. We walked around the gymnasium floor and out the back door, traveling down the covered walk that went to the cafeteria. There was less tension, at least on their part.

The cafeteria was brick, with several exhaust vents, and matched the main school with one exception. Attached to the side, extending out parallel and pointing downriver was a large Quonset-type structure, looking like a large tin can cut in half longways and placed open side down, on the ground. It was covered with rounded, corrugated metal sheets, starting at the ground and curving over the top, then back to touch the ground on the opposite side. The space created was used for seating and had been acquired from the government as military surplus.

Assembled at the entrance door of the Quonset structure was what looked to be the rest of the football team. Butterbean was standing in the middle.

"We found him," the kid walking beside me announced.

Butterbean gave a nod and motioned with his hand for us to enter the door. Over the door were two large, slow-moving fans, drawing the air from the building. With me toward the rear, the group made a grand entrance. There were quite a few non–football students sitting randomly at the long wooden picnic-type tables that were in rows coming out from the walls. Each row extended out and stopped, leaving a pathway down the center of the building.

The students eating and talking lowered their voices and looked down at the metal food trays sitting in front of them. We strutted as a group to the line, and those ahead of us waiting in line moved. We went ahead, and each player pulled a tray from a stack and slid it down the stainless steel railings, reaching for the food. The women standing behind the counter were setting it in front of us. They were wearing black netting on their heads, which contrasted with the white bib aprons.

Jerry Joe had on occasion stopped in the back door of this building. One of these ladies, a Culpepper, would give him a paper sack full of cheese. "Surplus," is all he said. It was good.

Approaching the stack of trays, I looked high on the wall to see a large picture attached to what at one time was the outside of the brick building, before the Quonset addition was attached. The picture was a black-line cartoon drawing of a fish, displayed on a white, unframed canvas. The fish appeared to be walking upright and using its tail fins for legs. The upper fins, about chest high, were arms wearing boxing gloves and were being held in a fighting position. Its big head and bug eyes had a mean, determined expression, and drops of sweat randomly flew into the air as it leaned forward. It seemed to be traveling along at a fast clip. Add a cocked sailor's hat on the head and a short cigar, with smoke wafting back, hanging from the side of a mouth that was snarling and showing sharp teeth and we were looking at a rendition of "Skipjack," the Boaz Junior High School mascot. Below, in block letters and including the exclamation mark, was "GO SKIPJACKS!"

Red Jell-O, mashed potatoes, and a long, flat ground piece of meat covered in gravy lay positioned beside the cooked-till-mushy carrots. Another lady added to the tray a drinking straw, plus two half-pints of milk that said Schultz Dairy, along with a hunk of cheese on a paper napkin.

A student with our football group was up ahead. Short and heavyset, he stood by the lady at the end of the line who was collecting either money or the previously purchased tickets.

When I approached, he said to the lady, "He's with us." She nodded and waved me on. I followed him to the bench seat attached to one of the picnic tables at the front.

On the other side of the aisle, the first table was painted maroon with a large white *B* in the middle. On this side, the table where we were sitting was painted white with a maroon *B* in the middle. The rest of the tables in the lunchroom were plain, unpainted wood.

"The team sits at these tables," he said and pointed across the aisle, "first string over there and us here."

"What position do you play?" I asked, remembering my earlier conversation.

"You're new around here, aren't you?" he said, and was not intimidated by my question. "My name is Toby Blair, elected president of the Boaz student body, also the head manager for both the football and basketball teams."

He stuck out his hand, and I shook it in a very adult manner, feeling like I had just shaken the hand of an important person. His round baby face had a perfect complexion, including natural rouge marks on his cheeks that were framed by black, horned-rim glasses. His dark, short hair was supposed to be cut in a flattop, but his round head and a cowlick at the front hairline made it look more like just a short haircut.

"Why didn't I have to pay her the twenty cents?" I asked.

"Football team eats free during the season. Alumni pay the bills. That and some creative bookkeeping." He laughed at his joke. I did not get it but laughed along.

"If your parents don't know, don't tell them, and you can clear an easy dollar every week when they give you lunch money."

I understood that part. "OK."

"Get in the locker room as early as you can after school, and I'll suit you up."

While talking, he pulled from his shirt pocket a small spiral notebook and thumbed to a clean page. Then he reached for a mechanical pencil from the same pocket, extended the lead, and laid it beside the pad.

"Give me your sizes, and I'll do the best I can. Most of the good equipment is already handed out by now, but I'll give it my best shot," he said, winking at me.

I winked back by reflex, wondering what our secret was.

"One more tip, the insurance. The school buys a separate insurance for football."

"Insurance?"

"Here's the way it works." He looked around and leaned over confidentially. "It's like this, the insurance you took out with the school, the accident insurance, also covers football injuries."

I remembered the insurance. They gave me the forms during the library orientation, on the first day. Six dollars covered the accident medical expenses during the coming year. A broken arm, stitches, or other complications from injuries would be covered.

Toby continued, "The football insurance is with a different company. If you go see Dr. Corbett, across from the city building, that's who the football team is supposed to go see. He will bill both insurance companies and give you the check from one of them, and he keeps the other one."

"I get to keep the money?"

"Yes, kind of like scholarship money."

"And I go if I feel like any little thing is wrong?"

"That's right."

I didn't think Jerry Joe was aware of this money aspect of football, or he would be a star by now, with many injuries. I looked across and saw the cheerleading squad sitting at the next table behind the first team. Susan and Karen both waved. I realized that the wave was probably going to get me extra beat up if I went to practice. Still, while sitting there eating, the feeling of being in the midst of something important was in the air. I felt drawn; more like attracted, but had no conscious clue as to what caused the feeling.

We finished eating and my newfound friend and I parted company with a promise to meet in the equipment room after classes. The importance of me being around the team seemed to have diminished.

I took off running for the Texaco station as fast as I could go, wondering how much insurance money could be made on a sprained ankle. The "police car" was parked at the front of the station. Vernon was inside, leaning on the counter and listening to Cecil.

"Kay here?" I asked. With a big, messy grin, Vernon casually pointed to the back, not speaking because his mouth was stuffed with potato chips.

Cecil stopped pointing to the greasy piece of automobile he held in his hand and said, "Him an' Garvin went 'round back, fussin' 'bout somthin'."

Kay was sitting on a pop crate placed upside down and lying flat on the ground. He had a disgusted look on his face. When seeing me, it turned to anger.

"What the hell are you doing?" Kay pointed to Garvin, sitting against the wall holding the bag of dynamite. "I turn my back for a minute, and you give all our stuff to this wino!"

I tried to explain, "They're searching the lockers, few more minutes, and they woulda found it."

Garvin sat quietly holding the bag and looking at Kay. "Nobody told you to come nosing around here, you little turdbird. I told the Rooster here I'd keep it for him. That's what I'm doing, so don't blow a gasket. Now, both of you answer my question, what are you going to do with this?"

"We're going to dig a well, up at the dairy," I said off the top of my head.

"Bullshit, that farm has the best spring water in the county. It needs a well like I need a hole in the head."

"If you don't give us back what's not yours, I'll give you a hole in the head!" Kay threatened. "And another thing, I know stuff nobody knows, 'cause I been all over my house up there. Know every little place and read every little paper. You see, I know what your real name is, Buster, and don't mind tellin' people!"

Garvin got up awkwardly and handed me the bag, then squatted in front of Kay. "I figured you knew that, but it isn't anybody else's business but mine, you hear me?"

I was holding the dynamite and stooped to get the fuse cord. This seemed to calm Kay, so his next question to Garvin was more quizzical than anything: "Why don't you want anybody to know?"

"'Cause they're a real nice family, trying hard to do things right, and I don't want them to suddenly find they got a one-armed drunk to be ashamed of, that's why, don't you understand that?"

Kay's face was blank. He showed no indication of understanding except for the unexpected tears, one from each eye, sliding slowly down his cheeks. "You don't think I can understand something like that, you big dumbass?"

Kay struggled to stand and started around to the front of the station while giving me an order: "Put the stuff in the trunk." Then he yelled into the station, "Let's go, Vern!" while he stood yanking, trying to get the car door open. I helped with the handle, and then boosted him into the seat.

"Pop is coming up to get me in a little bit, and we're both comin' and talkin' to these Goddamn idiot school people. He's gonna straighten 'um out, we're gonna play football, Bob. I guarantee it, and you keep your mouth shut about Garvin 'cause it ain't anybody's business."

I opened the glove compartment and gently lay the wrapped blasting caps from my pocket inside and clicked it back shut. "Don't put these in the trunk with the stuff; they might explode it," I said.

Exactly what the "Garvin business" was had not sunk into my brain. It was all confusing except that we got the dynamite back and it looked like I was going to play football one way or another, whether I liked it or not.

Vernon had been asking Cecil questions, getting free advice about some small problem with his car. He walked out, nodding his head back in Cecil's direction. They drove off with Kay sitting and looking straight ahead. His arms were awkwardly folded across his chest.

Garvin came around the corner. "I don't know what you all got planned, but you better let me do it, whatever it is, because it doesn't make much of a damn what they do to me. You kids have your whole life ahead. Do you understand that Bob?"

I did not understand, but did realize that it was the first time he had ever called me Bob.

I shrugged, shook my head and said, "I don't know what's gonna happen," and took off running for the school.

Mike and Susan were talking, sitting inside the school on the lower steps leading to the second floor. They were laughing and whispering, and both seemed happy.

"Where you been all day?" Mike asked.

"Taking that test over."

"Why? And eating in the Boaz Slop House; what's going on there?"

"I do not know."

I wanted to tell Mike about my morning, but the first bell rang, so I headed in the direction of the library. The couple got up from their seat, and moving to a wall, they went back to whatever they were giggling about.

We finished the test before the afternoon was over. Penny and I, both spent, parted company shortly before the remaining class of the day. She walked with her head down. Occasionally she pushed her glasses back on her nose and carried the briefcase that looked heavy because it tilted her to one side. When walking she made a rustling sound caused by the petticoat under her beige skirt.

The last class was history. I managed to slide to the rear of the class. Most teachers by now had forgotten the instructions for me to sit in the front. Pulling the library book from the back of my pants, I tried but couldn't read, being too exhausted from the day's events, so I sat listening to the modulated voice of the young teacher as she talked about the atomic bomb.

"It has changed the way we look at warfare. When you see the horrible devastation of innocent women and children it caused in Japan, it makes us wonder what the government was thinking when they dropped it. The war was over, six more months' fighting, at the most. There should be inquires made about this terrible mistake. You are the generation that must ask important questions like this—if there are to be any satisfactory answers."

I sat with my arms folded, thinking about my father and wondering "how much longer till this class is over," and asked Mike the time. He looked at his watch and held up five fingers. The bell finally sounded. We walked into the hall.

Mike said, "Let me get this straight, first there was Pearl Harbor and then the bomb, right?"

"Yeah, I think so."

But before we could talk further, Toby, the head manager, appeared. "There you are," he said.

He stopped to look at Mike. "Hello, Mike, good to see you," Toby said, and then looked back at me. "We need to get you suited up before practice starts, so let's go," he said, with an authority that seemed final. I shrugged at Mike's frowning face and walked away with Toby.

The football locker room smelled of male sweat. It was full of team members, some walking around in jock straps and some almost dressed for practice. All were moving in a subdued manner. Toby opened the combination lock on a large walk-in metal cage at the end of the room. It had wall pegs and random piles of equipment. He looked at me with an appraising face.

"Try these," he said, holding out a wrinkled pair of football pants, along with foam rubber pads. He showed me how to stuff them into pockets under the knee area. We pushed hard plastic thigh pads into other pockets. A belt with two pads attached was to go around my belly and was supposed to ride over my kidneys. They fitted down inside the pants while a portion remained sticking out.

The shoulder pads restricted my arm movement, so he removed a couple of the straps, and that allowed me to raise my arms.

"I'm not supposed to take these off, so keep it quiet," he said.

The only helmets left were too big, but we settled on one that only wobbled some, and everything seemed to work except the shoes. The remaining equipment was mostly hand-me-downs from high school players and tended to be large, so all the remaining shoes were entirely too big. We tried stuffing paper into the toes, but I could hardly walk. He finally decided I could wear my tennis shoes from gym class.

"If you do a good job, Coach will go to the high school and come back with you a good pair, one way or another," Toby said, looking me up and down to admire his work.

We were standing around all dressed when one of the assistant managers came in. "Coach is up in the principal's office, said wait till he gets here."

Most team members found a spot on the floor and stretched out with little talk. I glanced over at Butterbean, envying his equipment, which seemed to be new and fit him perfectly, but he ignored me.

Toby motioned for me to follow.

We walked into the coach's office while he said, "Might as well take care of some business while we're waiting."

He searched to find a mimeographed sheet of paper for me to sign. He took it back, then handed me another from a different stack. "This is the insurance. Take it home for a parent's signature and bring it back to me tomorrow."

"Can I use the phone?" I asked.

He shrugged. "Sure."

Turning the circular dial, I put in our number, 21801, and Mother answered.

"Where are you calling from, Bob?"

"School."

"They let you use the phone?"

"Yes."

"Are you in trouble?"

'No, I'm going to stay for football practice and might be late for supper."

"We haven't discussed this football thing; you might get hurt. Don't you think of these things?"

"I'll be OK; practice is starting so I got to go now."

"The family is going to sit down and have a serious discussion about this. Be careful. I'll keep you something to eat."

"OK, bye."

Walking in my stocking feet to my school locker, I sat in the empty hall putting on the tennis shoes, and then walked back across the gym floor. There was yelling and banging coming from the dressing room. Approaching, I could tell that it was the coach and peeked through the door just in time to see him throw someone's helmet to the far end of the room. It banged against and made a new dent in an already dented locker.

"What the hell are they going do next? You're playing like a bunch of girls, and now we got to babysit some touch game after school! Has everybody gone nuts! Get off your asses, outside, outside. Run laps till I say quit! First one quits, I'm stickin' a Kotex up your ass!! Go! Go!"

They came in a swarm. I sidestepped away from the door opening and followed behind. We ran a large circle around the field that was still well lined at the edges, while the middle showed wear from the game last Friday. On the third lap the coach yelled, "Jumping jacks!"

We formed several lines and Butterbean, the defensive captain, and the coach's son, the offensive captain, stood facing us. They called the cadence and after a few repetitions, I developed the required rhythm to stay in sync with the rest. It was followed by push-ups and another tirade by the coach, but it was less threatening in the wide outdoors than from the confined dressing room.

The practice got under way with offense against defense. I, along with the second team, mostly seventh and eighth graders, stood as a group on the side and watched. The coach, in a wide stance with his hands on his knees, looked at the defensive team.

"You were playin' matador defense, just waving them by, blowing kisses and throwing roses down on the ground for them to run by on. You got to hit somebody!" he said.

A large lineman was caught off guard when the coach suddenly lowered his shoulder and threw his weight forward, knocking the player to his back on the ground. You could hear air leaving the lineman's lungs. He jumped back to his feet quickly. Everyone knew it hurt, but he was doing a good job of not letting it show.

They ran more plays and the coach continued explaining what they were doing wrong. My mind wandered. I was looking toward the river, trying to imagine what Jerry Joe and the gang were doing, when the coach said, "Parsons, get over here."

"You see, you missed the first two weeks of practice, before school started, when we could practice twice a day and three times when everybody's dogassin' around. So now you don't know what the hell is going on, do you?"

"No, sir."

He put his hand on the back of my neck and led me to the huddle and said to the quarterback, "He's going to play left end. Tell him his pattern before callin' the plays, if it's a pass."

We leaned over; all helmets were close in a circle. The quarterback said words and numbers that made no sense; then he said, "On two." He looked at me. "Take three steps down field and turn out and don't start till the second 'hut.' OK?"

I nodded my head. They all clapped one time, simultaneously, to indicate the huddle was over. Looking around, I got down into a three-point stance, imitating the lineman beside me.

"No, no, Parsons, stand up so you can see what the defense is doing. The only people who get down like that are these roothog linemen. You gotta use your head, son, now let's go," the coach said.

I preferred standing, and bent forward slightly, imitating the kid playing the opposite end position. When hearing the second "hut" from the quarterback, I followed the instructions and turned to look back. My head turned but the helmet did not, and there was a sudden loud noise when the ball hit the unturned helmet, about where my face was located inside. I got up, quickly adjusting the helmet, and assumed I was in trouble.

"Toby!" the coach yelled. "Where'd you get that helmet, off some watermelon or something? Get him one that fits!"

Everyone was smirking and looking down. One good thing about wearing a helmet, it can hide expressions unless the observing person is positioned directly in front of your face. Toby quickly walked among the second stringers, asking for helmets. After trying several, we found one that remained reasonably well positioned when I moved my head around quickly. I jerked my head back and forth to check, while everyone watched.

We huddled and there was another play called. "You go out two steps and turn across the center of the field. I will jump straight up and hit you in the belly. On the third hut this time, let's go!" the quarterback said to me, and we all clapped.

It appeared to me that the coach was trying to see if I was any good. That made me determined to show him that I was. I took the two steps and turned, and the ball immediately hit me in the stomach. I caught it.

What happened next is difficult to describe. It was like being in bed early in the morning, sound asleep, and Mother coming into the room to wake me for school. But in this particular case, the voice had a more husky tone, like someone who did a lot of yelling. I gradually became aware that something wasn't as it should be and asked myself a question: "Why was I floating in a foggy sleep when a minute ago I know I was doing something?" While trying to remember what that something was, I opened my eyes and looked up to a surrounding huddle of inquiring faces, bent over looking. I wondered what was so interesting, and suddenly I jerked my head from side to side, trying to avoid the terrible smell of the ammonium smelling salts that Toby was holding under my nose.

I could hear the coach yelling, "Did you see that? He didn't drop the ball! He didn't drop the ball!"

He reached over and grasped my belt and pulled it up and down. I could feel air rushing back into my lungs. "Good, Parsons, that was good! Now get up and run it off, and we'll try some more pass plays!"

The team as a group raised me to wobbly feet. Toby put my arm around his neck for support and began walking me down the field as the team resumed practice.

"What happened?" I asked.

"Butterbean creamed you."

"Oh."

It hadn't occurred to me what would happen after catching the ball. I soon began running back and forth and was still a little woozy but felt no specific pain. My entire body tingled. Toby said the tingling was a good sign. He thought I would be OK.

After several plays, the coach waved me into the huddle again. The quarterback told me, "Go out, fake left, and then go straight down the field. I'll throw the ball high, and you run under it." We clapped and ran to the line of scrimmage.

Bowlegged people have a low center of gravity. They can abruptly cut back and forth. It is an advantage in football, and the guy who was about to guard me was bowlegged. He played defense but also offense, as a scatback, and often carried the football because he could dart quickly in and out of danger.

I did the fake and took off. The ball came down in a perfect arc. I caught it like when Jerry Joe threw. The scatback, who could out-dart everyone, could not keep up with me when running in a straight line. I kept running, not looking back, and heard a whistle being blown. The fear of Butterbean catching me made my legs go faster. Finally, after covering considerable ground and hearing no more footsteps, I ventured a look back.

The coach, quite a distance away by now, was jumping up and down and waving me back to him, while everyone else, including the scatback, was standing with their hands on their hips, watching me and laughing.

I trotted back. "Good, Parsons! Good," the coach said. "But when I blow the whistle, that means stop the play. Quit running, OK? Thought for a minute there that we might have to fish you out of the river."

Everybody started laughing again, including me. We practiced awhile longer while I stood with the second string and watched; then the entire squad ran several short, fast sprints to improve our wind.

Practice was over, with a pep talk about the upcoming game. How we had to focus on doing what was necessary to win. "You got to learn how to slap people around!" the coach said.

In the locker room with my street clothes on, I started to leave. Butterbean waved me to where he was sitting, not yet fully dressed.

"I told these guys you don't need an initiation. Said you got one the other day in the restroom, remember?"

"Yeah."

"See you tomorrow, Parsons," he said.

I walked away, feeling that we weren't close personal friends, but it seemed he might let me live. I appreciated it.

Heading out the door, Toby lay in my hand several mimeographed pages stapled together, covered with *x*'s and *o*'s.

"Memorize these plays by tomorrow, the coach said." Toby smiled at this latest impossible demand made by the coach. He was used to it.

Walking toward the Texaco station, I saw Jerry Joe sitting smoking a cigarette. After watching me approach, he got up to descend the hill, and together we began walking the tracks downriver .

"You a football player now, are you?" Jerry Joe asked.

"They beat the hell outta me, but they didn't say don't come back. So I don't really know, guess I am."

"Don't tell Kay 'bout it. You're supposed to be on his team, so he'll get pissed for sure," Jerry Joe said.

"You reckon?" I had not thought of that.

"Know him like a book. He come past the club today, said we got a game tomorrow. Somethin' about his dad straightenin' everybody out. Guess there was a talk. Gave me five dollars and told me to be at school or he'd send Herky after me with a warrant. Said he had the dynamite too."

"He does. They almost found it in my locker."

We went a ways. "I ain't seen you, Jerry Joe, what you been doin'?"

"I caddied twice today. Need the money, I guess."

He seemed more somber than normal and had even refrained from smacking me on the back of the head.

"You want to stop at Gibson's and get a pop?" he asked.

"Yeah." I was thirsty. "Something the matter with you?"

"I guess there might be. I don't know for sure, but I ain't supposed to tell," he said.

"What?"

He didn't answer. The walks up and back down the hill from Gibson's were both quiet.

"I think maybe Gloria might be gonna have a baby," he said. We walked on in silence. I was stunned.

I had no idea what to say or even how to arrange my mind to think about this revelation.

"What are you going to do?" I asked.

"Maybe join the Army. That's what the old lady said my daddy did. She's never seen him again."

"You gonna do that?"

We walked along home, ignoring the coal chunks that we usually tossed into piles. I was listening to our feet strike the cross ties. There was no one around, so we sat in Garvin and Cecil's "party" chairs and stared at the river.

"I ain't leaving. We're gonna get married. Would you know how somebody'd do that?" he asked.

I shook my head no. This conversation was over my head, I knew it, and asked, "Can I go to it? When you get married?"

He grinned for the first time. "I suppose. I don't think a Culpepper ever got married before. Do you have to go in a church?"

"I don't know, I'll ask Dad."

He started laughing. "Don't think they's been a Culpepper in a church before either. If we all went in at once, the roof would cave right in, for sure."

We both started laughing hard. Jerry Joe stood and motioned me up the hill, and we went to the road. He began thumbing a ride to Sharpsburg for his evening job at the skating rink. We stood waiting as several cars swished by.

"My great-grandparents, Mattie and Joseph, married themselves in front of God."

"How you do that?" Jerry Joe was interested.

The story was told. They had known each other since they were small children. Joseph's mother was originally from the Netherlands and spoke almost no English. She had migrated to the Fred's Creek area with her American husband and a young Joseph. The reason they came was never clear. Soon after arriving, Joseph's father was shot in a dispute over the ownership of a pig.

Mattie's father had also died the year before, from what was said to be "the grippe." Her twelve- and thirteen-year-old brothers were digging coal from the side of the hill that held Bone Marrow Branch. They used a pick and shovel and pushed the dug loads in a wheelbarrow, dumping the coal into piles where it could be shoveled into the horse-drawn wagon that came by periodically. The driver paid them a few cents for the considerable labor. In time they dug deep into the hill, and one day it collapsed, burying them both.

The women and children of both families moved in together and lived in a one-room, dirt-floor house. In the winter months they sometimes dug and boiled roots for food. Joseph was the only one that his mother could speak to because he was the only one who understood her Dutch language. The two of them sat and talked. He entertained her and made her laugh.

Mattie and Joseph were about thirteen when they decided to get married. With no one around to marry them, they decided to marry themselves. The area where they lived was named after the small creek that ran close to their house. It was called Bone Marrow because of the nearby cave. The cave had a high ceiling just past the entrance, and there were several large piles of long-dead animal bones, splintered and left by ancient inhabitants. The bones had been pounded and scraped, and the marrow eaten.

Joseph and Mattie climbed this tall hill that contained the cave and bones. The hill also had buried inside of it the bones of her dead brothers, who were still trapped in their homemade mine. The two stood on a level ledge close to its highest point, holding hands.

"If it be accepted, we will be married now," Mattie said.

There was no objection from the sky. They took this as God's blessing and a holy acceptance of their marriage. They had their honeymoon on the hilltop. Joseph picked her white wildflowers named Queen Anne's Lace.

"That could work I guess, but we want a piece a paper, all legal like," Jerry Joe said.

A car pulled to a stop for Jerry Joe. I watched as they drove away, then crossed the road and went into the gates of Maplewood. It was almost dark.

I suddenly felt the weight of the day. The energy spent in football practice made me tired and sleepy. Mother came into the kitchen when she heard the door and used a potholder to remove a plate of food from the oven.

She said, "Come in here and eat."

I washed my hands and followed her and sat at the dining table while she poured a glass of milk. I waved to father and my brothers who were in the front room watching *The Rifleman.*

Mother was studying her real estate books. She sat at the opposite end of the table. "You get hurt?"

"No, ma'am."

"You tired?"

I opened my mouth to say no but stopped and looked directly at her. "I'm a little tired."

"Bob, you look like you have the weight of the world on your shoulders. Do you know, honey, these will be the happiest days of your life? Carefree, no worries, you will someday look back on all this with fond memories." She smiled, thinking that she had cheered me up.

"Really?"

"Really."

Day Nine

Familiar voices transcend words. The tone, tenor, rhythm, and phrasing all convey a meaning the speaker may not be aware of and make insignificant the words used or even the topic. I could hear Mother's voice coming into my dream of sitting high on a hill on a cold, snowy night, by a comfortable fire with Smokey's ears perked and his all- knowing eyes keeping watch while I was carefully chipping flint to make hunting arrows.

"Bob, get up, you're going to be late for school. You need time to eat. I don't know how you're going to get up when I'm gone, you'll probably stay in bed till noon. You should start shutting your window at night; it's getting chilly in here."

I made a move to show I was getting up and felt soreness in my arms, legs, and stomach from the football practice, and made a conscious effort not to let mother notice that anything was wrong. In the bathroom I saw bruised ribs and legs, but after moving my arms and doing squats, the aches seem to subside somewhat, and the more I moved, the less noticeable it became.

Father's section at the plant was still shut down. He was sitting at the table and sipping coffee and watching out the opened front door for his later-than-normal ride to arrive. Mother placed in front of me two pieces of toast, lying side by side flat on a plate, with a poached egg jiggling on top of each. The eggs seemed to be staring at the ceiling and were accompanied by a pile of dark-brown fried potatoes on the side. I turned the plate and playfully arranged the potatoes to make a mustache for the imagined eyes. A small glass of hand-squeezed orange juice sat beside my milk, and I downed the juice, tasting and chewing the thick pulp, and started slicing up the eggs.

"Dad, what do you got to do when you get married?"

Father was staring out the front door and sitting perfectly still, a habit of his, and now turned his head slowly to look at me. Mother, who was making a trip back to the kitchen, stopped with the spatula in her hand pointing to the ceiling. She returned and took a seat at the table. She was wearing an apron with ruffles that matched her dress. She was ready for a trip to the real estate agency to find out details about her upcoming test.

"You gettin' married, are you?" Father asked, looking down his nose at me with squinted eyes.

Mother's eyes were wide, and she pressed a hand to her mouth in what looked like an effort to keep in words.

"No," I said, grinning and stuffing some of the eggs into my mouth, thinking he was joking. "I'm never gettin' married, but this fella I know said he wanted to. But he don't know how, so I'm helping him find out."

"I think you go to the courthouse and give them two dollars for a license, and then a judge or preacher can do the job."

Mother was concerned about my hearing, but occasionally I thought she missed a lot of what I was saying. "Bob, do you have a girlfriend we should meet?" she said.

"No."

"Is there a girl you have been seeing a lot of that we don't know about?"

"No."

"Well, who is this friend of yours who wants to know this stuff?"

"Somebody at school. You don't know them."

"So you're not getting married?"

"No. I'm gonna be late for school, so I better go."

I crammed the remainder of the egg-soaked toast into my mouth and picked up my library book with the football plays folded inside. I eased out the front door, leaving them looking at one another.

"You playing football tonight?" she yelled.

"U-u-umm." I turned to nod yes and waved, not being able to answer with my mouth full.

The usual gang stood waiting for the bus this morning. They were standing with all heads looking across the Maplewood entrance to the opposite side, staring at something I could not see behind the matching pillar. The group of kids waiting gave the appearance of grazing animals standing in a herd. They all had their heads cocked and were watching something at a distance that was giving them cause for concern but not yet enough concern to run.

I peeked around the square pillar to where their gaze was aimed and saw Garvin sitting propped against the mortared fieldstone rocks. He rolled to a standing position when he saw me and said, "Hi, Rooster. Thought I missed you. Mind if I walk along with you on this fine morning?"

Nodding my head in agreement, I was taken aback by his sudden friendliness. We crossed the road to walk the sidewalk that was overlooking the river and train tracks, traveling at a moderate pace.

Garvin suddenly stopped and turned around, saying, "Who are you?" to my classmate who was following closely on his heels.

"Mway Cwamel."

Garvin looked at me and I clarified, "May Campbell."

"Why are you following us, May?"

"Awah cwan wakawa if I wantow."

"I guess you can," he answered, with a little less agitation.

She pushed her way between us, and I—with the help of her nudges—stepped sideways off the curb and continued walking in the street.

"Bob, you got to tell me what you all are planning," Garvin said, after we went farther.

"I promised, so I can't."

We walked in silence. Anticipating more questions, I asked Garvin, in an attempt to change the subject, "Why won't you go see Big Kay?"

"How do you know about stuff like that?" Garvin asked, frowning.

"Heard them talkin' when I was caddyin'. He wants you to come and talk to him and you won't. Why not?"

"'Cause I'm through with that whole family," he said, getting more irritated with me.

"That don't tell anybody why," I said softly.

He caught himself and laughed and shook his head. "You ought to be a lawyer, young Rooster. You have a devious mind. I'll tell how come if you really want to know."

The story was told. Garvin had been caught in the girl's dormitory at Edger College and was about to return to school with the trouble smoothed over when his adoptive father started a scene by yelling and calling him a little bastard.

Booger, as Garvin's adoptive father was called behind his back, was a bully and not a happy man, mainly because he could get little positive feedback from his own father, King Kay. King Kay was a good judge of humans and knew that his son Booger was obtuse and would use his future position to feed his own ego, to the detriment of the Schultz Empire. To King Kay, the most important thing in the world was making money.

"King Kay liked me," Garvin said. "Well, he felt pride, the same as he would for a prize cow up on the farm. He knew I was smart and could be an asset to the family business and gave me a lot of attention and that infuriated old Booger."

But King Kay was getting old and failing in health, so he had less and less control over Booger and toward the last had no choice but to relinquish more of the day-to-day duties. King Kay made sure that the larger part of the fortune was put into trust, out of Booger's reach.

A number of employees that Booger had held petty grudges against for perceived slights had already been fired. When Garvin had his brush with the college authorities, it enraged Booger because he was approaching a critical point in his control of the company, and like all people who become drunk with power, he was demanding total control of everything.

In spite of Mrs. Schultz's pleading, he grabbed a brass floor lamp and swung it at Garvin, who caught it with both hands and pushed Booger slowly to the floor with superior strength and held it across his throat like a length of pipe.

Garvin slowly said, "I'm leaving this place, you disgusting pig, but if you lay a hand on anyone in this house, I'll come back and pinch your head off. Do you hear me?"

Booger, afraid at this point and not breathing very well because of the lamp pressure on his windpipe, agreed by shaking his head as best he could. Garvin stood and threw the lamp, breaking a leaded-glass window. They were in the room of the house that had been used for years as a home office by King Kay. Booger had now taken it for his own use. Garvin turned and walked out.

Garvin called Big Kay at college. Big Kay sounded scared and said fretfully, "I don't know what to do."

"Your a big help!" Garvin answered, and slammed down the telephone. He packed a small bag and left.

We three continued toward school in silence and finally stopped to sit three in a row along the front of the Texaco station, leaning against the outside wall in a shaded area. May sat between us, and she immediately reached over and squeezed Garvin's empty knotted sleeve, then looked up at him.

"What are you doing there, young lady?"

"Nwothwn."

"Open your mouth," Garvin said to her.

She did and he bent around where he could get a better look.

"Lift your tongue up," he said.

She tried but there was only marginal movement.

"I was in the army with a guy like you. Doctor clipped some skin under his tongue, and he could talk a lot better," Garvin said and sat back against the wall.

She quickly clamped her jaws shut and frowned at the suggestion that someone should cut in her mouth.

"Don't think he'd ever get a job as a radio announcer, but he could talk pretty good." He looked at me and said, "Take her to see Dr. Masters."

He looked at May again. "You ever been to a doctor?" She shook her head, flipping her hair back and forth but still keeping her mouth tightly closed.

"So you left?" I said, trying to get Garvin's events straight in my mind.

"Yes, I did, hitchhiked around, picked cotton in West Tennessee, took care of a swimming pool at a hotel in Biloxi, Mississippi, even worked on a shrimp boat for a while, but got to thinking about my family, my real natural family that I hadn't ever before thought about much and came back here and went down to St. Catherine to ask around."

Garvin found out that his family was probably migrant itinerant farmers and raised other people's tobacco crops. These farmers survived on funds borrowed against the share of money they agreed to receive at the end of the growing year, when the tobacco was sold.

The share would be paid to them, minus the money borrowed during the year, and the farm family usually ended back where they started, which was broke and no place to live. So they would move on to a next place and work themselves into the ground to break even or maybe come out a little ahead if they had a good year. Sometimes they just sneaked off at night while still owing money to the tobacco farm owner.

Garvin finally found a lead from an older lady who thought she remembered a child being taken to Pittsburgh. This triggered his memory of Veada telling him a story when he was barely old enough to walk about how she thought the nuns had taken his sister away. He put the two stories together and decided right then to leave the next morning and go searching for her.

The next morning before he left St. Catherine's, he was sitting in a café reading a two day old *Sharpsburg Sentinel*. On the front page was a long article and large picture declaring King Kay's death. Without thinking it over, he hitchhiked back upriver for the funeral. He watched from a distance when they lowered the old man into the ground, cried, and left town the same night after talking privately with Veada, Della, and Mrs. Schultz in the kitchen at the farm. They told him that he knew about as much as they did about his sister. Before he left, they made him promise that he would call, collect.

He attempted several times to make his way to Pittsburgh but could not find the nerve for some reason, and spent the next few months traveling with a carnival, helping to put up and take down the tents and drinking cheap wine. The weather was starting to cool, and the carnival owners decided to work their way back to the South and eventually to winter quarters.

They were in Evansville, Indiana, and Garvin parted ways, starting upriver on his delayed journey to Pittsburgh, catching a ride with a trucker to Cincinnati. Then he hitchhiked up the Ohio side of the river and knew when he had arrived at the spot across from Schultz Dairy.

He sat on the bank looking over the river to the old house where Veada and her family lived, and even though the day was chilly, he suddenly, on an impulse, stood and undressed and rolled his clothes into a ball. He tied them around his neck with shoe strings and waded into the mud and cold water and slowly began to swim sidestroke at a measured pace like he and Big Kay had done when they were younger. The effort of the swimming warmed his body, and the crossing was comfortable.

The river was almost a mile wide at this point, and misjudging the current caused him to land about a half mile downstream. He climbed the hill and lay naked and exhausted in a meadow used to grow hay and felt good as the clear fall sun took away the chill. It dried both him and his outspread clothes. After resting and dressing, the clothes still a little damp, he walked back upriver to the big house.

The swimming pool was yet to be built, and he entered directly into the kitchen and walked softly over to sit at the corner desk. Veada looked around from cooking at one of the stoves.

Garvin said, "Got anything to eat around this big old barn?"

Veada smiled and looked back at what she was doing. "Reckon I could find somethin' maybe, if you're not particular."

She poured coffee from a slow-perking pot and sat it in front of him.

"I'm not," he said, smiling back.

Della came through the door and walked over and smacked him on the head with dirty sheets. She had been changing beds.

"Where the hell you been, youngin'!" she said.

She continued on to the laundry room with Jerry Joe's mother-to-be, then almost thirteen, following her and grinning back at Garvin. Della returned and frowned at Garvin in false disgust.

"Better tell the Missus," she said, and she left looking for Mrs. Schultz.

Jerry Joe's future mother peeked around the laundry door, glancing at Veada who was still at the stove stirring a pot, and walked to stand by Garvin and asked, "What you doing?"

Garvin shrugged.

"Got some whiskey hid out back," she whispered.

"Where did you get something like that?" he said.

She leaned over. "Stole it from the cabinet," she said and held a finger to her lips.

Mrs. Schultz burst into the kitchen and hugged Garvin. "I'm so happy you're back."

"Just passing through."

"We need to have a long talk about things, Garvin," she explained.

She was leaving to go with her husband to a friend's summer home that was located upriver. She knew she could not beg off but wished she could. "Please stay till we can talk. I promise things are going to be different. Please?"

"All right," he agreed reluctantly.

He sensed something different about her. Normally she was well groomed and dressed fashionably, but her hair was not quite in place and the dress she was wearing to the party was slightly wrinkled and hung a little crooked. Her makeup was not perfect as he remembered, and her eyes had a vacant, sad look.

The plunge of the vehicle over the hill killing Mrs. and Mr. Schultz happened later that same night, while Garvin slept on a cot located in a small room of a barn.

This morning several school buses made the turn and sat in line waiting to let out passengers along the driveway around the school's parking lot. The bell rang.

"We better go," I said.

We all got up and walked to the end of the building closest to the school.

"You worried you might get in trouble by being late?" Garvin said.

"Yeah."

"How much trouble you going to be in when you blow a big hole in the roof?"

May's head quickly turned several times from me to Garvin and then on to the school roof in the distance.

I started walking but turned back around, almost bumping into May. "Did you see Big Kay then?" I asked and walked back closer.

"Yes, I did," he said.

Big Kay returned from college in shock and asked Garvin to please stay and help him. They had the funeral and buried their parents together, in a grave close to King Kay's. Big Kay then asked Garvin what they should do next, and he suggested they get drunk.

They walked down the hill from the Sharpsburg Cemetery, past the "Closed for Mourning" sign at the Sharpsburg Savings and Loan and on to Pinky's. They got drunk. Late in the night Pinky called Vernon's father, and he came and loaded them into the car for the trip home.

The next several days were a repeat performance, and they added the Nightingale bar and several roadhouses located up and down the river to their evening itinerary.

Big Kay told Garvin one morning soon after, "We're almost out of money."

Garvin suggested they go by the savings and loan and get some more. Garvin further advised Big Kay that they needed "a pocketful," when the bank teller asked them how much they wanted.

A young secretary named Birtie, who had gone to high school with them, caught the two just as they and the pocketful of money were getting back into the car. She had a phone message from Big Kay's girlfriend at college, announcing her arrival at the Cincinnati train station.

"What should I do?" Big Kay asked Garvin.

"Go get her."

He rode the train back to college with Kay's future mother without returning home, and from the station called Garvin asking him to stay around and help. Garvin said he would and rode with Vernon's father to bring Big Kay's car from the train station. Garvin soon moved into what used to be King Kay's large bedroom and went to work with Vernon's father and the good-sized farm crew. It felt strange being the only Schultz in the big house, and he drank late into the nights.

May and I were late for homeroom after hearing the end of the story. I quickly spotted Jerry Joe with his long legs extended into the aisles from the too-small desk, and his eye was now an array of colors ranging from purple to yellow with even a touch of green. He was sitting by Mike in the back of the room, and they both laughed when I entered with May.

"Where have you two been?" Jerry Joe asked, in an insinuating tone.

I shook my head in disgust and did not answer. They both laughed again as I took a seat close to them, accompanied by May. She sat beside me, glancing first at the ceiling and then at me.

"What you doin' here?" I finally asked Jerry Joe.

"Got five yesterday and get five for showin' up today and five more after we play the game. I'm on the payroll, son."

"We playin' a game for sure?" I asked.

"After school," Mike said. "He called me twice this morning. Didn't he call you?"

"No, but I left early so he might of tried."

"He said he found out that the intramural teams all have to have seven players, so he has to recruit some more people," Mike said and shrugged. "That's what he said. He's going to be here. So wait and ask him all your questions, OK?"

"OK."

We changed rooms for class. The teacher was new, and she asked Jerry Joe during roll call if he was a new student.

"Yea, ma'am, new to these here parts. Thought I'd drop by and see how things are doin'."

The class broke up laughing. Jerry Joe loved the audience, and the teacher was embarrassed. As the period progressed, it became obvious that Jerry Joe was not suited for academic life. He made faces when the teacher turned to the board, and again the class laughed.

Finally disgusted, and remembering the training speech about how she should maintain control of the class, she called him to the front, and with a heavy wooden ruler smacked him across the knuckles of one hand. Then she reached for the other hand, and the continued cracking of wood against the knuckles was loud. She put her best effort into the punishment, and several curls fell across her face as she swung. She was breathing a little hard when the punishment finished, and she looked at Jerry Joe for a reaction.

"This here knuckle got one more hit than the other, so you might ought to even them up," he said with a deadpan expression while pointing to the slighted knuckles.

"You're being smart-alecky, aren't you, young man?"

"I'm snot sneither."

"Get out of my classroom and don't ever ever come back in here again!!"

He shrugged and gave a fake expression of hurt feeling and walked slowly from the room. For the rest of the class there was not a length of time that passed without someone snickering. Mortie made it clear to everyone, including the teacher that in his opinion licks to the knuckles did not count on a student's total yearly accumulation. He was worried about competition.

Kay had explained to Jerry Joe that as a condition of his professional football contract, he was required to attend classes. Kay was afraid that Jerry Joe would be disqualified from playing if he was absent from classes on the day of the game.

Jerry Joe, after going to the restroom for a cigarette, settled down during the rest of the morning classes so there would be no question that he deserved the next five dollars that Kay had promised. He settled down too much and at one point had to be poked in the ribs to stop the snoring.

Between classes, walking the hall, I recognized three people in the crowd coming toward me. Butterbean looked directly at me and nodded his head ever so slightly to acknowledge my presence.

Karen beside him waved, jiggled, and said, "Hi, Bob!"

Beside her was Toby, the head manager. He grabbed my arm while the other two walked on. He looked around with importance to see if anyone was listening and confided in a serious tone.

"Coach got you a pair of shoes last night from the high school." He looked at his watch. "If we hurry, you can try them on."

"OK."

We turned into the gym and ran across the floor. He rolled his short, round body in a fluid motion. His sweater that flopped from being too large had the words "Head Manager" embossed in white thread across the large maroon letter *B*. Once we were inside the dressing room, he fished a set of keys from his pocket and unlocked the coach's office.

The shoes were beautiful. New, black, and low cut for less weight. The shoebox contained an extra set of longer cleats to replace the existing ones, in order to gain more traction in wet weather. I tried them on and they fit perfectly. When walking around the dressing room, the cleats made the same sound as golf shoes make walking across concrete. I actually giggled, feeling like Cinderella, and wanted to keep them with me, but Toby insisted we return the shoes to the box and let Coach hand them to me himself before practice.

I just made it to my next class, which was study hall and held in the library. The only student looking at a book, other than me, was Mortie. He sat reading *A Cat in a Hat* and picking his nose. The teacher spent her time trying to reduce the noise level, and the students poked each other, squealing and talking. Between trips patrolling the tables, she dropped into the chair beside me and asked how my book was going.

"Why does he call the Indians savages all the time?" I asked. "My Uncle Lester's grandma was an Indian, and she wasn't a savage."

"I don't know. That's a good question. Indians are like other people, some good and some not," she said.

"It's a good book, though. This fella Hurry is prisoner of the Indians right now, and the Deerslayer might be going to rescue him. Don't know yet."

"You better come up and let me check it out for another week. You don't think you will finish today, do you?"

I thumbed the pages. "I'm on ninety-eight and it goes on closer to six hundred pages. Don't think so."

She laughed and reached for the book. I followed her to the front while Umpteen Hendershot curled his fist into a ball and stuck his nose between his thumb and forefinger indicating that I was brownnosing the librarian. He got a laugh from several students around him.

The modern world tends to divide lives into compartments, such as home and family, school and classmates, work and fellow workers, and even gangs and gang members. So when I walked into the hall at the end of class and saw Herky standing and being entirely out of his normal compartment, it took a second to recognize him.

Mike, Jerry Joe, and I formed around him, and he spoke in a serious tone. "Got a message from Kay. Bring people to him at lunch so's he can hire them on his team," Herky said, and started for the door quickly.

"Wait!" Mike yelled, and Herky reluctantly retraced his steps. "It might help if we knew where he is, Herky."

"Oh yeah; on the boat."

"Where's the boat?"

It was Herky's turn to look sarcastic. He was not as easygoing as Vernon. "Boat's on the river, down to the swimmin' hole."

Mike started laughing at the news. That started Jerry Joe and I, and even Herky finally started laughing at the thought of Kay sitting on his boat waiting for recruits. Herky made his exit to get back to the city building. The three of us sat down in the hall and leaned against the wall and laughed. The other students walked by grinning and staring.

We began the recruiting. "I want a bulldozer for playin'," Umpteen Hendershot told Mike.

"I want a truck," Homer said, indicating his price to play.

"You will have to talk to him," Mike said, trying to keep from laughing. "So at lunchtime we'll go find out what kind of deal he'll make you."

At the lunch bell I sneaked quickly out a side door and ran over the hill, across the tracks, and into the corn patch, just in case the football team was looking for me to go eat with them. The others soon caught up. We walked in single file for the swimming hole.

The sailboat was tied to the big oak tree, stern first with rubber bumpers hanging between the boat and tree roots. A rope ladder with wooden steps hung down to the exposed roots and made the boarding easy. Kay was on the foredeck in his low deck chair with a light blanket over his lap. He was studying his clipboard that contained the usual scribbles. Seeing us approach, he waved us aboard in a serious manner. He was on his best behavior because he wanted something.

Vernon was in the cockpit by the wheel, watching a fishing pole that dangled overboard. He was eating one of the many ham-and-cheese sandwiches that Veada had prepared for the business luncheon and recruitment that was about to take place.

The nurse, sitting in the cockpit on a built-in bench behind Vernon, was knitting from the bag lying on the deck between her legs and drinking a red cream soda that came out of the large, built-in ice chest.

Kay's good humor didn't last long.

"Is this all you could get!" he said.

He was pointing to Mortie, Homer, and Umpteen. They were the only ones who were the least bit interested except for May, who followed us aboard uninvited. She was back beside Vernon and removing the wax paper from the sandwich that she had yanked, without asking, from the big wicker basket.

"What's she doing here?" Kay asked me.

"She just came," I said and shrugged.

Mortie wanted a camera for his services. On Kay's instructions, Vernon went below to unlocked a storage locker and came back with the old box Kodak camera that Kay's mother had kept on board for years.

"This is the best made," Kay said.

Mortie turned up his nose to study it slowly and carefully. "Maybe ten years ago it was!" he said.

Mortie finally accepted, mainly because he was not able to part with it and sat contentedly disassembling and examining the parts.

Umpteen wanted a bulldozer.

"I don't carry a bulldozer around in my back pocket!" Kay said, trying to control himself, and after some quarrelling he wrote an IOU for the bulldozer.

"When am I gonna get it?" Umpteen wondered.

"Tomorrow," Kay said casually.

"It don't say tomorrow."

Umpteen was studying the IOU and looking for loopholes. Kay motioned for the sheet of paper back and scribbled "tomorrow," which seemed to seal the deal.

Homer wanted a truck but settled for five dollars in hand. Homer was not as dumb as he looked.

"We need one more to make the seven," Kay said.

The touch intramural teams played with seven team members on the field.

"I'm the coach and shouldn't be playin'," he said, ignoring his physical condition. "But I'll put myself down to be a member anyway, just to make it all legal."

"What about May?" I asked.

"She's a girl! We'd be a laughingstock in this whole town with a girl playin'!!"

"We could say she's a cheerleader. But what if somebody gets hit real hard and can't play--what then? And you can't stay on the field all the time and still be the coach," I pointed out.

"We'd be disqualified for not havin' enough players," Kay said, realizing his dilemma.

Out of desperation, he finally hired her for two dollars. He gave her a lecture about staying out of the way, and she promised to say she was a cheerleader if anyone asked. Concentrating at printing, he then added his and her names to his list of players and then instructed the nurse to hand out the Boaz Browns uniforms.

Noticing the papers folded inside the library book still sticking in the back of my pants, he motioned for them and studied the x's and o's intently.

"This is all their plays. Where'd you get this stuff?" Kay asked.

"The manager let me look at them," I said vaguely, not wanting to tell him about my practicing football with another team.

He was fascinated by the plays, and looking at them he dismissed the meeting with an order to be at the field immediately after school. Anyone who was late or did not have on their uniform would be fined.

"Who we gonna play?" I asked. He was ready for me.

"The managers. The football team managers. See, they got seven or eight assistant managers, and we're going to play against them! Me and Dad worked it out with the coach," he said in triumph. Now he had everything he needed to play.

Jerry Joe tried to get out of attending school for the afternoon. "Been to ever class all mornin'—gives me a headache."

But Kay said he had to go. "We can't take any chances now. We're too close, no school, no pay!"

We all ate while climbing around the boat, pointing and daring each other to jump in the river, but no one did. Kay ignored us while studying my papers with the *x*'s and *o*'s.

We heard the first bell and were traveling back to school and walking among the cornstalks when I asked May, "How you feel; bein' on the team?"

She shifted her gaze several times between the direction of the sailboat and myself and said, "Fwabwagastwd!"

I slowed my walk, waiting for Jerry Joe to quit complaining to Kay and catch up with us.

"Did you tell Mike about Gloria?" I asked when he did catch up.

"Yeah."

"What did he say?"

"He asked Susan. She said we could go over to Virginia to get married. No questions asked and it'd be legal. It's called elopin'," he said.

He explained to me that women knew about these things. We looked at May, who had a deep frown on her face.

"When you goin'?" I asked.

Mike had dropped back to where we were and heard the last part of our conversation.

He interrupted before Jerry Joe could answer me and said, "You asked her yet?"

"Ask't her what?"

"If she wants to marry you, dumbbutt."

"No." Jerry Joe had not considered this.

"Maybe you should do that first."

"Yeah, I'll do that, after I get paid for the game."

The afternoon classes were passing normally with heavy eyelids and gazing out the window, punctuated by Umpteen dropping his pencil occasionally and trying to look up the girls' dresses. The routine was interrupted by a visit from the principal, with our teacher using the standard famous-visiting-dignitary introduction. A lady who came in with him was introduced as a guidance counselor. She was visiting from the high school. He was showing off for her benefit.

"Now, Mrs. Bonner is here. Let me see, I guess your test time will be sometime next week. She will be giving you an aptitude test to see what you might like to do after your schooling."

Everyone groaned. "No, no, this will be a fun test. It will tell you what sort of things you would be good at. See? Like you, Homer, what do you think you want to do?"

"Drive a truck."

"OK, OK, this test might indicate that you might do well as a forest ranger, for example. See?"

"I don't want to be no ranger. I want to drive a truck."

"Yes, I know, Homer. You see this is an example job, for exploratory purposes, see?"

"I ain't going to be no ranger; I'm going to be a truck driver."

The principal quickly changed the subject and directed his statements to the guidance counselor. She was standing with her arms crossed. He now wanted to impress her with his educational skills.

"For example, Mrs. Bonner, these students, this very day after school will be participating in athletic events, to round the body and mind like the ancient Greeks have taught us. I personally emphasize this practice each and every day, yes, yes," he smiled.

They went on to the next classroom. The principal was glowing.

Sometime during the day's last period, it dawned on me: I could not play in the class game and attend football practice at the same time. I decided to talk to Toby to see if I could delay practicing till after the game.

School let out and the Boaz Browns as a group traveled to the gymnasium dressing room and changed into shorts and the uniform T-shirts, except for Mike. He pulled his team shirt over his regular clothes. Jerry Joe fished a pair of shorts from someone's bent storage basket and put them on. Except for his clodhoppers with no socks, he did not look too bad. May was waiting outside the door of our dressing room wearing the blue pantaloon-type uniform that girls were required to wear during gym class. The school loaned uniforms to girls when they could not afford them. She had her Boaz Brown's T-shirt pulled on over the top.

We walked outside and saw Vernon's car across the field, followed by the Buick. Both were parked along the fifty-yard line, in a place we all knew automobiles were not allowed. We could see Kay waving us over from where he was sitting in the open door of the old car's backseat. He slid from the seat, and with whistle and clipboard, he was all business.

Vernon waved from his spot leaning against a front fender. The nurse was sitting in a lawn chair behind the Buick, back out of the way, with her knitting bag between her legs. Jerry Joe and I put our long pants in the backseat of the Ford and asked Vernon to watch them.

"I picked this side of the field so I could make game plans without any spies being around," Kay said, obviously nervous. His lips had a blue tint to them. He was fighting fatigue and with concentrated effort would reopen his eyes when they began to drift shut. He began making his coaching points.

We all saw the football coach coming our way, and he did not look happy. I was waiting for him to say something about the cars being parked on the field, but he ignored them and started in on Mike.

"You can't play dressed like that! Go put on shorts. If you're not dressed right, you're off the field!" The coach saw his chance to enforce the school rules on Mike, and he pointed to the school for him to go change.

"I don't have any shorts," Mike said defiantly.

"See Toby, he'll fix you up. If you don't change, you're not playing. That's final!"

248

Mike was caught off guard. He looked at me, then Jerry Joe, then to Kay who was standing with worry in his eyes.

Mike finally said, "OK, I'm going to change."

He actually took off running for the locker room to find Toby.

The coach's attention turned to me. "What the hell you doing out here, Parsons? You need to get changed for practice. I got something for you in my office."

"Can I come after the game?"

"NO! You can't play interscholastic football and intramurals both. It's against the county athletic rules! Didn't anybody tell you that?'

"You mean I can't play?"

"You can play one or the other, but not both."

I felt on the verge of a shaking spell. I wished I were somewhere else, less complicated, but I was here and heard myself say, "I was on this team first, so I guess I'll just stay."

"So you're a quitter, huh? If you quit, you can't come back. That's my rule and everybody knows it, so don't come a whining!" the coach said.

"Yes, sir."

"I'm really disappointed, Parsons. I thought you could do better than this."

He turned to walk away, and then turned back to Kay, and while pointing up and down the field, said, "Just play the fifty yards on this end of the field. We're going to practice real football down there, if you don't mind—little man!"

"What if we want to make an extra point?" Kay said, frowning, and not liking the little man remark. He was still trying to understand what the coach and I were talking about.

"Turn the teams around, you both run it for the same goal line. That'll be the day, when this team needs to make an extra point," he said. "Ask Toby, he'll show you."

The coach was done with us and started for the other end of the field, where some of the school football players were already dressed and standing around.

Toby and his team came running from the school, yelling and wearing the Boaz football team game jerseys that were tucked into basketball shorts. All were wearing the new white socks that Toby had just handed out. They were trying to intimidate us. It worked at first, but their team consisted of three managers chosen from each of the seventh, eighth, and ninth grades. They were not physical specimens, but at least they knew what was going to happen next, while on our side Homer was ducked behind the Buick and sneaking a smoke. Jerry Joe motioned for Homer's cigarette and took a drag while everyone was watching the opponents doing jumping jacks. They all were keeping in rhythm except for one guy.

Mike returned from the gymnasium in shorts and carrying his pants rolled under an arm. His white legs were skinny but not that skinny. He stopped to talk with Toby and pointed. They both trotted across the field. There were several arguments about procedure, and finally the nurse was trusted to keep the time clock. It crossed no one's mind that she knew nothing about football, much less when to start and stop the clock. Next came referees—there were none.

Toby went down the field. We all witnessed the coach slam his clipboard into the ground and heard him yelling some things that were unrepeatable. It made the Boaz Skipjacks drop their heads and laugh. Kay, in the meantime, was trying to give instructions on how we should hold our arms when blocking.

Jerry Joe and I were exchanging glances about Mike's maroon shorts. They were worn with black socks and Italian shoes. His team shirt was on over the long sleeves. Neither of us said anything.

Toby soon returned with Butterbean and the coach's son. They had removed their practice jersey, shoulder pads, and helmets, and around their necks were dangling whistles. They would referee. Kay argued against them being the referees, but there was no alternative. We knew it would not be good for our side.

Kay and Toby discussed the rules of play, and unnoticed by us, at least at first, a crowd slowly began to gather. First came Garvin and Cecil, standing on the field's opposite side. Then Big Kay walked from the parking lot to our side. Also arriving were parents of the managers, along with other curious people who came either walking or driving in. Some parked their vehicles along the sides facing the field and then sat on the hoods.

Kay waved me over and we went to the trunk of Vernon's car. I pulled the rope and lifted the trunk lid.

Kay said, "Find the ball cap."

The trunk was full of stuff, including Kay's helmet and what looked like a framed picture wrapped in newspaper, tied with white string.

"What's this?" I asked.

"None of your beeswax. Put it down!"

My pistol was in the holster with the belt wrapped around and wedged in a corner beside a paper bag holding several bottles.

"What are these?" I asked.

"Champagne for the celebration when we win," Kay said.

"Oh?"

I pulled one from the paper bag and it said "Dom Perignon 1948." Looking further, I came across a box of cigars and held them up. I was trying Kay's patience.

He said, "Cuban—Dad and Mom were down there last year. Will you quit messing around! We got to get back! Find the cap!"

Searching quickly, I came across the bag of dynamite and roll of fuse cord, and there mashed beneath them was the Cincinnati Redlegs baseball cap he wanted.

"Give it to that girl. Tell 'er to keep all that hair stuck up under it so we don't get laughed off the field." Kay was thinking about the team's image.

Kay grabbed my arm on the way back. "What was that coach talking about? You were going to be on the school team?"

"He wants me to but I don't want to, so he's mad."

"You're on the Boaz Browns, right?"

"Right."

It took some cramming, but May got most of her hair up under the hat. Kay looked at her, then tilted back to look up to the heavens and said, "It's got to do."

The coin toss took place on our side of the field. Butterbean borrowed a nickel from Vernon and flipped.

Kay called, "Heads!"

It was tails, so Toby chose to receive the ball. Our teams took the field, and Jerry Joe stood holding the ball casually against his leg on about our ten-yard line with the main road to his back. The managers were spread out along the forty-yard line of our abbreviated playing field. The rules of intramural said that you must punt all kickoffs. So as a few more people slowly gathered, Jerry Joe took three long steps and with a loud smack put his brogan into the ball. It sailed over everyone on the other team and with several bounces ended up in the middle of the football practice. A third stringer brought it back and tossed it to Butterbean, who placed it on the proper yard line, and the game began.

It was not a pretty game. The referees called holding on most plays because Umpteen or Mortie would each grab a manager and then throw them to the ground with bear hugs. Once Umpteen added a kick that got an additional penalty. The ball was sitting at our ten-yard line with nothing more then penalties when Jerry Joe intercepted a pass looped high into the air. He ran almost for a score before he was touched.

Mortie's natural running method was to lean his head forward. It was attached to a wrestler's neck, and he would ram people with it. Toby complained that this constituted illegal blocking. That caused another delay and argument.

We finally scored on a run by Jerry Joe. He caught the ball centered back from Mike and faked to May, the other backfield member. Kay thought that May standing in the backfield was a good way to keep her out of the way. After the fake, Jerry Joe quickly ran off tackle for the touchdown. We ran the same play for the extra point.

Kay was ecstatic, waving his arms and yelling encouragement, but after another long kickoff, the referees were blowing the whistles even more often. This upset Jerry Joe and caused him and Butterbean to have words.

The two of them had generally avoided one another over the years. Not that they weren't aware of the other's presence. They had their first fight in early grade school when Jerry Joe only missed school about once a week. Butterbean had run to the teacher and cried after being hit by Jerry Joe. She scolded Jerry Joe for being too rough. The last fight between them had taken place the previous year in the middle of the gym floor, after Jerry Joe accidentally hit Butterbean in the face with a dodge ball. This fight lasted a while longer than any of the earlier ones. Butterbean got in a couple of good licks, but

Jerry Joe finally hit him one too many times. Butterbean didn't run, but he walked away from the fight. Jerry Joe was glad he did.

Since then he and Jerry Joe had not spoken, until now. Kay came onto the field for the first time and argued, leaning back and looking up to point at Butterbean. Mike and I led Jerry Joe to the sideline.

"If you fight him, they'll kick you out and we'll lose," Mike said.

Jerry Joe nodded agreement and calmed down. After more discussion things resumed, and several plays later something happened that could be interpreted by some as a sign that God was on our side.

The managers ran a reverse. This is where the entire team runs in one direction, and the ball is given to someone running the opposite way. After being tricked, Mortie reversed directions in order to catch up to the person running with the ball. Butterbean was standing relaxed with his hands on his hips and the whistle sticking from his mouth. He was amused by the play and watched the ball carrier as he ran by. Mortie, with head down and running at full speed was looking ahead, at the person with the ball. He didn't see Butterbean and inadvertently caught him just below the breastbone with the full force of his head. It made a dull "thunk." All eyes went to the collision.

The manager who was carrying the ball continued on to score. Not many noticed the touchdown except the ball carrier and the other referee, who was already downfield holding up his arms to give the touchdown signal.

Mortie quickly jumped to his feet and started rubbing his head. A crowd gathered. Butterbean tried to stand up but finally quit trying and lay on his side, rolled into a fetal position, holding his stomach and having spasms like he was going to be sick. Toby was horrified and ran for the coach. I noticed the crowd for the first time as it gathered around Butterbean. I felt a pull on my jersey and looked around to see both of my brothers beaming. Tuffy was standing close behind and grinning along with them.

"What you doin' here?" I asked.

Tuffy shrugged. "We come to see you practice football. Just a watchin'."

May was now tugging at my shirt. She pointed across the field to Kay. He was waving us over. He was trying to assemble the team for some instructions and to take advantage of the break in play. I waved to the family and went running with May to huddle around Kay.

"When we get the ball, we're going to pass," he announced. "You two go get the ball from the car and practice." Kay motioned to Jerry Joe and me.

We went to the trunk. After showing him the champagne, we ran our down and out patterns with him passing and me catching while they carried Butterbean from the field. His arms were draped around the shoulders of the coach and another big football player.

The nurse, after checking Butterbean and sending him on his way, pointed out to the coach's son that she thought her stopwatch showed that the time had expired. Worried about the injury, he agreed with her and said they would run the extra point at the start of the second half. He blew his whistle and officially declared the first half ended.

At halftime Kay instructed his team to rest. He then walked to the Buick with the nurse in the lead and Big Kay following. The three got into the back seat. Kay was seated in the middle and they shut the doors.

Dr. Masters was going by the school, headed home, and pulled over to park when seeing the crowd. He approached the circle of people. They were standing around talking, while waiting for the second half to start. He looked around and noticed the teams.

Then seeing Mike in shorts, Dr. Masters said to a parent that he knew who was standing close, "I never thought I would see Mike playing football."

Mike had seen his father park and walk up and overheard the remark. He grinned back across the distance and said loudly, "Me neither!"

They both laughed.

Someone came and asked Dr. Masters to go to the Buick. He talked to Big Kay and the nurse through the window, then headed for the school to examine Butterbean when one of the managers came over and urged him.

They took Butterbean on to the hospital for x-rays, but Dr. Masters returned to the field and announced to the crowd that he thought Butterbean would be sore but otherwise just fine. We prepared to start the second half.

The managers changed strategy in the second half. After scoring their extra point, they decided to concentrate on Jerry Joe and me. They just ignored the rest of the team. They began grabbing my jersey to keep me from running to catch passes. The rest of the managers swarmed after Jerry Joe when Mike centered him the ball, and it worked.

The coach's son was now refereeing by himself and was not calling the managers for holding me. I showed him the orange piece of felt with the team name that had been partially ripped loose and was now dangling from my shirt, but he just shrugged. On one play Jerry Joe, in desperation, pitched the ball in a lateral to Homer, standing with his hands in his pockets. It hit him in the chest and bounced on the ground. One of the managers grabbed it and ran for a score.

This made everyone on our team upset with Homer. He stood his ground by claiming that Kay had told him he would only be required to stand out on the field. Everyone looked at Kay, and he threw up his hands and turned away. Jerry Joe rushed the managers' backfield on the extra point play and blocked the attempted pass by decisively slapping the ball into the ground while the intimidated passer ducked out of the way.

Toby, now that he was ahead by six points, became interested in how much time remained and consulted with the nurse. She was now standing along the sideline with the rest of the spectators. Kay joined the discussion, and after another argument, they decided to let Dr. Masters keep the time clock for the rest of the game. No one realized that he knew little more than the nurse about when to start and stop the stopwatch, but he took it anyway. He decided to let it run because Kay was, in his opinion, overtaxing himself.

Kay called time-out after the ball had changed hands several times. He moved me to the backfield and switched May to the end position. This way they could not immediately grab me and keep me from going out for a pass. Jerry Joe ran one way with the ball, and I ran the other. I finally broke loose and ran under a long pass, and while concentrating on catching the ball, I heard someone closing ground behind me. I caught it and ran as fast as possible. Glancing to my side, I saw another person running almost beside me.

I heard, "Won Bwob, Won!"

She was quickly swinging her thin arms and matching me stride for stride. Her hat had blown off and the now-loose hair bounced around with a life of its own. We ran across the goal line together.

Lining up for the extra point, Toby announced that we had only six players on the field. We looked around and someone pointed to Homer in the distance, walking away on the sidewalk in front of the school. He was headed home and not looking back.

"He's quit," Umpteen said and shook his head. Kay called another time-out.

"You have got to come out here and stand," Mike said to Kay.

Kay pointed to me. "Get my helmet."

He started trying to roll up his bib overalls pant legs to create shorts. The nurse stooped and did it for him, while I ran to the trunk and back. I pushed the helmet onto his head.

"You heard what the doctor said about getting too excited," the nurse said.

"I have to go out there and just stand, or we'll be disqualified," Kay told her.

Mike tapped me on the shoulder and motioned out to the field while the nurse tried to talk Kay into staying on the sidelines. May and the rest of the team were straightening Kay's clothes like mothers. We walked, accompanied by Jerry Joe, toward the coach's son standing by himself and waiting with the whistle in his hand. Toby was at a distance and on one knee giving encouragement and instruction to his team.

Mike walked to the referee. They stood almost touching, face to face.

"You blow that whistle this play, and this guy here is going to yank your pants down," he pointed to Jerry Joe. Then he pointed to me, "And this guy here is going to cram that whistle so far up your ass that every time you breathe you're going to sound like a Tweety Bird. Do you understand what I'm telling you?"

The referee looked around for some teammates, but almost all had left. Being the coach's son, he lived every day with the peer pressure of other students on one side and the parent pressure of his father on the other. He was always trying to avoid trouble. He quickly decided that the best way to handle this situation was to slowly hand the whistle to Mike.

In the huddle out on the field, Kay was flustered and said nothing about the extra point play.

Finally Mike said, "We're going straight ahead, up the middle. Kay, you carry the ball."

"Me?"

"Yes, you. It's going to be a surprise play. The rest of you, knock them--just grab somebody and drag the bastards to the ground. Do it any way you can, and don't let go till I tell you."

"Any way?" Umpteen asked.

"Any way. Just keep them off our boy here," Mike said.

"You sure I should take it?" Kay was afraid.

"You're too scrawny to block," Jerry Joe said, looking down and grinning.

Jerry Joe's calm attitude rubbed off on the rest of the team. His personal remark about Kay did what he thought it would do. It made Kay angry enough to forget everything in the world except running with the ball.

Mike centered the ball to Jerry Joe. He handed it to Kay and ran ahead of him. With his arms extended, Jerry Joe grabbed two managers at the same time, one in each arm, and with his arms wrapped tightly around their necks, he dragged them to one side and out of the way. May jumped on a manager's back and held her hands over his eyes, while he wandered around trying to remove them. I grabbed and held the jerseys of the two people watching me. It surprised them, because they had been grabbing and holding me for most of the game. Umpteen and Mortie detained the two remaining managers. Umpteen held one by his hair and legs. Mortie was using both hands and had a firm grip between the legs of the other manager, who was now frantically trying to run backwards.

Mike turned and motioned his arm for Kay to run. Kay bent forward and moved his legs in the quick steps that were trying to keep up with his body. He held the football on his chest, wrapped with both arms. No one was near him. He lunged in a straight line past Mike and eventually was tripped by his own feet. His fall landed him and the ball about three yards ahead, just over the goal line.

"Was it good?" Mike yelled to the referee while walking directly at him.

"Good!" the referee indicated and held his arms up.

Our team jumped up and down in delight, but Kay was still lying in the same spot and shaking. We rolled him over, and he was laughing out loud in his high-pitched laugh with tears running down his cheeks. A wad of gouged dirt and grass, caused by his fall, was sticking from the helmet.

Dr. Masters ran onto the field and knelt beside Kay and said, "The game's over."

Meaning that Kay would not be allowed on the field any longer, but those around thought he meant the game had ended, since he was holding the watch in his hand.

The Boaz Browns started yelling, "We won! WE won!"

Toby, even with all his intelligence and ability to handle major situations, was overwhelmed. He stood there not knowing to whom he should launch a protest. Both teams started off the field. Toby decided to follow the coach's son, arguing to no avail. The referee was washing his hands of the whole mess and took off for the dressing room with his hands in the air. Toby ran alongside, still making his case.

Kay was helped up to his feet, and he walked off glowing, still holding the football with both hands. It belonged to the school, but he was not going to part with it, and in the confusion, no one noticed that the school's ball was leaving. It looked like the only way he would put it down was if someone asked him for an autograph. The smiling and laughing continued while the crowd milled around. Mike introduced his father and Big Kay to Tuffy. They shook hands. Garvin and Cecil were standing back a ways and watching.

Tuffy waved and said, "Hey, Cecil." Cecil nodded back.

"You know Cecil?" I asked.

"Ain't seen him in years. Knew him some, back in Sharpsburg," Tuffy said.

Tuffy looked off into the distance and focused his eyes at about a thousand yards, a sign that he did not wish to speak further about it, so I dropped the subject.

Finally Kay decided we should start the celebration.

Tuffy said he would clear things with Mother. He said that I should not stay out too late and "cause her to have a fit."

I promised. The Black Ace Gang, with Vernon driving, prepared to pull out.

Kay was promising the nurse, Big Kay, and Dr. Masters that he would go straight home.

We finished loading into the car, while Big Kay and Garvin looked at each other and laughed.

"He's got a set of them, don't he?" Garvin said.

Big Kay nodded and wiped an eye.

"We're not going home" was the first thing Kay said while we rode across the field to the sidewalk.

We bounced over the curb, into Main Street, and turned upriver.

"They're plottin' to put me in bed. They're going to drug me up and make me stay there. I'm not going to do it! They can all go to hell! Vernon, you got any shots?" Kay asked.

Vernon nodded his head and looked down at Kay, displaying a rare frown, but said nothing.

Kay sat in the middle of the front seat, and he was still wearing the helmet and holding the ball. Jerry Joe sat by the window, occasionally holding his cigarette out and letting the wind blow the ashes away.

"Where we goin'?" Vernon finally asked.

"Go to the caves," Kay said.

"You might get cold." Vernon was uneasy.

"I'll build a fire," Kay said.

We traveled on to the caves. Kay talked and replayed the game to the rest of us like we had not been there.

It was dusk and we searched the area for wood, finding small to medium dead branches and one large tree limb that we dragged to the middle of the boulder and built a fire by using Mike's Zippo. A few of the Cuban cigars were pulled apart and used as kindling to ignite the carefully arranged pile of small sticks.

Vernon carried the folding chair and a blanket to the fire for Kay. Kay sat and watched us with the football in his lap and the blanket draped around his shoulders. While the fire grew, the rest of us sampled the champagne after Mike demonstrated how to pop the cork.

Kay wanted one of his shots, but Vernon resisted, knowing Kay had had several shots during the course of the day, including one at the halftime of the game. Vernon had been instructed not to give the shots he carried except in unavoidable circumstances. He said he thought Kay should go home and get a shot from the nurse. But after an outburst from Kay, Vernon gave in as usual and gave the shot while the rest of us walked out to the edge and looked down at the river. Dusk was turning to night.

Kay had assembled his usual outfit, which included my gun and holster across his chest and his pistol pushed into the Browns jacket pocket. He sat quietly, still wearing the football helmet, while the rest of us discussed the champagne. Mike and Jerry Joe liked it, but to me the taste somehow made my teeth hurt. I was thirsty and drank some anyway, swallowing quickly to avoid the taste.

After giving the shot, Vernon carried his bottle of champagne to the fire. He found a rock to sit on. He and Kay watched while the rest of us talked and walked around. Mike sneaked behind me and got down on all fours, and Jerry Joe pushed me back over him. I dropped and broke my bottle and hit the boulder with my back and one elbow. This was an old trick we pulled on one another; it was my turn to be caught. It hurt, but I got up laughing and kicked the broken bottle glass out of the way.

Kay was in a tired and serious yet happy mood, and watched us while sitting beside the now-substantial fire.

"We need to have a meeting," he said. "Vernon, you're not supposed to be here when we have meetings. Just stay where you are, but keep your mouth shut."

"I will," Vernon said with a grin.

Kay began searching, peering down into his bib overalls pockets. Finally, he pulled out the ace of spades and holding it up between two fingers, he waved it around in the air so everyone could see it and handed it to me.

"Put it on the ground and put yours down there too," he said.

I removed the ace from my billfold. The other two came over with theirs. We arranged them so they were in a row, equally spaced, lying on the smooth surface and pointing to the fire.

"Now we got to settle things. Jerry Joe, here's your money." Kay rolled to one side and pulled folded money from his lower pocket. "Here," he held out the substantial amount.

"I liked beatin' the managers' ass, so just pay me for goin' to school."

"You don't need the money?" Kay asked.

"I can use it."

"I just thought so. I know lotsa things people don't think I know. Like I know you got a bank savings." Kay laid the money on his lap and was searching in his pockets again while talking. He awkwardly removed and unfolded a small piece of paper. "Two hundred and sixty seven dollars and sixteen cents," he said.

"You a nosy little shitass, ain't you?" Jerry Joe said, and started laughing.

We all laughed, not quite sure what we were laughing about. To me it was a gigantic sum of money.

"Don't ever tell nobody that. Ever Culpepper in the country would be wantin' some of it. How did you know that?" Jerry Joe was surprised.

"I called down to that bank I own and asked them, that's how." Kay held out the money and the paper with the savings account total written on it. Jerry Joe reached from his reclining spot on the boulder and took them.

Kay waved his hand like he was shooing the money away. "Keep it all for me. I might lose it out here or something; we'll settle it up later."

"If you're so damn smart, who's my daddy then?" Jerry Joe asked in a challenging tone of voice, while he crammed the money and paper into his front pocket.

"I swear I don't know that exact thing," Kay said, and looked over at Vernon. "Vernon, who do you think it was?"

Vernon, sitting and leaning forward on his rock stool, had lit one of the cigars and was puffing with one hand while holding a celebration bottle in the other.

He said, after first explaining that he meant no disrespect about Jerry Joe's mother, "Coulda been a lot a folks, JJ."

The hands working in the barns had called him JJ when he was young. Back when he, his mother, and Della were living on the farm.

"It weren't me," he grinned. "I'd a married her in a minute, but she'd not have a thing to do with me." Vernon looked away a while, then continued.

The story was told. There was some disagreement among people who were present at that time, but it was generally thought that a man named Jerry, who worked for a short while in the barns at the dairy, was his father. This Jerry had first become the new boyfriend of the long-missing younger sister of Della Culpepper. He was, according to the story, sleeping with her but also sneaking around with her daughter. Her daughter was now Jerry Joe's mother. Not that long after he had arrived, this Jerry left and at the exact same time Della's younger sister left.

Herky witnessed them getting into the big rowboat that was kept along the river below the old house. After flipping it right side up and shoving it down the bank into the water, they loaded an old black suitcase and a long rope that was wrapped around a cement block.

"And her and this Jerry fella rowed out on the river," Vernon said.

Neither was ever seen again. The rowboat was found downriver on the Ohio side, empty and tied to a tree.

"Some people think he killed 'er and others think they both went away for good," Vernon said.

"What do you think happened?" I asked.

Vernon thought they went away together, but Herky, who at an early age wanted to be a policeman, thought that Jerry had killed her.

"Why?"

"'Cause when me and Herky went after the rowboat, that cement block weren't in there, and Herky says Jerry tied it to her and dumped her in the river."

"You sayin' my daddy kilt my grandma?" Jerry Joe said.

"No, I ain't sayin', Herky's sayin', and I don't know."

"Why didn't he just leave?" I asked.

"That's another story," Vernon said.

"Tell it," Kay said.

"I always thought Big Kay was his daddy because they look a little bit alike," Mike said.

"No, that ain't it, but they's a reason all right." Vernon suddenly stopped telling the story.

He had been told many times not to mention any of this.

We begged, and then Kay threatened him several times. With the champagne he was drinking helping us, we convinced him to continue and promised over and over not to repeat anything that would get him in trouble.

It was said that Big Kay's father, Booger, had seduced Della Culpepper's missing younger sister. He somehow got her to sleep with him. So if that were true, Big Kay and Jerry Joe's mother were half sister and brother. Big Kay was Jerry Joe's uncle, not his father.

"And that's why they look alike," Vernon said.

Vernon continued the story. "This Jerry fellow" had learned from Della's sister the story of how Jerry Joe's mother had came into this world and that Booger was her father. He had listened to the whole story one night while they were in the hayloft. He immediately decided they should blackmail Booger for some money so they could go away together. She was afraid to try herself, so Jerry went to Booger alone. He threatened to tell the straight-laced King Kay the whole story.

"Veada heard them talk," Vernon said.

Booger went along with the blackmail but told Jerry that as soon as he was gone, there would be something found missing. If he ever came back, he would be arrested and sent to jail for the trumped-up crime. Jerry agreed to the terms, but Booger would not give him the money. Booger told him to send Della's sister for the money.

"Booger mumbled something, sorta like he was sorry for things turnin' out like they did, and she took the money and left, and we don't know to this day if she ever did know her daughter was gonna have Jerry Joe here, or not."

Vernon looked over at Jerry Joe. "Your mama called you Jerry, and Della called you Joe. So the rest of us, just to keep from fightin' about it, always called you JJ or Jerry Joe."

"Maybe if she knew he'd been foolin' with her daughter, she mighta killed him herself," I said. "Or maybe they killed each other?"

"Who tied up the boat?" Mike asked me.

"That's a good question," I said.

"And it could be that Booger was waitin' over there for both of them, and he did it," Vernon said. He had thought about this a lot.

"Della coulda killed him," Jerry Joe said, to unanimous nodes of agreement.

We sat looking at the fire in silence. Kay dropped the football on the ground beside the chair and turned to scoot out. He picked the football up and walked to stand a little closer to the glow, saying, "We beat their ass."

He cackled his laugh, but it was much quieter than normal. We laughed along and nodded our heads, all a little subdued.

"Yeah, we did," Mike said, with genuine feeling.

Kay walked behind his chair and then back. "You all played a real good game, and I'm proud to be your coach."

The tone was in the dignified manner that he thought suitable for a coach to use.

Vernon's behind was starting to hurt from sitting on the rock. He said, "I'm a gonna sit in the car. Kay, we gotta go soon, you know that?"

"I know," Kay said, and he carried the ball away until Vernon had left, then he walked back again and stood with his back to the fire looking off into the dark, toward the river, then slowly walked out a ways.

With time we became even more subdued. I was squatted with my knees in my armpits and poking the fire with a stick. For some reason I was remembering that my mother used to tell me, "Don't play in the fire, Bob. It will make you pee the bed."

I began thinking about the fire in the dream I had had while waking up that morning, where I was sitting on the mountain with Smokey and making arrowheads. Mike and Jerry Joe sat on the bare rock and puffed cigars. They discussed Gloria and the possibility of a trip over to Virginia to get married.

During our stay a breeze had come up, blowing into us from the water, making the fire glow hotter, and we heard the many rustling leaves behind us, up on the hill. I looked out to see the fire reflecting from Kay's back. He stood by himself at the edge of the boulder, looking off into the black that held the river. I saw his legs run forward, and he was gone.

I must have had a surprised look on my face because Mike and Jerry Joe stopped talking. The three of us stood slowly. They looked around the empty boulder then back at me, and that's when it happened.

We were not kids anymore. Beginning with that second, everything that we did for the rest of our lives would be looked at through the slued assuming gaze of adulthood, tinted by preconceived notions and the anticipation of consequences; always somewhere ahead there would be consequences.

FUNERAL

Kay was found the next day around noon. Downstream along the riverbank among the roots, just past the mouth of the Big Piney, where swirling eddies are caused by the confluence of the two river currents meeting almost at right angles. Volunteers searching from a large johnboat pulled Kay to them with a long pole used for probing and searching along the waterline. He was wearing his Boaz Browns shirt held on by the bib overalls. Everything else, the river had washed away.

Jerry Joe came to school early that same morning. Mike and I were glad he did. Mike's parents and mine, after a discussion, decided it would be best if we attend school and explained to us that the police and fire department were searching and doing everything possible. We three sneaked away from school before the morning homeroom

bell and sat at the swimming hole looking out, watching the water
flow by, all searching for Kay but not saying so.

"I think he jumped," I heard myself say and they looked at me.

"You sure?" Mike asked, in a low voice after a pause.

"He did."

"On purpose?" Jerry Joe asked. I nodded my head.

Jerry Joe snickered and shook his head, and tears were rolling
down his cheeks. We all started laughing and crying. Those arriving
at the caves last night after Vernon went for help had all assumed
he fell.

We looked at each other, and then sat quietly looking out over
the water. I do not remember the three of us ever again discussing
the possibility that he may have deliberately jumped. We all knew
he had.

Dr. Masters came to the school later that day. He told us that
Kay had been located and tried to console us as best he could. The
look in his eyes showed a genuine sadness. He offered to buy us all
something to eat after school, but we declined.

The funeral was held at one o'clock on Friday. Kay was a Baptist,
the result of a decision by King Kay many years before that his family
would join the First Baptist Church of Sharpsburg. The other leading
business and professional people were members, and he thought it
good for Schultz business.

People from the area would deny the assessment, but religion was
not that important until after the Civil War, when they could feed
themselves by working from daylight to dark six days a week instead
of seven. Religion became, in those days of new prosperity, the way
people joined together to enjoy this leisure. In the earliest days of
the area's settlement, a mention of religion would have received a
noncommittal look from most people. Even today religious affiliation
is a practical matter with a few exceptions, such as my grandfather.

The large Baptist church building was constructed of tightly
joined, large, gray oblong stones, and it stood about halfway up a hill
that rose away from the downtown area. The hill continued on up to
a wide level top, where the cemetery stood.

The cemetery was a vantage from which the whole of Sharpsburg
could be seen. The steel bridge that spanned the Ohio River rose and

fell in three graceful arches and was complemented by what seemed like a smaller imitation bridge pointing in a different direction and spanning the Big Piney. Both bridges climbed into the air from foundations hidden among the assorted buildings and houses of Sharpsburg, and from this hilltop the bridges took on an almost imaginary existence that was accentuated by the sun and water being reflected from the odd greenish tint of their light-blue paint.

Mr. Schultz called my house early Thursday morning before school and asked me, with the permission of my parents and at the suggestion of Mike, if I would be a pallbearer and mentioned that he had just called Della and asked her the same question about Jerry Joe. She said she would find Jerry Joe for him. They needed a fourth pallbearer and Vernon, being too shy on his own, volunteered through Veada and was immediately accepted by Mr. Schultz.

"I think Kay would like that," he explained to me about Vernon being the fourth and said, "thank you again" and hung up.

Mother was attending the funeral with me. Tuffy had to work. We rode along with her concentrating on driving, something she had only been doing for about three months, and she steered by holding tightly with both cloth-gloved hands while sitting up straight and stretching to see ahead. Her clothes were black; the dress was made of a shiny synthetic material, sleeveless, and pulled tight around her small waist, then billowing into large loose folds that hung to about her knees. It was contrasted by a mother-of-pearl necklace and matching earrings. A black pillbox hat, with an attached veil that had small black dots and was pulled down to about her eyebrows, completed the outfit.

"Bobby, you never seem to talk to me about things. Why?" she asked.

"I talk."

"Yes, but you never come and tell me how you feel, and tell me about your problems and let me help you try and solve them. I don't understand."

"I don't guess I got any."

"Have any, honey, you don't have any."

"Yes, ma'am."

She did not understand that as a fourteen-year-old I thought many of my problems only became problems when she found out about them.

She went on to say something about Kay's death, and I agreed. "It's all such a tragic shame," she said.

Herky had driven to the Cincinnati airport and returned with Kay's mother. She had been in California visiting a retreat where they were teaching her to meditate, eat properly, relax, and participate in the daily mud baths that were offered. She preferred Herky to Vernon because, on a percentage basis, he smelled better and shaved more often. She arrived at the farm, and the doctor was quickly summoned for medication to help her stop crying.

She entered the church for the funeral in a loose, black, flowing dress that touched the floor and a narrow-brimmed hat that had a full, dark veil that was gathered under her chin.

Kay's body was positioned below the pulpit among a great number of flower arrangements, in a dark wooden coffin of proportionate size to his body. People entered the church and came down the aisle to approach the open casket and stood for a few seconds to pay the customary respects, then retreated, searching for a seat in the almost-full building with some people already standing at the back.

We pallbearers received our instructions in hushed tones from an employee of the mortuary, and soon after the four of us walked to the casket while the large, quiet crowd watched. Jerry Joe was in a suit borrowed from Big Kay and at Mike's side. I walked at Mike's other side, and Vernon came behind us. Mike bent over, pretending to touch Kay's arm while hiding Kay's ace of spades in the palm of his hand.

Mike had picked it up from where it lay on the rock by the fire. Vernon had gone for help, and after trying to go down the hill beside the boulder and almost falling into the water ourselves, we had decided there was nothing we could do but wait for help. We three had stood silently crying and looking at the card in the dimming firelight as we listened to the Boaz siren calling the volunteers.

Today Mike leaned over Kay's body a little farther and slid the ace of spades under the folded, dark purple silk cloth that was covering Kay to the chest. We turned and sat in the first pew as directed.

The Boaz junior high principal had arranged for a school bus, and most of the 9-1s and some from other classes rode to Sharpsburg to attend the services. Arriving late, they stood as a group in the back of the building, except for May. She came bouncing down the aisle to the front and wiggled her way between Mike and me, wearing her homemade dress with her Boaz Browns shirt pulled on over the top.

The preacher was a round-faced man with a ruddy complexion and he said, among other things, "God works in mysterious ways. Kay is in a far better place now than when he was here on earth."

He held his hands to the heavens and asked God to forgive us all.

The casket was light. Mike and Jerry Joe carried the front. Vernon was clean-shaven for the first time that I had ever noticed and was wearing a black suit that had belonged to his father. Vernon and I carried the back. The outside of the church had a number of wide limestone steps that were holding the crowd that had exited before us. It parted to make way for the casket to descend.

We were to travel as a procession the short distance up the hill to the cemetery. The mortuary attendant walked backwards down the steps ahead of us, just in case. May walked directly behind the casket, frowning, and watched as we lifted it into the hearse for the slow ride. While going up the hill to the cemetery, we saw out the window of the funeral home automobile that we pallbearers and May rode in several people walking along uphill on the sidewalk, and they stopped with respect until we had passed. Some of the older men removed hats and held them to their hearts.

There was a large, dark purple tent with open sides erected beside the gravesite, and Big Kay, his wife, and a number of other people I did not know were sitting beneath it, while the large crowd stood outside and arced around the now-closed casket positioned beside the oblong hole that was dug not far from King Kay's large marker. The preacher said a blessing and prayer, and it was over.

"Is that it?" Jerry Joe asked, a little surprised by the brevity.

I nodded and noticed for the first time, sitting under the tent, a person I would not have recognized if it were not for the loose suit sleeve. Garvin stood and walked before us, shaved and with a haircut, and he was wearing a quite nice suit that was borrowed from Big Kay.

"You all did real well today," Garvin said to the pallbearers. "Hang around a minute, I need to talk to you,"

Mike's mother and father walked over to us, and Mike introduced them to Garvin.

"Have we met before? You look familiar," Mike's mother asked Garvin.

"No, ma'am, I do not think we have, but it is a real pleasure." Garvin answered.

The Masters went on to their car, leaving Garvin standing and smiling from ear to ear.

I lied to Mother and explained that I was required to stay and would ride home with Vernon. She protested but finally agreed. May did not get back on the school bus as she should have and was following me around. I explained to Mother that she had no way home.

Mother smiled at her and said, "Of course, she can ride with me."

She held the passenger door inviting May to join her for the ride back to Maplewood. They slowly pulled away in the Packard with Mother straining to see the road and May studying her intently.

The pallbearers and Garvin sat under the tent while Big Kay and his wife shook hands with a long line of distinguished-looking people. The cemetery emptied surprisingly fast for the amount of people attending.

Herky held his arm for Mrs. Schultz to hold onto while walking to the car for the ride back to the farm. Big Kay walked with them and promised her he would be along soon; he waved as Mrs. Schultz and Herky pulled away in the Buick.

Big Kay watched them until they were quite a distance down the hill, and then turned to approach the sitting group.

"Garvin, we need to talk. I need to tell you something," Big Kay said.

"OK," Garvin said, "let's walk to Pinky's and get something to drink. You remember how to get there, don't you?"

Big Kay, with sad eyes, smiled for the first time in several days. "I think I can find the place all right."

The pallbearers fell in behind Big Kay and Garvin, walking down the hill to Pinky's.

"You got any money?" Big Kay asked Garvin.

"I got a pocketful," Garvin said, and together they broke into a genuine laugh.

"You remember Birtie that works at the bank?" Big Kay asked.

"Yeah."

"She's always asking about you. I think she's been sweet on you since high school."

"She's married, isn't she?" Garvin asked.

"He died in the war. She has a son; he's a good kid."

We walked past the closed savings and loan and saw Pinky's ahead.

The story was told that Pinky returned to Sharpsburg broke and in poor health. He was a leading jockey for a time after fighting his way up the ranks to obtain the good horses necessary to become a top jockey. He did not wear success well.

Drinking, women, and a perpetual weight problem had made him careless, and he had taken several spills, the last of which broke numerous bones. He tried a comeback but had lost his edge, and even though five years earlier he had ridden a brilliant race by bringing in a long shot to place in the Belmont, one of the most prominent races in the country, he could no longer get good mounts and eventually gave up. When grooming horses was the only work he could find, he came back to Sharpsburg.

King Kay sent for him, and they had a talk. King Kay had a problem. Recently his bank had become owner of the land and building with a pool hall, when he foreclosed on a loan. He was having trouble finding someone to buy or even run the place.

"You run the place like it was yours. Keep the building in good repair. Pay the utilities and taxes," King Kay said.

Then King Kay named a nominal payment on a loan figure that was sure to keep the building and land in the Schultz family for many years. In return it gave Pinky self-respect and an income. He accepted.

"Anybody asks you, it's your place as long as you want it, you just bought it," King Kay said with finality.

They shook on the deal, and nothing was ever put into writing.

King Kay, knowing a pool hall was the last place to find someone with money, thought it a waste of time and never set foot inside the door, but Pinky, out of gratitude, even all these years later would not let Big Kay or anyone he was with pay for anything. This was Pinky's rule.

Big Kay came in less often as the years went by, but today as we entered he said, "They're with me."

I felt the same as the day I had entered the cafeteria with the football team, important, and we were going to play pool on the prestigious first table.

Big Kay, Mike, and Jerry Joe ordered a draft.

Garvin said, "Give me an orange drink."

We all looked at him, but he pretended not to notice.

"I'll have a orange too," I said, and he grinned at me.

There were only two people in the place besides Pinky and Motherload. Both were old men sitting together in chairs on the elevated platform, nursing beers in silence and watching us. Vernon ordered two fried baloney sandwiches with extra mayonnaise and a Pepsi-Cola.

Our group was too dressed up to be frequenting Pinky's, but he knew about the funeral and had sent flowers. Pinky would not set foot in a church, because it would require him to remove the hat that always covered his bald head.

Vernon joined me as a partner, and we played eight ball against Jerry Joe and Mike while Big Kay and Garvin sat together in the elevated chairs.

"You remember Tom Galloway? He played football with us in high school, defensive back most of the time?" Big Kay asked Garvin.

"Sure, I remember, everybody called him 'Kootie.' He's a cop now, isn't he?" Garvin asked.

"Kootie could possibly be Sharpsburg's next police chief. Anyway, we were at a Rotarian luncheon not long ago and the subject of Mom and Dad came up, about the wreck. He said he was a rookie on patrol with the county sheriff's department back then and was the first one to the car when it went over the hill."

"No kidding." Garvin now listened closely.

"He told me he climbed over the hill to see if he could help while others were on the way and found Dad laying several yards from the car."

"Must have thrown him out," Garvin said.

"That's what he thought and went on down and found the passenger door open and mother sitting behind the wheel. She was dead." There was a long silence. "That's what he told me, and I believe him. He said he was too scared, being a young fellow then, to say anything. You see, he said he pulled her out from behind the wheel to see if she could be still alive, and when the others arrived, they just assumed he was driving."

"She was driving?" Garvin said in a low steady voice, turning the information over in his mind.

"What do you think about that?" Big Kay asked after a while.

"It sure puts things in a different light," Garvin said.

"Just between me and you, I think she might have done it on purpose," Big Kay said. "That's strictly between the two of us."

"Why?"

"I've had some time to think about it, and I think she did it for you," Big Kay said, with uncharacteristic conviction in his voice. They sat in silence and stared at the pool table.

Vernon and I lost the game and sat down.

"Come on, we'll play these wet-behind-the-ears babies," Garvin said, not being a person who could be still for long. He reached for a pool cue. "I was the best one-armed pool player in the Veteran's Hospital, by far."

Big Kay and Garvin beat them three in a row. Garvin was pretty good even with resting the stick on the cushion and stroking with one hand.

Garvin and Big Kay quit trying so hard after that and were now just playing. Big Kay asked Jerry Joe the details about his black eye, and Jerry Joe was pointing to the back of the room and explaining.

"You're gonna miss Kay, aren't you?" I asked Vernon, who was sitting beside me. He dropped his head, and holding back a sob, nodded yes.

I said, "Me too." We sat in silence.

None of us noticed when Clyde and Lonny Piggott came into the poolroom through the back door. They had been drinking, even though it was early in the afternoon, and they were discussing something and did not notice who was at the front until they were almost face to face with Jerry Joe. The sudden close proximity was a surprise to us all.

Pinky was in his element and way ahead of everyone. He had reached under the counter for a baseball bat and walked to block the front door.

"Motherload!" Pinky yelled. "Don't let nobody out the back door." Everyone stood still.

Garvin spoke first, "'Well, well, said the spider to the fly, if it isn't the notorious Piggott brothers, Bonnie and Clyde. Er, I mean Lonnie and Clyde. Came to apologize, have you? Here, come on up to the bar," Garvin slapped the bar where he wanted them to stand, then walked behind the bar and sat a mug under the tap and filled it and sat it on the counter. "Here, Clyde my boy, have a beer on me."

Clyde inched for the beer with Lonny staying close. Garvin filled a second mug, and Lonny reached for it and took a drink, slowly, with his eyes darting from person to person.

"You know, Clyde, by all rights we ought to beat the snot out of you. Don't you know that?" Garvin said.

Clyde moved the mug away from his mouth and bobbed his head and spoke, "Yeah."

"Jerry Joe, you want to beat the snot out of them?" Garvin asked.

Jerry Joe walked close to Clyde. I noticed for the first time how much bigger Jerry Joe was than either Clyde or Lonny. Jerry Joe could only fight when he was angry, and at this moment he was the farthest thing from that. That was a lucky break for Clyde, but Jerry Joe did tell him how things stood.

"You come near me or my Mother again, and I'll beat the squirmin' dogshit outta both a you."

"I get you," Clyde said, and nodded. The tension broke and the pool game continued.

About halfway through the next game, Big Kay asked Clyde what he was doing for a living now.

"Caddyin', nobody'll hire a jailbird," Clyde said.

"You go on down to the streets department Monday morning and apply for a job. What do you want to do?" Big Kay asked seriously.

"I'll do any damn thing," Clyde said.

"You want to paint bridges?"

"That'd be just fine with me," Clyde said.

"You get in any more trouble, and I won't stand up for you. You understand?" Big Kay looked at him with a practiced steady gaze learned from arbitrating his business's and the town's problems for many years now.

"Yes, sir. Thank you. Can we go now?" Clyde asked.

"Sure. Give them another beer first, Pinky."

"OK."

Pinky expertly drew two more beers with more beer and less foam than Garvin's.

Big Kay said, "You get along with the people over there Clyde, and down the road sometime maybe they will hire your brother here. That's how things work, you see? Who knows what might happen."

The Piggotts left after quickly drinking the second beer. Clyde thanked Big Kay one last time before going out the door.

After awhile Big Kay said to the rest of us, "Let's get out of here before Vernon breaks Pinky up, eating all those sandwiches." We walked out into the street with a bright afternoon sun shining.

Garvin said, "Let's go over to the bowling ally and eat."

"OK," Big Kay agreed.

We pulled tables together and ate. Big Kay watched Vernon dig into a banana split and shook his head and asked Jerry Joe, "Why don't you stay with Della? I got her that house so you would have a good place to live—she even picked it out—but you spend your time in those dammed old houses down by the river in Boaz. Why?"

"I stay with her sometimes. Gettin' married, so I'll be living with her all the time then."

This was news to everyone but Mike and me. There was considerable discussion about who and when. Della was giving them the spare bedroom and was happy about having a baby in the house, another Culpepper.

"I love Della," Garvin said, "She's a good friend and you can count on her, and she sure does have a loud mouth."

Everyone laughed and agreed. "Always wondered why she never had any children?" Big Kay asked.

"Don't know for sure, but I don't think she ever liked a man that way; several tried, I hear. But she sure likes babies," Garvin answered.

"We're going to have to get you on one of those riverboats sooner rather than later, Jerry Joe," Big Kay said.

Big Kay sat back, touching little food, and clasped his hands behind his head. He looked at the ceiling and appeared to be thinking and after awhile said to Garvin, "What should we do, Garvin?"

"What do you mean?" Garvin looked puzzled.

"King Kay told me when I was a little boy to always ask you what we should do and listen when you told me. So what should we do?"

"About what?"

"Any damn thing, Garvin."

"Well, I got this idea for a scrap yard, over the hill behind the stockyard."

"Most of that floods," Big Kay said.

"We don't care. We just use it for junk car storage; we need to buy one of those car crushers and mash the junk cars up and sell them back to the steel mills in Pittsburgh. The railroad spur comes right to the land where they pick up the cattle; we can load flatbeds with little square cars."

Everyone laughed at the thought of little square cars.

"Here's the beauty of it. You can help by putting some political weight behind that abandoned vehicle bill that's in the State Senate. I keep reading about it in the paper. Then the state will pay me to go get them. Then the steel mills will pay us to reuse the metal. We get paid coming and going, all profit, see? Not to mention the scrap copper we can buy on the side—that stuff is selling at a premium as we speak—and recently totaled cars will come to us every time there's a wreck. We'll just want the ones nobody else will have anything to do with, see?" His eyes were flashing and his mind was racing to explain.

"Sounds good. OK, we'll give it close consideration. Come to the office Monday, and I'll find you a desk," Big Kay said.

"We'll put a trailer on that high spot at the other end of the yard, and Cecil can move in and drive the wrecker and watch things at night. Oh yeah, we need a big wrecker with a wench that can lift to a flatbed truck; we need the truck too." Garvin continued with his train of thought for a while.

After Garvin finally slowed down, Big Kay said, "OK, you stay over at the hotel for the time being if the farm's too far, and Garvin, buy some clothes, please."

"I will."

I listened and laughed along but was somehow removed from the present events. I was watching the proceedings from an emotional distance. I was no longer living in the moment. In the back of my mind, I was missing Kay, a comrade, and I looked at Mike and Jerry Joe and saw in them the same distance.

During a pause Big Kay said to Jerry Joe, "I've tried to get you to talk to me for a long time but every time I do, you run off. Why?"

Jerry Joe shook his head. "I was always afraid you'd make me do stuff."

"What stuff? Like going to school?"

"Yeah. That'd be one thing."

I spoke up for the first time. "Kay got him to go to school."

Big Kay looked at me with that where-did-you-come-from look and then asked, "How?"

"He paid him money to go," I said. Mike and Vernon started laughing.

Big Kay scratched his forehead. "Not a bad idea. Come on, Jerry Joe, I want to introduce you to some people down at the dock." He looked at his watch. "Then I have to get up to the farm and see about the missus."

He rose, motioned for Jerry Joe to follow, and put his arm around his shoulder,

"Paid you to go, huh?" Big Kay said.

Jerry Joe nodded. I could tell he did not like the direction that things were going and knew he would rather be going upstairs to talk to Gloria.

Back over his shoulder Big Kay said to Vernon, "Come on, I'll take you to your car."

Vernon stood and tried to wipe the different flavors of ice cream from the suit that Veada had told him not to get dirty.

"Wait a minute," Mike said to the departing three.

They turned back to the table and Mike continued, "I want to make a toast, to Kay."

We all automatically looked about the table for the remainder of soft drinks. We all stood up.

"A toast to Kay," Mike said, and looked around at everyone individually with tears in his eyes. "Here's to the guy who had more guts in one little finger then the rest of the world all put together."

Mike, Jerry Joe, and I surprised the rest when we said, "Hear! Hear!" and held our drinks high in the air, like at the Black Ace Gang meetings.

"Let's do it again," Big Kay said.

We all held our drinks high and said, "Hear! Hear!" in unison.

Big Kay took a sip and put down his soft drink and said in a quiet low tone, "Thank you guys very much." And they left.

We sat down and were quiet for a while. Mike and I discussed Jerry Joe and his new responsibilities. We felt it was about time that he had a taste of the family pressures we had been dealing with all our lives and giggled about it while Garvin, in a quiet mood, listened and watched the bowlers.

"You know what's wrong with men?" he said out of the blue.

"What?" I said after glancing at Mike.

"We made a trade with the devil, that's what."

Mike rolled his eyes, thinking "here we go again."

"What did we trade?" I asked.

Mike and I grinned at what we thought was Garvin's latest absurd thought.

"Feelings, we traded him our feelings," Garvin said, nodding his head and looking away.

"What did we get back?" Mike asked.

"Food. It's food, because back at the beginning we had to kill food to feed the tribe or clan or whatever, depending on where we were. So we had to lose our feelings to feed our family."

"We still go huntin'," I said. "You mean like that?"

"Yes, exactly Rooster, like that. You go hunting. OK, ever go deer hunting, say?" I nodded. "Do you remember the first time you killed a deer?" he asked. His eyes were serious, so I thought and remembered.

The story was told. I was nine years old and walking with Tuffy, Badeye, Grandfather, and my Uncle Paul up the hill and following the gully that held Bone Marrow Branch. We were deer hunting and it was the first time I had been allowed to go along with the men.

Uncle Lester wasn't along because he had quit hunting. He said often, "If I'z hungry I'd go in a minute. People bring me more meat than I need now, so them deer can just go on. They don't bother me none."

The men sat me against a tree looking uphill and then fanned out wide on both sides of the mostly dry creek bed. I did not realize it at the time, but they were going to herd deer downhill and into my sights.

It was a young buck with short spike antlers that had one small additional prong protruding forward from each horn. Deer have sensitive smell and hearing and can see any small movement, but otherwise, contrary to popular belief, their eyesight is average. The wind was gently blowing uphill, and I was frozen in my seat with gun raised. I heard him coming from quite a distance because the trees had recently shed many dry leaves, and even a squirrel would make a loud racket when on the ground. I was breathing hard, from excitement and nervousness. He saw my chest rising and falling about a second before I held my breath.

He froze and looked directly at me. We were staring into each other's eyes. It seemed from the penetrating look that he knew everything there was to know about me. He turned to one side quickly in order to jump from the creek bed and climb back up the hill. I shot him behind a front leg, at an angle that immediately penetrated his lungs and heart. He made the jump but did not land on solid footing and rolled back down the hill, bringing leaves with him, and was dead before he quit rolling.

I began a shaking spell and rose from my spot and walked to him and nudged the antlers with the barrel of my rifle to make sure he was dead, like I had been taught. His face was young and the eyes were open and still staring at me, and even dead they seemed to know my innermost secrets. I wondered why I had to shoot him and was about to cry when the other men arrived.

They patted me on the back and were laughing proudly. I relaxed and beamed at all the attention and felt good. We field dressed the deer with its back feet tied to a nearby tree limb. I helped carry it down the hill with everyone bragging on my good one-shot kill. Grandmother cooked the heart and liver that night and the whole family said, "You did good, Bob."

"So you felt good?" Garvin asked.

"Yes, I did."

"Did you have any feelings for the deer?"

"I've thought about it, if that's what you mean, but I had to shoot it." I explained.

"I know you did," Garvin said. "That's my point. You had to trade your feelings for the deer, in order for the tribe to live. See? You traded feelings, and they were replaced by admiration and praise and something to eat."

"What do we do for feelings now?" Mike asked.

"Women kept their feelings. So we mostly use theirs now," Garvin said with a satisfied smile.

"I got feelings," I said.

"I'm not saying you don't have feelings. I'm saying you fight them, push them down. They don't grow up like the rest of you. See? They're like small children. You're a man, but your feelings remain like a young child because you fight to keep them small.

"What if women traded their feelings?" Mike asked.

Garvin answered with a deep serious look. "We, all of us, would be in very very deep trouble."

"You mean women didn't trade nothin'?" I asked.

"They traded. They traded their individual wants for the good of the tribe and do, most of the time, what they think is best for us all.

That's something that's harder to do because with feelings women suffer. Men don't emotionally suffer for the good of all like women do. Men just go out the door with small emotions like anger and fear, to kill or be killed. It's much simpler. Men are much simpler people then women, Rooster. You remember that."

"OK," I said.

"When a woman asks you how you feel and you shrug and shake your head, they think you just don't want to tell them. They don't understand that you really don't know how you feel and are even somewhat mystified by the question. You see what I'm saying?"

I thought about mother, did not exactly see, but decided to give it some thought.

Garvin, moving around with the nervous energy that developed when he talked, looked intently at Mike.

He said, "I got to get this off my chest. I know I been running at the mouth too much, but this is important. You remember last Sunday when you said your mother was originally from around here and had a brother and I told you my sister was in New York?"

"Yeah."

"I was lying. I've told people for years that she's in New York. I think everybody but me believes that. I'm almost positive that your mother is my sister. I am positive," Garvin said.

"The nuns told her he died," Mike said, surprised. He tipped forward and set his chair back down on all four legs.

"They're lying, too. They told her that so she wouldn't run away and try and find me."

"How come you never talked to her? Or told her about this stuff?" Mike asked, a little upset, and we were again engrossed in Garvin's every word.

"I've talked to her. You were real young, riding in a stroller all bundled up, probably pissin' down your leg, up there in Pittsburgh. It took me several years to find her. I can't count the times I started to look her up but always found some reason to delay the trip up there."

The story was told. After the Schultzes adopted him and later when they were killed in the car wreck, Garvin stayed and helped on the farm and kept in touch by phone with Big Kay, who was off in college. They always talked about business first, but then they would just pass the time of day, and when Garvin learned that Big Kay was going to join the Coast Guard and later learned of his impending marriage, he drove to Connecticut for the wedding.

The experience made Garvin want to join the Army, but he stayed in Sharpsburg at Big Kay's urging and continued to help in several areas of the Schultz businesses. Big Kay came home on leave for an important business meeting, followed by his wife. Kay was suddenly born. The following ordeal taxed everyone, and Kay's mother with Veada's help went to Cincinnati and rented an apartment close to the hospital where Kay stayed on and off for almost a year.

After Big Kay went back to the Coast Guard station in North Carolina, Garvin, on an impulse, went to the Army recruiters' office and joined. He walked in and showed the sergeant his agricultural deferment paper, tore it up, and dropped it on the desk.

He was sent to New Jersey, and after completing basic training, was given two weeks' leave before being sent to England where the European invasion was being staged. He bought a bus ticket to Pittsburgh and began looking for his sister, walking the streets and spending the nights at the YMCA. He lay in bed looking at the ceiling, knowing he had little hope of finding his sister, but he knew he had to try.

Remembering that Veada had told him years before of the nuns who had taken her away, he could think of nothing else to do but stand outside the combined school and orphanage that someone at the Y had told him about. The first day he asked inside the reception building, and the days after he stopped people coming and going and asked if they could tell him anything about his sister. They all said no.

Finally, an old nun who was excused from most work because of age and went for a short walk each morning began having chats with him, and against rules that she never liked, searched and found his sister's records, using the last name and story that Garvin had given her. She seemed to do it at first mostly for her own curiosity, but finally, in a whisper, she told him that after asking around she thought his sister was married to a doctor named Masters, but there was no current address, and added that she thought his sister was more than likely still in Pittsburgh.

He and the nun found a listing in the telephone book for all the Masterses and after contacting several of them with no luck, he knocked on the door of one address that was within walking distance. Dr. Masters's mother came to the door and only understood what he was trying to say when he mentioned St. Catherine's and Sharpsburg.

She remembered these names from talks with her son when he told her, in Italian, about his new wife's history. She quickly gave the nice young man in the uniform a piece of paper on which her daughter-in-law had written an address.

Garvin followed his sister the next morning as she left her small apartment on the University of Pittsburgh campus; she would be allowed to stay there while her husband was overseas in the war. He had applied for and received a grant to study infectious diseases after completing his residency, and the apartment was part of the benefits. The school said she could stay until he returned.

She was pushing a stroller with newly born Mike, and her oldest, a girl, was pointing at things while walking and holding the middle brother's hand. Garvin followed from a distance and remained completely engrossed in every move they made.

They were on a trip to the grocery store. When they started back, he walked over and offered to carry the food sack. They made small talk. He told her he was from Sharpsburg and his name was Schultz and he was just in town to visit a relative before going overseas, but could not bring himself to say anything more.

She thought nothing suspicious of the stranger's help; it was common practice in those days. She was happy to have adult company on the walk home and talked quite a lot, and he listened and memorized each word.

She told him she thought she was originally from somewhere around Sharpsburg and St. Catherine's, but didn't remember much about it.

He asked casual questions, designed not to make her suspicious.

She told him, "All I remember is water and climbing up in a tree and holding my little brother. They told me later it was my brother;

he died. I remember watching fast muddy water running in through the doors of this big, black barn that was close to us."

"What happened then?" Garvin asked gently.

"They say I blocked it all out. I remember riding in a boat and having a blue ribbon in my hair. I still have the ribbon. I've looked the whole thing up in old newspapers since then. The figures vary, but there were almost fifty people drowned, and they didn't find the bodies of about half of the missing and they were never sure about the rest. I guess I was lucky."

"I'm glad you made it," Garvin said, still in a low voice.

"Thank you," she answered and went on to tell him that she was going to "one of these days" move there. Just so she could see what it felt like to live in a place where her relatives had lived.

"You've got your hands full right now, don't you?" he said.

They were at her door and the children were fussing. The middle child started crying, and Garvin handed her the bag. "He was a lucky little brother to have you. I hope you make it back there someday."

She looked at him for a long minute, in silence, and with a smile said, "Thank you."

He returned the smiled and walked directly to the bus station.

Garvin, with glazed eyes, looked across the Lucky Strike Bowling Alley table and said, "Mike, I just couldn't bring myself to tell her. I figured her husband might get killed and I could get killed too, and I just wanted to spare her the added grief. It was probably a wrong decision, but that's what I did."

"What about later?" Mike asked.

"Later? I couldn't just walk up and say 'hi, I'm your drunk, one-armed, crazy nuts brother.' I've spent the years since then sitting around drunk with my head between my legs. I've rode freight trains all over the country. Even rode a cargo ship to Europe and walked into the water where I lost my arm. I don't know, I thought it might help but it didn't."

He sat for a long time and then looked at me. "Rooster, you're the reader, ever read Pearl Buck?"

"No."

"Great American writer; ignored mostly, I don't know why, maybe because she writes mostly about China, I just don't know. But she said the Chinese always were buried where they were born because it made for a peaceful spirit. I got an arm buried in the middle of the Atlantic, so I probably don't have a chance at peaceful, but I'm going to try from now on to be as normal and boring as is humanly possible." He looked at Mike. "I can't promise a lot, but I'm going to try."

"You going to tell Mom now?" Mike asked.

"You think I should?"

"Yes, I do."

"Why?"

Mike looked all around while slowly shaking his head.

He finally said, "For one thing I might not have to be the black sheep in the family anymore." We all laughed louder than we should have. "And another, I think probably she's wondered about it a lot. She just should know."

Mike looked at his watch. "Dad's making rounds at the hospital right about now. Let's go see what he thinks about it."

They agreed, said good-bye, and headed for Market Street and the walk to the hospital. Mike was carrying the coat to his black suit. I noticed for the first time when they walked out the door that his white shirt was short sleeved.

I sat with a hand in my pocket, staring at the mess on the tables and trying to digest all of the things that had happened during the day, when a thought struck. How was I going to get home in time for supper? I walked out the door and started for the bus stop. Vernon pulled over and waved me into the car.

"She's runnin' a little hot. Had to give her a drink a water," he said, and we headed for Boaz in silence.

"You still got that dynamite in the trunk?" I finally asked.

He nodded his head.

I said, "Me and Mike are going to take it back up to Fred's Creek, here before long. Would you keep it hid someplace for me?"

He nodded again. I pushed the button to open the glove box and removed the wrapped blasting caps and pushed them gently into my pocket. We pulled into Maplewood, driving on the just finished new blacktop.

Vernon said, "Come here a minute," and got out and walked behind the car.

He pulled the rope to open the trunk, and then took out the picture-looking object that was wrapped in newspaper.

He handed it to me. "Kay told me the other day that he was sometime gonna give this to you because you was askin' him about it."

I was stumped. I lay it in the yard and cut the string with my pocketknife and pulled the paper away. It was the picture from his dining room wall of the ice-cutting crew standing on the frozen river beside the team of horses.

"What's this for?" I asked.

"He said you'd know when you read on the back," Vernon said, and shrugged.

I turned the picture over and neatly written in ink was a list of the names of the men posing for the picture. I read down the list. The last one was a name I had stood and stared at many times in the Fred's Creek graveyard, Joseph Spencer. He was Mattie's husband and my great-grandfather.

On the old brown paper attached to the back Kay had added in his unmistakable scratching, "Look" and had drawn a wavy arrow to the name. I turned it over to see Joseph's serene, smiling face looking at the camera. I thanked Vernon as he left.

I carried it in the house and showed my parents. They were more amazed than I was.

"What you gonna do with it?" Tuffy asked.

"Give it to Grandpa, I guess."

"He'll like that," Mother said, and with the picture leaning against the dining room wall, we soon gathered around the table to eat. We discussed the funeral.

Mother said, "Your little friend May is coming by tomorrow. I have some old skirts and blouses from high school put back that might fit her with just a little bit of altering. I'm going to try to do something with that hair, too."

Things were quiet for a while.

I heard myself say to mother, "You really looked nice today, for the funeral."

She looked over at me slowly and said, "Thank you."

Tuffy started grinning. He bent over his plate to hide his face and looked down at his food.

"Tuffy, sit up straight, and bring the food up to your mouth when you eat. It looks more civilized," Mother said.

"Yes dear."

He sat up and looked at me and wiggled his eyebrows and smiled.